PRESERVED

FOR THE END OF TIME

MORE UNCOVERED EZEKIEL PROPHECIES ABOUT CHRIST'S RETURN

Volume 2

Chapters 30 through 48

A. A. Kevas

and

W. I. Walker

Preserved for the End of Time

More Uncovered Ezekiel Prophecies About Christ's Return

Volume 2

Copyright © 2024 by A. A. Kevas and W. I. Walker

All rights reserved.

No portion of this book may be reproduced in any form or by any means, other than for quotations.

Self-published in the USA in 2024 by A. A. Kevas and W. I. Walker

CreateSpace Independent Publishing Platform, North Charleston, SC

ISBN 10: 8324295974

ISBN 13: 979-8324295974

Table of Contents

SECTION 1: Second Half of Book of Ezekiel Reveals More Hidden Prophecies About Christ's Return 4
SECTION 2: God Promises the Ending of Israel's and Russia's Oppressive Takeovers and Corrupt Lifestyles 10
    Ezekiel 33:21-22 11
    Ezekiel 30 12
    Ezekiel 31 18
    Ezekiel 32 24
    Ezekiel 33:25-33 32
    Ezekiel 34 35
    Ezekiel 35 41
    Ezekiel 36 45
    Ezekiel 38 54
    Ezekiel 39 60
SECTION 3: God Assures That the Dead Will Be Resurrected and Judged 68
    Ezekiel 33:1-20 68
    Ezekiel 37:1-10 73
SECTION 4: Jesus' Outings at Jerusalem's and Israel's Notable Sites 84
    Ezekiel 40:1-3 86
    Ezekiel 43:1-3 & 4b 87
    Ezekiel 44:1-5 88
    Ezekiel 43:4-5 90
    Ezekiel 40:4 90
    Ezekiel 43:6-27 91
    Ezekiel 45 95
    Ezekiel 46 101
    Ezekiel 40:5-49 105
    Ezekiel 41 113
    Ezekiel 42 118
    Ezekiel 44:6-8 122
    Ezekiel 45:4b 131
    Ezekiel 44:27 & 26b 131
    Ezekiel 44:26c & 44:9-31 131
    Ezekiel 47 136
SECTION 5: God Affirms That the Holy Land Inheritance Also Belongs to Israel's Arabs 141
    Ezekiel 33:23-24 141
    Ezekiel 47:13a & 47:15-23 143
    Ezekiel 46:16-18 145
    Ezekiel 45:8-11a 146
    Ezekiel 37:15-28 147
    Ezekiel 47:13b-14 150
    Ezekiel 48 151
CLOSING REMARKS 159
APPENDIX 1: Gregorian Equivalences of the Biblical Hebrew Months 162
APPENDIX 2: Biblical Measurement Conversions 163
REFERENCES 164
INDEX 170

SECTION 1

Second Half of Book of Ezekiel Reveals More Hidden Prophecies About Christ's Return

After publication of the first 29 Ezekiel chapters of a start-from-scratch Hebrew translation in 2014, it didn't seem possible to discover anything more amazing than the prophecies unearthed in the first half of *Preserved for the End of Time* (ISBN 13: 978-1483949710) that in recent times have been coming to pass. The in-depth study of the ancient Hebrew words that exist in Ezekiel chapters 30 through 48 (the same one used for the King James translation) continued to reveal prophecies not realized by earlier translators. After we finished dusting off each Hebrew word, the uniform theme from chapter to chapter seemed like a second letter from God. A continuous theme emerged from one chapter of Ezekiel to the next, that amazingly continued from the first half of the Book of Ezekiel. The prophecies foretold in this second half of *Preserved for the End of Time* are so detailed that the words seem to paint pictures, measurements included, of what Old City Jerusalem will look like during the timing of the false Messiah's appearance in Israel, and after the real Messiah returns. The images described appear to depict what Old City Jerusalem looks like today, including the various gates and several of its holiest religious temples, such as its most sacred church, mosque and sanctuary shrine located upon and nearby Temple Mount. The ordinance rituals that shall have been practiced at two of these temples by the followers of Israel's false Messiah at the time of the true Messiah's return are also described.

As previously explained in our translation of the first 29 Ezekiel chapters, many of the differences between this translation and the other ones stem from the earlier translators' incomprehension of events prophesied ahead of their time. For instance, the first half of the book uncovered several passages prophesying metallic flying things with wings, wheels, and lighting that could transport people by air or throughout the heavens. The earlier translators could not have even imagined that this was describing future space- or aircraft. In this book, we also located prophecies that have more recently begun to transpire, such as the continuing wars of Gog, which the reader will discover pertains to a Russian leader (Gog) and his massive army conquering more of its neighboring lands (like what has been happening in Georgia and Ukraine). It also discloses about the Israeli Zionists led by the prophesied false Messiah (leader of the Magog people), whose massive army will continue to plunder and seize the lands of their neighboring Arab territories. All of the other existing translations of the Bible completely miss these miraculous prophecies, and many more that we retrieved.

As explained in the first book containing the first half of Ezekiel (*Preserved for the End of Time, 2014*), prophecies such as the ones we have uncovered have remained hidden for so long because of the fear and taboo of straying from the current translations of the canonical Bible. However, all of our research reveals that not only is "seeking knowledge" not a taboo, but it is, in fact, required. Many have argued that the translation of God's inspired words depend on faith alone, forgetting that the ancient Hebrew words comprise the only inspired words. The English translations of the Old Testament (Tanakh) were constructed hundreds of years later by scribes attempting to record it in terms that they fathomed.

Additionally, it is crucial to understand that the ancient, biblical Hebrew words had no vowels; only consonants. After ancient Hebrew had ceased to be a spoken language, several systems of vowel signs were invented by Jewish grammarians to help the public read Hebrew accurately. The present vowel mark system was adopted around the ninth or tenth century CE. [1] This is where our translation becomes markedly different from the other existing translations. In looking for continuous themes, it was important to be open to every possible vowel pronunciation of the same Hebrew letters. Keeping with the context of the sentences, in many cases, the same definitions were used as in other translations, but there were other instances where common sense drove the selection of another word with the same Hebrew consonants recorded by the scribes. We attribute this to being one of the primary reasons that we found prophecies others missed. We did not depend on a vowel mark system invented in the ninth or tenth century; and it is also crucial to note that the Dead Sea Scrolls do not have any vowel marks attached to its words.

Another reason why our translation is so different is because of where our sentences begin and end. Ancient biblical Hebrew did not contain punctuation marks, [2] therefore, it was easy for the earlier scribes and translators to create different sentences by punctuating wherever they desired. Although the resulting biblical passages in many of the prophecies contained the same sequence of Hebrew (Old Testament) words, they no longer disclosed God's true revelations, but instead were stated in a way that hid the actual message. Therefore, in an attempt to reconstruct the original message, we employed <u>asterisks</u> to indicate where two verses from the King James translation and the Hebrew (Old Testament) translations should run together.

Amazingly, after re-connecting the Hebrew sentences in the book of Ezekiel, by punctuating the same word sequence differently, we unearthed sentences from the first half of our Ezekiel translation (published in 2014) prophesying that the sentences in God's message shall have been split apart and altered by the ancient Israelites, hiding what God had actually relayed. Thus, this would lead many of its future descendants astray, as well as many of its gentile readers, who would be depending on their Hebrew speaking neighbors to correctly translate for them. We also noted that because this scripture was revealed to Ezekiel through God's messenger spirit, it is apparent that God is speaking in the first person to those specifically addressed such as, to the Son of Man (Jesus; Iyesh), the imposter Jesus, the House of Israel, the gentiles, Gog, and so on. Also, we found evidence of the deliberate rearrangement of words by the earlier scribes and translators to form sentences that incorrectly favored the Israelis. According to the message in our translation of the first half of Ezekiel, it was stated multiple times that the altered scriptures also included the integration of the idolatrous beliefs of many of the Israelites, who had embraced several of the pagan customs and beliefs from the idol-worshipping, non-Hebrew gentiles. For instance, in our investigations, numerous books illustrated how the ancient Egyptians' pagan tenets shaped the Old Testament, and how the idolatrous Greek and Roman beliefs and myths influenced the writings within the New Testament, as well as their translation. We referenced these books throughout our comments, designated by a note number (N:#) for each comment.

In addition to the difficulty of translating future events by earlier scribes, many of the Hebrew words possess more than one meaning. We spent numerous hours evaluating every potential Hebrew definition for each word. Every word constituted a piece of the puzzle used to decode this message from Ezekiel's revelation. To avoid the confusion of the current Bible translations, we analyzed those Hebrew words which have more than one meaning, and selected the definition that flowed with the context of the sentences, paragraphs, and chapters. In some cases, it made more sense to leave the Hebrew word as a proper noun, and in other cases it was more fitting to translate as the words major meaning. For example, David (Dawid), which literally means "beloved," can either be translated as "beloved," or can remain as the name "David."

Although this translation is a bit easier to read than the current versions of Ezekiel, because it is a literal translation, the reader may encounter several complex sentences, particularly where all of the prophesied measurements within Jerusalem's Old City are recorded. During our 25-year study, it has always been our intention to unveil God's true message. It seemed logical that God would provide the warnings stressed throughout *Preserved for the End of Time* because he expected the latter generations to understand the warnings and the signs of the Messiah's return. To us, careful analysis and utilization of the actual verb tenses recorded by the scribes was crucial in obtaining these warnings from God.

In the Hebrew language, a pronoun is attached to the verbs as prefixes or suffixes, where its position indicates the verb tense. These were used to more accurately reflect the original meaning, as translators of the current King James Version had done, with the exception of what is known as the "waw-conversive rule." [3] Unlike most of the other existing Hebrew Bible translations, we specifically translated the future, past, and present tenses according to the <u>actual</u> verb tense recorded by the scribes. Contrary to this, Israeli rabbis have been teaching their followers, and the learners of biblical Hebrew, to <u>reverse</u> the actual verb tense in each Bible sentence that begins with the Hebrew prefix, "waw" (Strong's Hebrew Concordance number coded as 2050.1), which has always represented a conjunction (such as; *and, also, so, but, that, moreover, indeed, because, thus,* etc.). According to these Jewish scholars, this "waw-conversive rule" of time-reversal only applies when reading the Bible, yet, <u>not</u> when reading the newspaper or any other document written in Hebrew, either now or from that time period. [4] We, therefore, strongly disagree with this supposed rule, and have found at least one other scholar, Robert Young (Young's Literal Translation of the Bible; 2005) who also translated using the literal verb tense, even when a conjunction preceded the sentence. ⁵   In Hebrew, the "imperfect tense" indicates that the action has not been completed, and can be represented in either the <u>present</u> or <u>future</u> tense. When God reveals a future prophecy, or warning, in the incomplete tense (present or future), it is illogical to expect His believers to understand that the event foretold had already happened (complete tense) just because the sentence started with "and" or another conjunction; particularly when it is clearly not their language practice. Hence, we did not apply this rule and translated <u>exactly</u> as it was written. By translating using the actual verb tenses recorded by the earlier scribes, it was easier for us to find the hidden prophecies that current KJV readers see as past events.

    Moreover, in Hebrew, many of the words are spoken in the reverse order of English. For instance, where the Hebrew or Greek phrase would literally state "not you should have oppressed neighbors your gentile," the English translation would read "You should not have oppressed your gentile neighbors." In cases such as this, we reported the numbers in the original Hebrew order, with semicolons between them, but translated in the appropriate English order. In many instances, Strong's dictionary would define a particular Hebrew word as a group of words. In these cases, we also used the entire dictionary phrase in our translation, and underlined the collective words. Whenever the group of words was continued on the next line, we typed the abbreviation "<u>cont</u>." (i.e., continued) above the underlined word(s) that occurred in the row that followed. In some cases, if only one or two words were at the end of a line in our translation, and the remaining group of words was continued on the next line, we typed "<u>below</u>" above the word(s) at the end of a line, and then included all of the Strong's Concordance numbers on the following line.

    In this book, also included, are various researched comments or explanations that are provided in a different font style than the translation, to clearly distinguish it from the Ezekiel passages. It is important to read these comments in order to better appreciate the actual historical events that have occurred or are now occurring that fulfill the revealed prophecies. Within many of the translated sentences, brief explanatory words, or a reminder of who or what a particular pronoun is in reference to, have been included in <u>brackets</u>. These bracketed words are <u>not</u> part of the translated sentence, and only serve to aid the reader.

    The Masoretic Hebrew texts existing today are copies of copies, with nearly a millennium between the time they were revealed and the time they were recorded. ⁶   In translating, there is also the added difficulty of whether to use the Hebrew word(s) or verb tense(s) that exist in the text (called the Kethim), or the ones corrected in the margin by the earlier scribes (referred to as the Qere). ⁷ As a general rule, we used the same Hebrew words selected by the translators of the King James Version, but in most cases, it did not matter whether the Kethim or Qere were applied, since the resulting message was comparable. Although the original Hebrew Scriptures are nonexistent, the closest that we have to the original Hebrew are the ancient Dead Sea Scroll fragments found in 1947, and the Genizah scroll fragments found in 1898 (referred to as the First Dead Sea Scrolls). An example of some of the difficulties encountered is found in the Genizah fragments. Early scholars considered the book of Sirach to be illegitimate, and omitted it from the current Hebrew writings in the Bible. [8] However, this particular book appeared in the Genizah collection, and now scholars realize that it should have been included. Since this Ezekiel translation agrees remarkably with the Dead Sea Scroll fragments, we feel confident that the majority of Hebrew words occurring in the book of Ezekiel were recorded correctly, in spite of the fact that some of the other books are missing.

As in the first 29 Ezekiel chapters, this latter half of the book translation is equipped with supporting evidence of this translation, as well as Strong's Hebrew Concordance numbers coded above each biblical word, to verify the translation. We used the concordance numbers taken from *The Strongest Strong's Exhaustive Concordance of the Bible*, by James Strong, LL.D., S.T. D., as a reference guide to aid the reader. For the Strong's numbers representing a particular verb tense, the reader can find a description of the verb tense online at http://www.lexiconcordance.com by simply entering the Hebrew Strong's Concordance number for that particular verb tense. For example, if one were to enter the verb tense number "8799," a description would emerge of what an "active, imperfect tense" indicates. In addition to providing the Strong's Concordance numbers, in order to aid the reader in confirming the prophesies uncovered in this translation, we also extensively studied and included excerpts from other supporting documents, such as the Dead Sea Scrolls, *The Didache*, the Old- and New Testament revelations, *The Gospel of Barnabas*, and the Koran (Qur'an). These additional resources strongly support the astonishing divinations unveiled in this translation.

Recall that the first book of *Preserved for the End of Time*, published in 2014, specifically featured the return to the Middle East of Jehoiachin's descendant, Jesus (Iyesh), who was referred to throughout the Ezekiel prophesies as the Son of Man (a descendant of Adam, i.e., human), God's prophet, and the Royal Leader of Babylon (i.e., of Iraq, Syria, and the other neighboring allies). It also revealed that Jesus had escaped crucifixion and was instead transported in a metallic spacecraft to a rocky earth-like planet by some pious celestial beings, following his first advent, and that he had not died for the atonement of his followers' sins.

Also highlighted in the first book were the prophesies about the emergence of Israel's false Messiah, who will be an imposter Jesus (the false prophet of Nazareth), and who shall appear on earth first; possibly around six and a half to seven years prior to the actual Jesus' return (deduced from Ezekiel 8:1a and 20:1 in the 1st book). The imposter Jesus will claim to be God, the Son of God, and to have died like a sacrificial lamb for the atonement of his followers' sins; confirming the incorrect beliefs and practices of many of today's people.

This second half of Ezekiel is, therefore, a continuation of the first half of *Preserved for the End of Time*, and in addition, informs of characteristics of the tyrannical Gog and Magog leaders, as well as their destined destruction for brutally invading more lands of the Arab gentiles that will be opposing the imposter Christ and Zionist Israelites for their cruelty and violence against the Arabs. Because of the ongoing controversy between the Israelis and their bordering Arab neighbors over the rightful ownership of the Promised

Land, God, in this second half, also reveals which territories in Israel, Palestine, Jordan, Syria and Lebanon were actually inherited to Jacob's sons and Joseph's two sons, as well as who today's rightful owners shall include. While in the first half of *Preserved for the End of Time,* it is prophesied that Israel's army shall eventually invade and occupy Egypt, it is further prophesied in this second half that Israel's imposter Jesus will also become Egypt's ruler, and shall claim it as part of Israel's property; contrary to what God had actually stipulated.

Preserved for the End of Time contains God's unique message that we uncovered in the book of Ezekiel, which had until now remained hidden for over 2,600 years behind the Hebrew letters. As revealed in the first 29 chapters of Ezekiel, and stressed throughout this second book, at the time of Christ's return, the Holy Land is prophesied to become exceedingly corrupted, where the true Messiah, Jesus, will dispel the falsehoods attributed to him, and will re-implement the correct teaching of the Oneness of God and the importance of praying solely to God in God's Name [Yahweh or Eloah (Hebrew), Alaha (Aramaic), Elah (Chaldean), or Allah (Arabic)]. In this second half of Ezekiel (chapters 30-48), God further warns the Israeli and gentile supporters of the imposter Jesus, as well as the Russian ruler (Gog) and his troops, of their upcoming destruction for their blasphemous beliefs, abominable religious practices, and for filling the Promised Land with bloodshed in order to plunder and obtain more land from the Arab gentiles that will refuse to accept the imposter Jesus.

Again, it is extremely important to read the comments and historical data supporting the events foretold in this book. We hope both parts of *Preserved for the End of Time* will enlighten those seeking knowledge, and will prepare the Jews, Christians, Muslims, and people of other faiths for what is to come in the approaching decades. We are confident that this translation of Ezekiel is the closest to the truth than all other Ezekiel translations based on the fulfilled prophesies and the confirmations obtained from the Dead Sea Scrolls and other supporting, religious documents; as well as the fact that we translated in the actual verb tenses recorded by the earlier scribes. With this more exact translation, it is now more apparent what occurrences will be taking place, as well as what the intended warnings are to the latter generation upon Jesus Christ's return.

SECTION 2

God Promises the Ending of Israel's and Russia's Oppressive Takeovers and Corrupt Lifestyles

The following Ezekiel passages reveal further information concerning the <u>future destruction</u> of Israel and its annexed lands (which will also eventually include Cairo and other parts of Egypt, as well as the Gaza Strip, the West Bank, western Jordan, southern Syria, and southern Lebanon); and also prophesizes about the eventual annihilation of Israel's imposter Jesus (ruler of the Zionist Magog people), Gog (ruler of Russia and Georgia at the time of Christ's return), and their massive armies. Recall from Ezekiel chapter 29 in the first book of *Preserved for the End of Time*, that despite a peace treaty between Egypt and Israel (such as the one agreed upon in September of 1978 and finalized in March of 1979), Israel would again be sending troops to Egypt by the treaty's 40th year, and then sometime after the 40th year, people from Israel would eventually begin occupying parts of Egypt. Although we speculated from the uncovered Ezekiel prophecies in the first book that Israel's imposter Christ might be the cause of Israel again attacking Egypt by 2019 (the 40th year of the Israel-Egypt Camp David Accord), we see now that this was not the case.

Instead, fulfilling this prophesy, we learned that from early 2016 through 2019, Israel, presided by Prime Minister Binyamin Netanyahu, had carried out over 100 airstrikes over the Sinai region in Egypt, but it was conducted in secrecy using unmarked drones and aircraft. [9] At the time of the initial air raids, Cairo accepted Israel's intervention and allowed Israel to help them defeat the brutal ISIS (Islamic State of Iraq and Syria) militants that had infiltrated the Sinai, fiercely attacking Egypt's military, its police, and its Muslim and Christian citizens, and posing a threat to Israel. Because Egypt's military and police apparently could not handle the ISIS militants without Israel's involvement, senior Israeli officials are now seeing that Egypt is dependent on Israel's military for their country's security, [10] and this could very possibly lead to Israel eventually seizing regions of Egypt as prophesied in Ezekiel 29 and 30. According to Ezekiel 29:6-17 (in the 1st book), after the 40th year of the Israel-Egypt peace agreement, "by the 27th year" (Ez. 29:17) from "when Egypt was relying on Israel for security, Israel will break off all ties with them" (Ez. 29:7), and in due course, will invade Egypt; and the imposter Jesus will eventually rule his

Israeli and gentile followers from Cairo sometime after Prophet Jesus and his militia shall have captured Jerusalem (Ez.33:21).

Also recall from the first book that evidence was found in the Dead Sea Scrolls that several of the chapters were out of order compared to the King James Version. After studying the following sections, it was apparent that again several of the passages and chapters had been moved out of place by the earlier scribes. When we discovered the uniform theme throughout the Book of Ezekiel, it became much more obvious when events described were out of place. Hence, in this particular section, to restore the sequenced events within the given topic described, Ezekiel chapters 38 and 39 were moved back to follow Ezekiel chapter 36. Also, a few passages from Ezekiel chapter 33 were noticeably misplaced and moved back here to complete the same subject material.

Ezekiel 33:21-22

33:21   2050.1; it; 1961, 8799   871.1; 8147; 6240; 1886.3; 8141   (below)
This, indeed, shall come to pass by its twelfth year of our exiles, by the fifth

871.1;6224;871.1;2568;1886.3;3807.1;2320;3807.1;our;1546 – See Appendix 1 for Gregorian equivalences of Bib. Heb. months
of the tenth month [Tevet; i.e., a few days before Christmas]:   This one who had

(he;935,8804;413;2967.1;1886.1;6412;4480;3389; see Ez. 15:3, 21:29, 24:7-8, and N:28 (1st book)) ...   cont.
escaped [i.e., the actual Jesus who had escaped crucifixion] shall have come from

cont.   559, 8800   it; 5221, 8717; 1886.1; 5892
Jerusalem to Mine, saying; *"The city (of Jerusalem) has been stricken!"*

33:22   2050.1; 3027; 3068   1961, 8804   (413; 2967.1; 871.1; 6152, 6153, or 6154)...
Hence, the (helping) hand of God shall have been upon Mine throughout the Arab

cont.   3807.1; 6440   1886.1; 6412; 935, 8800   (below)
(populace), who shall have been in the presence of the returning escapee since

2050.1; he; 6605, 8799   853 or 854; 6310; 2967.1   Ez. 29:21 & (N:52) of 1st book (below)
when he shall open up (and recite) from My Own Testimony [i.e., the Qur'an] during

5704; his; 935, 8800; 413; 2967.1; 871.1; 1242   refer back to Ez. 1:24-28, 8:1b-2, and N:10 of the 1st book
his arrival to Mine at dawn [as he, the four celestial beings, God's messenger spirit,

also refer to Ez. 43:3 & 44:4b in Section 4   (below)
and some Muslims at a mosque in Syria were praying the dawn (Fajr) prayer]. After

2050.1; he; 6605, 8799 or 8735   6310; 2967.1   (2050.1; 3808; mine or I; 481, 8738; 5750)...
he shall open up (and read from) My Testimony, then never again shall Mine have

cont.
been silenced.

11

Ezekiel 30

30:1   _{2050.1; 1961, 8799; 1697; 3068   413; 2967.1 559, 8800}
<u>Indeed, the Word of God shall come to Mine, saying</u>:

30:2   _{1121   120   5012, 8734   2050.1; you; 559, 8804}
"<u>Son</u> of <u>Man</u> [Jesus]; <u>let it be prophesied what you had (formerly) relayed</u>."

_{3541   559, 8804; 136; 3069   per Ez. 30:4-19}
"<u>This is what</u> <u>Lord Yahweh said</u> [regarding the upcoming destruction of Israel's imposter Jesus and his massive army, several years after Israeli troops shall have invaded Cairo and other regions of Egypt, and he also becomes Egypt's ruler]:" ^(N:1)

^(N:1) Bear in mind from Ezekiel 17:12-19 in the first book of *Preserved for the End of Time*, that this particular Israeli takeover of Egypt is to occur sometime after Jesus (who shall have been ruling from Babylon, i.e., from Iraq and Syria) and his militia shall have counter-invaded Jerusalem, seized the imposter Jesus, and transported him to Babylon; after which time, Prophet Jesus shall have made a treaty with him to become a part of Jesus' "humble kingdom, without ever again exalting himself." But unfortunately, after agreeing to these terms and returning to Israel, the imposter Jesus will, instead, sometime afterwards, break the treaty made with Jesus and will send his troops to invade Egypt. He then will become the ruler of Egypt and shall tend to his Israeli and gentile followers from Israeli occupied Egypt. It is revealed later in Ezekiel 38 and 39 that sometime after this prophesied invasion of Egypt, the Russian ruler (Gog), who will be a follower and supporter of the false Messiah (imposter Jesus), will go to Israel, along with his massive army, with the intention of invading the Arab refugee territories and plundering their wealth and possessions. But as prophesied in the following chapters, both tyrannical leaders and their armies will instead be met with God's wrath. After their demise, the real Jesus will then be recognized and accepted by all monotheists to be the true Messiah and prophet of God.

30:3*   _{3213 (w/o marks), 8685; him or his   1929; 3807.1; 3117   (3588; 7138; 3117)...}
[Jesus:] "<u>Make him (and his multitudes) wail</u> <u>on the Day of Woe</u>! * <u>For the time is</u>

_{cont.   2050.1; 7138; 3117; 3087.1; 3068   3117   6051}
<u>near</u>! <u>Indeed, Yahweh's Day is near</u>! <u>It's the day</u> <u>the smoke cloud</u> (will occur over

<small>per Ez. 30:17-19, 32:7-8, 34:11-15, 38:16   6256   1471 plur.   per Ez. 30:4-6</small>

Israel and its annexed lands) at the <u>time when</u> <u>the foreign nations</u> [opposing Israel]

<small>it; 1961, 8799   2050.1; it; 935, 8804; 2719 sing.   871.1; 4714   (below)</small>

30:4*   <u>shall come (there)</u> * <u>after a destructive weapon shall have entered</u> <u>into Egypt</u>, and

<small>2050.1; it; 1961, 8804; 2479 sing.   871.1; 3568</small>

<u>had caused anguish</u> <u>throughout Cush</u> [11] [Saudi Arabia, Sudan, and Ethiopia] because

<small>5307, 8800; 1886.3; 2491; 871.1; 4714   2050.1; they; 3947, 8804   1995; 1886.3   (below)</small>

of <u>its slain falling in Egypt</u>, and because <u>they seized</u> <u>its wealth</u> <u>when their (buildings)</u>

<small>2050.1; they; 2040; 8738   3247; 1886.3   3568; 2050.1; 6316; 2050.1; 3865   2050.1; 3605; 1886.1; 6152 or 6153</small>

30:5*   <u>were torn down</u> to <u>its foundations</u>. *<u>Cush, Libya, Lud</u> [12] [Turkey], <u>and (in fact) all of the</u>

<small>cont. 1285 as follows   2050.1; 3552 or kab (variant of 3513); 2050.1; 1121 plur., possv.   776 sing.; 1886.1; 1285</small>

<u>Arab (League)</u> <u>that have honor, including the offspring of</u> <u>the league's dominion</u>,

<small>854; 3963 1   871.1; 2719; they; 5307, 8799</small>

will be <u>against them</u>. (N:2) <u>They shall fall by a destructive weapon!</u>"

(N:2)   According to Ezekiel 30:3-5, when Israel eventually invades Egypt, killing many of the inhabitants in Egypt and plundering their wealth, this will further anger Yahweh, Jesus, the Muslim nations, and anyone who will be heeding God's warnings throughout this translation of Ezekiel, and will oppose Israel's imposter Jesus. The nations prophesied in Ezekiel 30:5 that will eventually be uniting in a defensive attack against Israel are revealed to include Turkey and the nations belonging to the Arab League. There are currently 22 nations affiliated with the Arab League. These include the countries of Saudi Arabia, Palestine, Jordan, Egypt, Syria, Iraq, Libya, Morocco, Tunisia, Sudan, Algeria, Somalia, Mauritania, Oman, United Arab Emirates, Qatar, Yemen, Bahrain, Lebanon, Comoros, Djibouti, and Kuwait. [13] At the time when this prophesy is to occur, the real Jesus Christ shall have united and lead these predominantly Muslim nations in the final counter-invasion against Israel that had captured and occupied Egypt. Moreover, as revealed later in Ezekiel 30:9-19, Jesus and his Arab and Turkish militia will be aided by God and His angels during the final counterattack.

<small>3541   he; 559, 8804; 3068</small>

30:6   "<u>This is what</u> <u>Yahweh said:</u>"

<small>2050.1; they; 5307, 8804   they or those; 5564 (support), 8802   4714   (below)</small>

"<u>After they have fallen</u> by <u>those defending</u> <u>Egypt</u>, then its arrogance (and) its

<small>(2050.1; it; 3381, 8804; 1347 sing.; 5797; 1886.3; 4480 prefix; 4024; 5482)…</small>   <small>cont.</small>

power from Migdol[14] (to) Syene[15] [i.e., from the Sinai Peninsula to Aswan], shall

<small>cont.   871.1; 2719 sing.; they; 5307, 8799; 871.1; 1886.3   (below)</small>

have diminished. They shall fall by their own destructive weapon; for it was (clearly)

<small>it; 5002, 8803   136   3068 or 3069</small>

stated in the Oracles; 'The Lord is Yahweh.'"

<small>   2050.1; they or theirs; 8074, 8738   871.1; 8432   776 plur.; 8074, 8737</small>

30:7   "They, indeed, shall have been destroyed in the midst of the desolated lands,

<small>2050.1; 5892; 2050.2   871.1; 871.1; 8432   5892 plur.   2717, 8737; they; 1961, 8799</small>

and their cities will be in the midst of the cities they (themselves) will be ruining!

<small>   2050.1; they; 3045, 8804   3588; 589; 3068 or 3069</small>

30:8*   *For they should have known that I (Yahweh) am God."

<small>   871.1; I or mine; 5414, 8804 or 8800; 784   (871.1; 4714; 2050.1; they; 7665, 8738; 3605; 5826, 8802; 1886.3)</small>

"When Mine shall have had the fire set in Egypt, and theirs, (as well as) all of their

<small>   cont.   (871.1; 3117; 1931; 3318, 8799; 4397; 4480; 3807.1; 6440; 2967.1)…</small>

30:9*   supporters, were crushed *during that time, angels from amongst My presence will

<small>cont.   871.1; 6717 plur.   2729, 8687   853; 3568</small>

arrive in (space)ships to cause the trembling [in Israel and Egypt]; but Cush [Saudi

<small>   983   (2050.1; it (fem.); 1961, 8804; 2479 (fem))…</small>

Arabia, Sudan, and Ethiopia] will be safe. Because anguish shall have been

<small>cont.   871.1; 1992   871.1; 3117; 4714   3588   2009   it; 935, 8802</small>

caused by these in Egypt at that time, then, behold; it is coming to pass!"

<small>   3541   559, 8804; 136; 3068 or 3069</small>

30:10   "This is what Lord Yahweh said:"

<small>   2050.1; I or mine; 7673, 8689; 853 or 854; 1995 sing.; 4714   871.1; 3027 sing.   (below)</small>

"After Mine, along with Egypt's army, have put an end to the power of the false

<small>5019 (or deriv. of 5029; 3538 (lacking 'b'); variation of 5139)   4428 sing.; 894 (Iraq & Syria)   (below)</small>

30:11*   prophet of Nazareth [Nebu-ked(ab)-Razar], the Royal Ruler of Babylon * and his

<small>1931; 2050.1; 5971; 2050.2   854; 2050.2; 6184 plur., possv.; 1471 plur.   935, 8716   (below)</small>

people will then be against his oppressors' gentiles that will be brought there to

	7843, 8763; 1886.1; 776	2050.1; they or theirs; 7324, 8689	2719 plur.; 3963.1

destroy the region (where) theirs had (previously) emptied out their destructive weap-

cont.   5921; 4714   2050.1; they; 4390, 8804; 1886.1; 776   2491sing.

ons over Egypt, and had filled the country with the slain."

30:12   2050.1; I; 5414, 8804   2975 plur.   2724

"So after I have caused the rivers [in Israel and its invaded lands] to be dry land,

2050.1; I; 4376 or 4377, 8804   853; 1886.1; 776 sing.   (below)

I, consequently, shall have devalued the (Promised) Land that had been under the

871.1; 3027 sing.; 7451 plur.   I; 8074, 8689   776 sing.   (below)

power of evil ones. After I have caused the destruction of the (Holy) Land, and all

2050.1; 4393   871.1; 3027 sing.; 2114 plur.   (589; 3068; I; 1696, 8765)

that is therein, it will be under the control of the alienated ones, as I, Yahweh, have

cont.

warned!"

30:13   3541   559, 8804; 136; 3069

"This is what Lord Yahweh said:"

2050.1; I; 6, 8689   1544 (N:18 of the 1ˢᵗ book)   2050.1; I; 7673, 8689   457 plur.

"After I have destroyed the crucifixes and have put an end to the idolatrous images

4480 prefix; 5297 (Noph) ¹⁶   2050.1; 5387 sing.   4480 prefix; 776 plur.

(that originated)from ancient Memphis, and after the exalted one is off of the regions

4714   3808; he; 1961, 8799; 5750   2050.1; I; 5414, 8804   3374   (871.1; 776 sing.)...

of Egypt because he shall no longer exist; I, thus, shall have put fear throughout the

cont.   4714   2050.1; I; 8074, 8689   (853 or 854; 6624; 2050.1; I or mine; 5414, 8804)...

30:14*   the country of Egypt * that I had made desolate, when Mine within southern Egypt

cont.   784 sing.   871.1; 6814   (below)

had set the fire in Zoan¹⁷ [a region in northern Egypt, including the Sinai]. I, also,

2050.1; I; 6213, 8804   8201 plur.   871.1; 4996   2050.1; I; 8210, 8804 (below)

30:15*   shall have executed punishments in No¹⁸ [Luxor and Karnak] * and poured forth My

2534; 2967.1   5921; 5512 (refs. 15, 22 & 23)   4581 sing.   4714   2050.1; I; 3772, 8689   853; 1995 sing.

wrath upon Syene [Aswan], a refuge in Egypt. ⁽ᴺ:³⁾ After I have cut off the multitude

15

                    4996 (No)   2050.1; I or mine; 5414, 8804; 784; 871.1; 4714   2342, 8800   (below)
30:16* at Luxor and Karnak, *when Mine shall have set a fire in Egypt, tormenting Aswan as

        it; 2342, 8799; 5512 (Syene)   2050.1, 4996 (No); it; 1961, 8799   1234, 8736   871.1; 5297 (Noph)
it grievously falls; Luxor and Karnak shall also be rent asunder, along with Memphis".

                                6862 plur.   3119   970 plur., possv.   206   2050.1; 6364
30:17*   "(Because of causing) afflictions daily, * the young men of Aven¹⁹ and Pi-Beseth²⁰

                                          871.1; 2719 sing.; they; 5307, 8799   2050.1; 2007 (below)
[both in the vicinity of Cairo, Egypt] shall fall by a destructive weapon, after those in

        871.1; 7628   1980 (or 3212), 8799   2050.1; 871.1; 8471   (below)
30:18* captivity shall move out *and (be) in Tahpanhes²¹ [a northern border of Egypt] on the

             it; 2821, 8804; 1886.1, 3117; 7665, 8800; 8033   853; 4133 sing   4714   (below)
day it shall have grown dim there while destroying the oppression in Egypt; as well

           2050.1; 7673, 8738; 871.1; 1886.3; 1347; 5797; 1886.3   (1931; 6051; 3680, 8762)...
as its power (and) arrogance that was put to an end, wherein the smoke cloud shall

          cont.   2050.1; 1323 plur.; 1886.3 (fem.)   871.1; 7628; they (fem.); 1980, 8799   (2050.1; I; 6213, 8804)
30:19* cover.   When its settlements under captivity shall move (to safety), * and I have

          cont.   8201 plur.   871.1; 4714   2050.1; they or theirs; 3045, 8804   (below)
executed the punishments in Egypt, it is because theirs had (once) known that I

       3588; 589; 3068 or 3069
(Yahweh) am God." (N:3 cont.)

(N:3) According to Ezekiel 30: 3-19, after the troops of the "exalted," imposter Jesus shall have invaded Egypt, which shall have occurred sometime after Jerusalem had been captured by the real Jesus, Israel and its annexed territories (including the Israeli occupied regions in Egypt) will eventually be counter-invaded by Jesus and his militia defending the Egyptians and Israel's Arab refugees. During the final battle and "Day of Woe," it is later revealed in this section, that Israel's imposter Jesus will be killed by the prophesied mass destructive weapon, along with his army and many of his followers in Israel, Egypt, and the other Israeli occupied Arab territories.

In Ezekiel 30:15, Aswan Egypt (the ancient city of Syene) is mentioned as being a refuge city that will be seized by the Israelis and then later counterattacked by Jesus and his militia. Within the past fifty years, Aswan Egypt has accommodated hundreds of thousands of Sudanese refugees (from "Cush") that fled their war-torn cities during Sudan's civil war of 1983, [22] and more recently, since April of

2023, that fled to Aswan due to military conflicts in Sudan. The United Nations has reported that between the months of April and June 2023, over 450,000 Sudanese have fled to Aswan for refuge. [23]

30:20   (2050.1; it or this; 1961, 8799)...   [deduced from Ez. 33:20-21 & 40:1]   cont.
So, [~11 years after Jerusalem had been stricken by Jesus and his militia] this

   cont.   871.1, 259; 6240   8141; 871.1; 7223; 871.1; 7651; 3807.1; 2320
shall come to pass by the eleventh year, on the seventh of the first month [Nisan];

   1961, 8804; 1697; 3068   413; 2967.1; 559, 8800
the Word of God shall have come to Mine saying:

30:21   1121   120   (853; 2220; 6546 (w/o marks) or 6547; 1886.3; 4428; 4714; I; 7665, 8804)...
"Son of Man [Jesus]; I have broken the arm of its leader (who is also) the ruler

   cont.   2050.1; 2009   3808; it (fem.); 2280, 8795 or 8804   5414, 8800   7499 plur.
of Egypt. Thus, behold! It has not (yet) been bandaged to grant healings (any-

   7760, 8800; 2848 sing; 2280, 8800; 1886.3   2388, 8800; 1886.3
time soon). Casting a splint wrapping on it (will also hinder) it to be strong enough

   8610, 8800   2719 sing.
to take hold of a destructive weapon."

30:22   3807.1; 3651   3541   (he; 559, 8804)...   cont.   136   3068 or 3069
For certain; this is what he [Jesus] had relayed; "The Lord is Yahweh."

   2005; 2967.1   413; 6546 w/o marks or 6547; 1886.3   4428; 4714   (below)
Behold Me going against its leader (who shall also be) the ruler of Egypt, when I

   2050.1; I; 7665, 8804; 853; 2220; 2050.2   853; 1886.1; 2389; 1886.3   (2050.1; 853; 7665, 8737)...
have destroyed his forces that were its (nation's) strength, which was causing (all of)

   cont.   2050.1; I; 5307, 8689; 853; 2719 sing.   (4480 prefix; 3027)
the destruction. Thus, when I have caused the destructive weapon to fall out of his

30:23*   cont.   2050.2; 2050.1; I; 6327, 8689; 853; 4714   871.1; 1471 plur.   (below)
control, * after I had caused the Egyptians to scatter into the foreign nations, or had

30:24*   2050.1; 2219, 8765; 3963.1   871.1; 776 plur.   (2050.1; I; 2388, 8765; 853; 2220 plur., possv.)...
dispersed them throughout (other) regions,* I then shall have strengthened the forces

          cont.   4428 sing.; 894 (Iraq & Syria)   2050.1; I or mine; 5414, 8804   (853; 2719 sing.; 2967.1)…
of the Royal Leader of Babylon, after Mine shall have delivered a destructive weapon

          cont.   871.1; 3027; 2050.2
of Mine into his hand.

        2050.1; I; 7665, 8804   853; 2220 plur.; 6546 (w/o marks) or 6547; 1886.3; 2050.1; he; 5008, 8804
Once I have destroyed the forces of its leader, and he shall have groaned over

     5009 plur.   2491; 3807.1; 6440; 2050.2   2050.1; I; 2388, 8689   853; 2220 plur.
30:25* the cries of the slain in his presence, * I, indeed, shall have strengthened the forces

     (4428; 894 (Iraq & Syria); 2050.1; 2220; 6546 (w/o marks) or 6547; 1886.3; 5307, 8799; 2050.1; they or theirs; 3045, 8804)…
of the Royal Leader of Babylon, while the forces of its leader shall fall because theirs

        cont.   3588; 589; 3068 or 3069
had (once) known that I (Yahweh) am God.

     871.1; I or mine; 5414, 8804 (or 5414, 8800)   2719 sing.; 2967.1   871.1; 3027 sing.
And when Mine shall have put the destructive weapon of Mine into the hand of

     4428; 894 (Iraq & Syria)   2050.1; 5186 (spread out), 8804; 853; 1886.3   413; 776 sing.
the Royal Leader of Babylon, and it shall have exploded upon the (annexed) land

     4714   2050.1; I; 6327, 8689   853; 4714 plur.   871.1; 1471 plur.   (below)
30:26* of Egypt * after I had scattered the Egyptians throughout the foreign nations, or had

     2050.1; I; 2219, 8765; 853; 3963.1; 871.1; 776   2050.1; they; 3045, 8804; 3588
dispersed them into the (other) regions [to safe havens]; it's because they knew that

     589; 3068 or 3069
I (Yahweh) am God.

Ezekiel 31

     2050.1; it or this; 1961, 8799   871.1; 259; 6240   8141   871.1; 7992; 871.1; 259; 3807.1; 2320
31:1   Thus, this shall occur by the eleventh year, on the first (day) of the third month

     [deduced from Ez. 33:21 & 40:1]   (1961, 8804; 1697; 3068 or 3069)…
[after Jerusalem had been stricken by Jesus and his militia]. The Word of God shall

     cont.   413; 2967.1   559, 8800
have come to Mine, saying:

31:2

¹¹²¹ ¹²⁰ ^{559, 8798; 413; 6546 (w/o marks) or 6547; 1883.1} ^{(4428; 4714)...}

"Son of Man [Jesus]; relay this (that follows) to its leader, (who is also) the ruler of

cont.

Egypt [i.e., to Israel's imposter Jesus, who is also referred to throughout Ezekiel as

^{2050.1; 413; 1995 sing.; 2050.2}

the false prophet of Nazareth and Israel's god]; and, also, (convey this) to his army."

31:3*

^{413; 4310} ^{you; 1819, 8804} ^{871.1; 1433; 3509.2} ²⁰⁰⁹ ⁸⁰⁴

"To whom have you compared yourself in greatness? *Behold Assyria [Turkey,

Syria, Iraq and Iran], 24 (and contemplate on the following allegory):"

^{730 sing.} ^{871.1; 3844} ^{3303; 6057 sing} ^{2050.1; 2793 sing.} ^{6751, 8688}

"The cedar in Lebanon has a beautiful branch and a forest providing a shade

^{2050.1; 1362 sing.; 6967 sing.} ^{2050.1; 996} ^{5688 plur.} ^{1961, 8804}

because (it has) a lofty height; yet, (it) is amongst thick foliages that have existed

31:4*

^{6788; 2050.2} ⁴³²⁵ ^{they; 1431, 8765; 2050.2} ⁸⁴¹⁵ ^(below)

(beneath) its treetops. * Water has kept them growing deep (into the ground), lifting

^{7311, 8790; 2050.2; 854; 5104; 1886.3} ^{it; 1980, 8802; 5439} ^{4302; 1886.3} ^(below)

it high near its rivers; and, also, it is circulating about its planting ground because of

^{2050.1; 853; 8585; 1886.3} ^{7971, 8765; it} ⁴¹³ ^{3605; 6086 plur.} ^{1886.1; 7704}

its irrigation trenches that have kept sending it out to all the trees of the cultivated

31:5*

^{cont.} ^{5921; 3651; 1361, 8804; 6967; 2050.2} ^{4480 prefix; 3605; 6086; 1886.1; 7704} ^(below)

land. * In fact, its height has risen up above all of the cultivated land's trees, and its

^{2050.1; 7235, 8799; 5634 plur. (boughs); 2050.2} ^{2050.1; 748, 8799} ^(below)

main branches will (continue to) grow out and lengthen because of the abundant

31:6*

^{2050.1; 6288; 2050.2; 4480; 4325; 7227 plur.; they; 7971, 8763} ^{871.1; 5589 plur.; 2050.2; they; 7077, 8765; 3605; 5775 plur.}

waters. (As) its branches were growing, * in its boughs nested all the (various) birds

^{1886.1; 8064} ^{2050.1; 8478} ^{6288 plur.; 2050.2} ^{they; 3205, 8804; 3605; 2416 plur.; 1886.1; 7704}

of the sky, and beneath its branches, all (variations) of the land animals bore their

cont.

young."

31:7*

^{2050.1; 871.1; 6738; 2050.2} ^{3427, 8804} ³⁶⁰⁵ ^{1471 plur.; 7227} ^(below)

"Also in its shade, dwelled each (branch) of the numerous gentiles * because it

19

_{2050.1; it; 3302, 8799; 871.1; 1433; 2050.2; 871.1; 753; 1808; 2050.2   3588; it; 1961, 8804; 8328; 2050.2}

is lovely, on account of the majestic length of its branches'. Thus, its root has existed

_{413   4325; 7227 plur.   730 plur.   (3808; 6004, 8804; it; 871.1; 1588 possv.; their; 430)…}

31:8*   *because of the abundant waters. * The cedars in their god's garden has not been*

_{cont.   1265 plur.   3808; 1819, 8804   413; 5589; 2050.2   (below)}

equal to it. The cypresses have not compared to its branches; nor have its chest-

_{2050.1; 6196; 3808; 1961, 8804; 6288; 2050.2; 3605; 6086; 871.1; 1588 sing.; their; 430   3808; 1819, 8804; 413; 2050.2}

nut trees' boughs. Every tree in their god's garden has not compared to it, or to

_{3308; 2050.2}

its beauty."

_{3303; I; 6213, 8804, 2050.2   871.1; 7230; 1808; 2050.2   (below)}

31:9   "*I (Yahweh) made it beautiful with its abundant branches, and all of the trees of*

_{2050.1; 7065, 8762; it; 3605; 6086; 5731; 834; 871.1; 1588; 1886.1; 430}

the 'Eden' that is at their god's garden, envy it."

_{3807.1; 3651   (3541; he; 559, 8804)…   cont.   136   3068 or 3069}

31:10   *Assuredly, this is what he* [Jesus] *had relayed;* "*The Lord is Yahweh.*"

_{3282   834   his; 1361; 6967}

Hence, [regarding their god, the imposter Jesus] *because of his exalted stature,*

_{2050.1; I; 5414, 8799   per Ez. 31:11-12   6788 (bough); 2050.2   (below)}

I shall, indeed, assign (him and) *his highest branch, as well as the branches whose*

_{413; 996; 5688; 2050.1; 731; 3824; 2050.2; 871.1; 1363; 2050.2   per Ez. 31:14 & 16; Ez. 32:18, 23, 25, 26, 29, 30}

heart he lifted by his loftiness, to (be) *amongst* (those going down to the Pit [Hell]),

_{2050.1; I; 5414, 8799; 2050.2   871.1; 3027   352 (not 410)   1471 plur.   6213, 8800; 2050.2   (below)}

31:11* **after I deliver him into the hand* of the *mighty one's nations to deal with him. I shall*

_{I; 6213, 8799   3807.1; 2050.2   871.1; his; 7562   I; 1644, 8765; 2050.2}

execute (this) *against him because of his wickedness.* (After) *I have cast him out,*

_{2050.1; 3772, 8799, 2050.1; 2114, 8801   6184 possv.; 1471 plur.   (2050.1; below)}

31:12* **and the alienated ones shall cut him off, the foreign nations' oppressors shall then*

_{5203, 8799; 2050.2}

forsake him.

        413; 1886.1; 2022 plur.   2050.1, 871.1, 3605; 1516 plur.   (they; 5307, 8804; 1808 plur.; 2050.2)

Towards the mountains and upon all the valleys, his branches shall have fallen,

    2050.1; 7665, 8735; 6288 plur. (boughs); 2050.2   871.1, 3605; 650; 1886.1; 776

and his main branches will be destroyed nearby each waterway of the region.

    2050.1; they; 3381, 8799   4480 prefix; 6738 (shade); 2050.2   2050.1; 3605; 5971 plur., possv.; 1886.1; 776

When they depart, away from his [supposed] protection, then all the nations of the

      cont. 2050.1; they; 5203, 8799; 2050.2   5921; 4658; 2050.2   they; 7931, 8799; 3605; 5775; 1886.1; 8064 plur.

31:13* world shall also forsake him. * Upon his carcass, each bird of the skies shall settle,

        2050.1; 413; 6288 plur.; 2050.2   (they; 1961, 8804; 3605; 2416 plur.; 1886.1; 7704)...

and amongst his (fallen) branches, will be all the land creatures that shall have

      cont.   3807.1; 4616   per Ez. 32:3-6, 33:27, 34:5, & 39:17-20 (834; 3808; they or theirs; 1361, 8799; 2050.2)

31:14* remained * for the purpose of (devouring the remains), so that theirs will no (longer)

       cont.   871.1; 6967; 3963.1

exalt him with their (lofty) stature.

   3605; 6086 plur.   4325 plur.   3808; 2050.1; they; 5414, 8799   853 or 854; 6788; 3963.1

All the trees and bodies of water will, thus, not provide for their highest branch

        413; 996; 5688 plur.   2050.1; 3808; they or theirs; 5975, 8799   (below)

(when they are bound) in the midst of fetters, nor shall theirs stand before their male

352; 1992 (or 451; 3963.1); 871.1; 1363; 3963.1 per Ez.12:10-11; 12: 22-23; & 22:8-12 (1st book) (below)

'lamb', in their loftiness [who had allegedly died for their sins]; or are going to have

    3605; 8354, 8802; 4325 plur., possv.; 3588; 3605; 3963.1   they; 5414, 8738

anymore drinks of water, since all of them [i.e., their souls] shall have been delivered

    per Ez. 31:15 & 31:17; 3807.1; 4194; 413; 776; 8482   871.1; 8432   1121 plur.; 120 (below)

to (Sheol,) the place under the ground at death, in the midst of the humans that are

  413; 3381, 8802   953 sing.

going down to the Pit [Hell]. (N:4)

          3541; 559, 8804; 136; 3068

31:15   "This is what Lord Yahweh said:"

    871.1; 3117   3381, 8800; him or his   7585; 1886.3

"On the day of his (people) going down to Sheol, therein [where the souls of the

                                                                   (I; 56, 8689)...

dead remain until their sentencing on the Day of Judgment], (N:4 cont.) I shall have

<u>caused grief</u> after <u>Mine have covered the depth of the earth over him</u>. <u>Also, I shall</u>

<u>hold back</u> <u>its water sources</u>, <u>so that the abundant waters will be stopped</u>. <u>When</u>

<u>I cause Lebanon to mourn over him</u>, <u>and all of the cultivated land's trees</u> <u>to collapse</u>

31:16* *<u>from the loud sound</u> during <u>his fall</u>, <u>I shall have caused the (remaining) gentiles to</u>

<u>tremble</u>. And after <u>I have caused him to descend</u> to <u>their Sheol</u>, to be <u>with theirs</u>

<u>going down to the Pit [of Hell]</u>, <u>they, then, shall repent</u> <u>in the place beneath the</u>

<u>ground</u>. (N:4 cont.) For <u>all of the trees of Eden</u> were for <u>the choicest and morally best</u>

<u>of Lebanon</u>, as well as <u>all the water they were drinking</u>."

31:17 "<u>Those also</u> <u>with him</u> <u>that shall have descended down to</u> <u>their Sheol</u> <u>for the ones</u>

<u>slain (by) the destructive weapon</u>, <u>and for his armed force</u>, will be <u>theirs who shall</u>

<u>have dwelled</u> <u>within his protection</u>, <u>in the midst</u> of <u>the foreign nations</u>."

(N:4)   In the Old Testament (Tanakh), there are 65 occurrences of the single, Divine Hebrew word, "Sheol" (Strong's Hebrew Concordance # 7585). [25] However, the translations into English range from simply "grave" in 31 occurrences, to "Hell," in another 31 instances. [26] Yet, in 4 of the places where "Hell" was construed, it indicates "grave" in the margins. Additionally, there are 3 places where "Sheol" was translated to "Pit," but in these 3 instances, it is clear that "grave" is implied. [27] Thus, the predominant Hebrew understanding of the word "Sheol" was "grave," indicating death.

Other sightings of the Hebrew word "Sheol" can be found in several Dead Sea Scroll documents, including 1QMIV, 1QHIV, and 4Q184 fragment 1. Most of these Dead Sea Scroll occurrences of the Hebrew word Sheol were translated to indicate "Hell" or an eternal fire. [28] Even more complicated is the fact that the Greeks translated "Sheol" as "Hades," and they used this translation in various places of the New Testament to coincide with their previous understanding of the underworld from Greek mythology. [29] There are 11 occurrences of "Hades" in the New Testament. [30]

These various translated words from the single, Hebrew word "Sheol," have vastly different meanings, and therefore, it is critical to understand what the actual Hebrew word (Sheol) represents. In E. W. Bullinger's studies found in his book entitled *Sheol and Hades* (ISBN: 978-1-78364-553-4), the actual word denotes a "state of death" beneath the ground, for a duration of time until "resurrection" occurs, which, according to Hosea 13-14, Psalms 16:10, and Acts 2:27, 2:31 & 13:35, is the only exit out of Sheol. Bullinger's understanding of Sheol is the same as described in Ezekiel 31:14 and 31:17, where Sheol is "the place under the ground at death," wherein each soul awaits its resurrection and sentencing on the Day of Judgment. According to the uncovered Ezekiel prophesies in this section, those in Sheol to be shunned by God for their unholy, abominable ways, and for worshiping someone other than Him, and not praying solely in His Name, will be sent down to the Pit of Hell, while the righteous people of God will have an eternally, blissful life in God's presence after being resurrected out of their Sheol for the righteous. This understanding of Sheol also appears to be synonymous with the meaning of the Arabic word "Barzakh," [31] which, in Islam, is a phase (beneath the ground) between death and resurrection, and is somewhat analogous with the Roman Catholic word "Purgatory," [32] which represents a state after death, of purification prior to entering Heaven (before resurrection).

31:18 [Imposter Jesus:] "(Again,) to whom have you compared to in this manner; in glory and in greatness, when you and the trees of Eden shall have been brought down? At the lowest depth beneath the ground, with the trees of Eden, you shall lie

         871.1; 8432; 6189; you; 7901, 8799   854; 2491, plur., possv.; 2719 sing.

in the midst of the uncircumcised ^(N:5) with the ones slain (by) the destructive weapon."

     1931   6546 (w/o marks) or 6547; 1886.3; 2050.1; 3605; its; 1995   (below)

This (unfortunately, will be the fate of) its leader and its entire multitude. (For) it

        it; 5002, 8803   136   3068 or 3069

was (clearly) stated in the Oracles; "*The Lord is Yahweh*."

Ezekiel 32

    (2050.1; it; 1961, 8799; 871.1; 8147; 6240; 1886.3; 8141; 871.1; 8147; 6240; 2320; 871.1; 259; 3807.1; 2320)...

32:1   This (that follows) shall, indeed, come to pass in the twelfth year [after Jerusalem

     [deduced from Ez. 33:21 & 40:1]   cont.

had been stricken by Jesus and his army], by the first of the twelfth month [Adar].

    1961, 8804; 1697; 3069 (or 3068)   413; 2967.1 559, 8800   1121; 120   5375, 8798

32:2*   The Word of God shall have come to Mine, saying;* "Son of Man [Jesus], carry

    7015 sing.; 5921; 6546 (w/o marks) or 6547; 1883.1; 4427 or 4428 sing.   4714 (below)

the (following) lamentation over to its leader, (who is also) the ruler of Egypt, which

  2050.1; 559, 8804   413; 2050.2

you had (formerly) relayed concerning him:"

    (3715; 1471; you; 1819, 8738)...   cont.

"You [imposter Jesus] have been compared to a young lion (among) the gentiles,

2050.1; 859   3509.3; 8577 871.1; 3220 plur. 2050.1; you; 1518, 8799   871.1; 5104 plur.; 3509.2

but you are like a monster in the seas when you upsurge (the water) in your rivers,

2050.1; you; 1804, 8799   4325 plur. 871.1; 7272 plur. per Ez. 32; 13 (below)

but you stir up (their) water sources by the feet (of your people and livestock), and

2050.1; you 7515, 8799 5104 plur.; 3963.1 see (N:28) in 1st book about Israel contaminating Palestinians' water

you muddy up their streams [polluting the exiled Arab's water supply]."

    (3541; he; 559, 8804)... cont.   136   3068 or 3069

32:3   "This is what he [Jesus] had relayed; '*The Lord is Yahweh*.'"

     2050.1; I; 6566, 8804   5921; 3509.2; 853; 7568; 2967.1   871.1; 6951 sing.

"Thus, I shall have spread out My net over you, by (way of) the assemblage of

                    5971; 7227; 3963.1   2050.1; they; 5927, 8689; 3509.2   871.1; 2764; 2967.1
          their Commander's people.   For they shall have caused you to ascend into My trap,

                 2050.1; I; 5203, 8804; 3509.2   871.1; 776 sing.   (5921; 6440 (face); 7704 sing.; I; 2904, 8686; 3509.2)
32:4*   *and then I shall have cast you onto the ground. I shall hurl you upon the surface

                    cont.   (2050.1; I; 7932, 8689; 5921; 3509.2; 3605; 5775 sing.; 1886.1; 8064 plur.)...
          of the cultivated land, and shall have caused each bird of the skies to settle upon

                cont.   2050.1; I; 7646, 8689; 4480; 4480; 3509.2; 2416 plur.; 3605; 776 sing.
          you. I shall have also caused all the land animals from amongst you to be full,

                 2050.1; I; 5414, 8804; 853; 1320; 3509.2   5921; 1886.1; 2022 plur.   2050.1; I; 4390, 8765   1886.1; 1516 plur.
32:5*   *after I have cast your flesh upon the mountains, and have filled the valleys with

                7419; 3509.2   2050.1; I; 8248, 8689   (776; 6824; 3509.2; 4480; 1818; 3509.2)...
32:6*   your remains. *Furthermore, I shall have moistened the ground from your oozing

                cont.   413   1886.1; 2022 plur.   2050.1; 650 plur.   (they or these; 4390, 8735; 4480; 4480; 3509.2)...
          blood. Upon the mountains and ravines, these (creatures) from amongst you shall

                cont.
          be satiated."

                                  2050.1; I; 3680, 8765; 871.1; 3518, 8763; 3509.2; 8064 plur.
32:7   "When I have covered over the sky regions (with the smoke cloud) after having

                   cont.   2050.1; I; 6937, 8689; 853; 3556; 1992   (8121; 871.1; 6051; I; 3680, 8762)...
          quenched yours, and I have darkened its stars, I shall (also) cover the sun with the

                 cont.   2050.1; 3394 sing.   3808; 215, 8686; it; 216   (below)
32:8*   cloud, and the moon shall not give off its (reflected) light. *I shall cause all of the

          3605; 3974; 216; 8064; I; 6937, 8686; 3963.1   5921; 3509.2   2050.1; I; 5414, 8804   2822   (5921; 776; 3509.2)
          heavens' shining light to dim above you, once I have caused darkness upon your

               cont.
          land."

                         it; 5002, 8803   136   3068 or 3069
          "It was (clearly) stated in the Oracles; 'The Lord is Yahweh.'"

                   2050.1; I; 3707, 8689   3820 sing.; 7227; 5971   (871.1; I; 935, 8687; 7667; 3509.2)...
32:9   "Thus, I shall have troubled many people's heart after I have caused your de-

                cont.   871.1; 1471 plur.   5921; 776 plur.   834   (3808; you or yours; 3045, 8804; 3963.1)
          struction, along with the gentiles on the lands where yours lacked the knowledge

25

32:10* <u>of these</u> (others). *<u>So after Mine, who are against you, have caused the desolation,</u>

<u>numerous people</u> <u>and their leaders</u> <u>shall tremble in horror over you,</u> <u>because I shall</u>

<u>have caused the destructive weapon of Mine to fly</u> <u>above, before them.</u> When they

<u>shall have trembled</u> <u>during their moment</u> (of fear), <u>Jesus</u> shall (only) be <u>liable for his</u>

<u>own life</u> <u>on the day</u> of <u>your downfall.</u>"

32:11 <u>"Assuredly,</u> <u>this is what he</u> [Jesus] <u>had relayed</u>; '<u>The Lord</u> is <u>Yahweh</u>.' "

"<u>A destructive weapon</u> of <u>the Royal Leader</u> of <u>Babylon</u> [Iraq, Syria, and the other

32:12* allies] <u>shall target you!</u> * <u>By (way of their) mighty warriors' destructive weapons,</u> <u>I</u>

<u>shall cause your army (and) all of the foreign nations' oppressors to fall!</u>"

<u>Consequently, they shall have destroyed</u> <u>the arrogance</u> in <u>Egypt,</u> <u>after all of its</u>

32:13* <u>multitude have been annihilated.</u> *<u>I, also, shall have caused the destruction</u> of <u>all of</u>

<u>the livestock</u> <u>from beside</u> <u>the abundant water sources,</u> <u>and never again shall the foot</u>

32:14* <u>of man muddy them up</u>; <u>nor shall the hooves of the livestock muddy them.</u> * <u>Then,</u>

<u>at that time, I shall cause the waterways of these</u> (oppressors) <u>to descend,</u> <u>and shall</u>

<u>make their rivers flow like oil.</u>

it; 5002, 8803   136   3068 or 3069
It was (clearly) stated in the Oracles; "<u>*The Lord is Yahweh*</u>."

871.1; I; 5414, 8800 or 8804   853; 776 sing.   4714   8077   2050.1; it; 8074, 8737; 776 sing.

32:15   When I have made the land of Egypt desolate and the country becomes destitute

4480; it; 4393   871.1; I; 5221, 8687 or 8804   853; 3605; 871.1; they; 3427, 8802
of all that was therein, and when I have struck down everywhere they were dwelling;

871.1; 1886.3   2050.1; they; 3045, 8804   3588   589; 3068 or 3069
(it's) because theirs, indeed, had (once) known that I (Yahweh) am God.

7015; 1931 (it)   2050.1; they; 6969, 8790; 1886.3   (1323; 1886.1; 1471 plur.; they; 6969, 8787)

32:16   There will be lamentation when they have deeply mourned. The gentiles' women

cont.   853; 1886.3; 5921; 4714   (2050.1; 5921; 3605; 1995; 1886.3)...
shall wail over (the destruction of) their (annexed) Egypt, and over (the deaths of) all

cont.   it; 5002, 8803   136   3068 or 3069
their multitude.   (Again,) it was stated in the Oracles; "<u>*The Lord is Yahweh*</u>!"

2050.1; it or this; 1961, 8799   871.1; 8147; 6240   8141

32:17   This (that follows) shall also come to pass in the twelfth year [after Jerusalem

[deduced from Ez. 33:21 & 40:1]   871.1; 2568; 6240   3807.1; 2320
had been stricken by Jesus and his militia], by the fifteenth of the (same) month.

1961, 8804; 1697; 3069   413; 2967.1   559, 8800
The Word of God shall have come to Mine, saying:

1121   120   per Ez. 30:3   5091, 8798; 5921   1995 masc.; 4714

32:18   "Son of Man [Jesus]; (On the Day of Woe) only mourn over Egypt's army men

(2050.1; 3381, 8685; 1992; 853; 1886.3; 2050.1; 1323; 1471; 117; 413; 776; 8482 plur.; 853; 3381, 8802; 953 sing.)...
and their noble gentile women that these (oppressors) going down to the Pit had

cont.   4480; 4310   you or yours; 5276, 8804
32:19* caused to descend beneath the ground. * For whom have yours been pleasing?

(fem. you; 3381, 8804 or 8798)   2050.1; 7901, 8689   854   (below)
(Your Sistren) shall have descended also, and shall have been laid amongst their

27

　　　　　　　　　　6189 masc.; 3963.1　　　　　　871.1; 8432　　2491 sing.　　　　　2719 sing.; 5307, 8799
32:20*　uncircumcised men　(N:5 cont.)　*amidst the slain that shall fall (by) the destructive

　　　　cont.
　　　weapon."

　　　　　　　　　　　　2719 sing.　　　　　　5414, 8738　　　4901; 2050.2　　　　　　　　　　(below)
　　　"The destructive weapon has been given its extension (long enough).　These

　　　　　　853; fem.; 2050.1; 3605; 1995 masc.; 1886.3　　they; 1696, 8762　　(3807.1; 2050.2; 413; 2967.1; 1368; their)…
32:21*　(women) and all of their multitude*that would call out to him, their mighty one, will

　　　　cont.　　　　　　　4480; 8432　　　　7585　　　　　　854; 5826, 8802; 2050.2
　　　(call out) to Me (Yahweh) from the midst of Sheol, with those that were helping him,

　　　　they; 3381, 8804　　　　they; 7901, 8804　　　　1886.1; 6189 plur. (having foreskin)　(below)
　　　who shall have descended and been laid amongst the uncircumcised (men) slain

　　　　　　　2491; 2719 sing.　　　　　　8033　　　804　　　　　　　　　　　(below)
32:22*　(via) the destructive weapon.　*Where Assyria was (once located), will also be the

　　　　　　2050.1; 3605; it; 6951 plur.; 5439 plur.; 2050.2; 6913 plur.; his　　　3605; 3963.1; 2491 plur.; 5307, 8802
　　　grave sites of all its congregation that were his neighbors.　All of theirs that are going

　　　　cont.　　　　　　　　　871.1; 2719 sing.　　　　　　　　(834; they or the ones; 5414, 8738)…
32:23*　to fall down dead by the destructive weapon are *the ones who shall have been

　　　　cont.　　　6913 plur.　　　　　　1886.3; 871.1; 3411 plur.　　　　　953 sing.
　　　placed at the grave sites of theirs (who will be) within the far ends of the Pit."

　　　　　　　　　　2050.1; it; 1961; 8799　　　　　　　6951; 1886.3 (fem.); 5439 plur.; 6913 sing; 1886.3
　　　"When this (prophesy) occurs, the burial site of their congregation that are the

　　　　cont.　　　　　　　　　　　　　　　　　　　　　　　3605; 3963.1　　　(below)
　　　neighbors [of Israel and overthrown Egypt] shall include all of theirs that are going

　　2491; 3963.1; 5307, 8802; 3963.1　　871.1; 2719　　834　they; 5414, 8804　2851　　871.1; 776
　　to fall down dead by the destructive weapon, who had caused terror in the land of

　　　　2416; 3963.1　　8033　　5867
32:24*　those living*where Elam 33 was [i.e., in a western and southwestern area of Iran, and

　　　　　　　　　　　　　　　　　　(2050.1; 3605; 1886.3; 1995 sing.; 5439 plur.; 6900; 1886.3)…
　　　a portion of southern Iraq].　Also, the burial place of all its (congregation's) army that

　　　　cont.　　　　　　　　　　　　　　　　　　　(3605; 3963.1; 2491; 3963.1; 5307, 8802; 3963.1)
　　　are neighbors [of Israel and Egypt], shall include all of theirs that are going to fall

    cont.   871.1; 2719   834 they; 3381, 8804   6189 (below)
down dead by the destructive weapon, who shall have descended uncircumcised to

   413; 776; 8482 plur.   834 5414, 8804; 2851; 3963.1 871.1; 776 2416; 3963.1
the place beneath the ground, and who had caused terror in the land of those living."

   2050.1; they; 5375, 8799   3639; 3963.1 (854; they or those; 3381, 8802)...
"Thus, they will bear the penalty of their own disgrace, with those that are going

  cont. 953 sing. 871.1; 8432 2491; 3963.1 5414, 8804; 4904 (below)
32:25* down to the Pit; *amidst their dead that had (casket) bedding placed for theirs, in

   3807.1; 1886.3; 871.1; 3605; 1995; 1886.3; 5439; 2050.2; 6913; 1886.3; 3605; 3963.1; 6189 (below)
the grave(s) of all its army of uncircumcised (men) that were his neighbor(s) slain

   2491; 2719   3588; they 5414, 8804 2851; 3963.1 871.1; 776 (2416; 3963.1)
(by) a destructive weapon. Because they had caused terror in the land of those

  cont. 2050.1; they; 5375, 8799   3639; 3963.1 (854; they; 3381, 8802)...
living, they, indeed, will bear the penalty of their own disgrace, with those that are

  cont. 953 871.1; 8432 2491; 3963.1 they; 5414, 8738 8033
32:26* going down to the Pit, in the midst of their dead that shall have been placed *where

  (4902; 8422 (Tbil or Tubal); 2050.1; 3605; 1995; 1886.3; 5439; 2050.2; 6913 plur.; 1886.3)... cont.
the graves of all its Meshech [Moscow] and Tbil [Tbilisi] army will be, that were

  cont.
his (far north) neighbors."

  Tubal [34] or Tbil is a region lying southeast of the Black Sea, which could include north east Turkey and/or Georgia. We believe that in these particular prophesies, however, that Tubal or Tbil is explicitly in reference to Georgia's capital, Tbilisi.

   3605; 3963.1; 6189 plur.; 3963.1   2490, 8790; 2719
"Each of these uncircumcised (men) shall have been killed (by) the destructive

  cont. 3588; they; 5414, 8804; 2851; 3963.1 871.1; 776 sing. (2416 plur.; 3963.1; 2050.1; 3808; 7901, 8799)
32:27* weapon because they had caused terror in the land of the ones living *that would

  cont. 854; 1368 (5307, 8802; 4480; 6189 plur.)...
not lodge amongst the mighty warrior(s) of uncircumcised (men) that were going to

29

| cont. | 834 | 3381; 8804 | 7585 | 871.1; 3627; 4421; 3963.1 |

fall, who shall have descended to Sheol by means of their weapons of war." (N:5 cont.)

| 2050.1; they; 5414, 8804 | 853; 2719 plur.; 3963.1 | (8478; 7218 plur.; 1992)... |

"Since they had set off their destructive weapons under (the commands of) their

| cont. | 2050.1; they; 1961, 8799; 5771; 3963.1 | 5921; 6106 plur.; 3963.1 (below) |

top leaders, they, indeed, will be liable for their sinfulness during their lives. Be-

| 3588 | 2851; 1368 | 871.1; 776 | 2416; 3963.1 (below) |

32:28* **cause of the mighty warriors' terrorization throughout the land of those living,** *yours

| 2050.1; 859 | 871.1; 8432 | 6189 | (you; 7665, 8799)... |

shall, consequently, be in the midst of the uncircumcised (men) that you [Jesus] must

| cont. | 2050.1; you or yours; 7901, 8799; 854, 2491; 2719 |

destroy. Thus, yours shall lie amongst (those) slain (by) the destructive weapon,

| 8033 | 123 |

32:29* ***where Edom**[35] **was [i.e., in the southern region of Israel and Jordan that's south of**

| 4428; 1886.3; 2050.1; 3605; it; 5387; 1886.3; 834 (below) |

the Dead Sea to the Gulf of Aqaba]. Its rulers and all of its leaders, who had been

| 5414, 8738 | 871.1; 1369; 3963.1 | (854; 2491; 2719)... |

appointed because of their power, will be among (those) slain (by) the destructive

| cont. | 1992 | 854; 6189 | (they; 7901, 8799; 2050.1; 854; 3381, 8802)... |

weapon. They will be with the uncircumcised (men) that will also lay with those

| cont. | 953 | 8033; 5257; 6828; 3605; 3963.1 (below) |

32:30* **that are going down to the Pit;** ***where all their leaders of the north will be, and also**

| 2050.1; 3605; 6722 plur. | 834 (below) |

all of the Sidonians[36] **[i.e., those located in the vicinity of Saida, Lebanon], who shall**

| 3381, 8804 | 854 | 2491 | 871.1; 2851; 3963.1 | (4480; 1369; 3963.1)... |

have gone down with the slain, because of them (causing) terror on account of their

| cont. | 954, 8802; 3963.1; 2050.1; they; 7901, 8799 (below) |

power. They were acting shamefully, so they shall lie amongst the uncircumcised

| 6189; 854; 2491; 2719 | 2050.1; they; 5375, 8799 (below) |

(men) killed (by) the destructive weapon. Thus, they will bear the penalty of their

| 3639; 3963.1 | 854 | 3381, 8802 | 953 sing. |

own disgrace, along with those that are going down to the Pit."

| | 853; 3963.1 | he; 7200, 8799; 6546 (or 6547) | 2050.1; he; 5162, 8804 (w/o marks or 8738) (below) |

32:31   "Their Pharaoh(-like) leader shall (eventually) realize, after he has grieved over

5921; 3605; 1995; 1886.3; 2491; 2719   (6544 or 6546); 2050.1; 3605; 2428; 2050.2)...

all of their multitude slain (by) the destructive weapon, and also (over) all of his aveng-

cont.   it; 5002, 8803   136   3068 or 3069   (below)

32:32* ing army, that it was (clearly) stated in the Oracles; '*The Lord* is *Yahweh*.'   *Thus,

3588; I; 5414, 8804   853; 2851; 2050.2   871.1; 776   2416; 3963.1   (below)

I shall have caused his terror, in the land of the ones to live.   Then, afterwards, the

(2050.1; he; 7901, 8717; 871.1; 8432; 6189 plur.; 854; 2491; 2719; 6546 (or 6547); 2050.1; 3605; 1995; 1886.3)...

Pharaoh(-like) leader, and all of their multitude, will be laid in the midst of the un-

cont.

circumcised (N:5 cont.) with those killed by the destructive weapon."

5002, 8803   136   3068 or 3069

It was (clearly) stated in the Oracles, "*The Lord* is *Yahweh*."

(N:5) Recall from Ezekiel 16:59-61 and Comment (N:32) in the 1st book of *Preserved for the End of Time* (p.134) that it is prophesied that anyone who breaks God's Covenant made with Abraham would be put to shame and despised, while those keeping God's Covenant would be His people. Thus, even up to today, God has required "every male child" believer in God to be circumcised as prescribed in Genesis 17:1-11.

Throughout Ezekiel chapter 32, God identifies the non-Jewish congregation serving the imposter Jesus, who shall, consequently, also be destroyed along with the prophesied Israelis via a destructive weapon, as being the gentiles, whose men are not practicing the Abrahamic ordinance of circumcision. At the time of this publication, amongst the three main monotheistic religions (Judaism, Christianity, and Islam), the only one that does not promote male circumcision is Christianity. The Abrahamic Covenant between God and His people, who are to devoutly obey God's Commandments and Ordinances, including the observance of male circumcision, was deemed unnecessary by Paul. In Galatians 5:6, Paul wrote, "For in Jesus Christ, neither circumcision, nor uncircumcision, count for anything." Hence, the male circumcision ordinance has not been observed by most of the Christian denominations.[38]

Ezekiel 33:25-33

33:1-20   [Relocated to Section 3, since it relates to the resurrected being judged]

33:21-22   [Relocated in this section preceding Ezekiel 30]

33:23-24   [Relocated to Section 5, since it relates to the Holy Land inheritance]

                              3807.1; 3651; 559, 8798; 413; 1992

33:25   [Jesus:] "<u>Rightly convey (the following) to these</u> [Israelis and gentiles serving the imposter Jesus]."

                3541; he; 559, 8804; 136; 3068 or 3069
      "<u>This is what Lord Yahweh said</u>:"

                    5921; 1818; 398, 8799   (2050.1, 5869, 3509.2 plur.; 5375, 8799; yours; 413; 1544)
    "<u>Yours shall devour (lives) by bloodshed</u>, <u>and shall lift up your eyes towards the</u>

        cont.   2050.1; 1818; 8210, 8799   2050.1; 776; yours; 3423, 8799   (below)
33:26* <u>crucifix(es)</u>. <u>Also, yours shall shed blood</u> <u>so that yours can possess the land</u> of *your

      5975 (A'mad; or 5975, 8804); 3509.2   5921   2719 sing.; 3509.2   (below)
    <u>(neighboring) A'madian(s)</u> [i.e., the Muslims] <u>with</u> <u>your destructive weapon(s)</u>. <u>Yours</u>

        yours; 6213, 8804   8441; 2050.1; 376; 853; 802; 7453; 2050.2; 2930, 8765   (below)
    <u>have committed abomination(s)</u>, <u>and have even defiled one's neighbor's wife</u>, <u>so</u>

          2050.1; 1886.1; 776; yours; 3423, 8799
    <u>that yours could take possession of (their) land</u>."

                    3541; you; 559, 8799   413; 1992
33:27   [Jesus:] "<u>You must (also) relay (the following)</u> <u>to them</u>:"

                3541; he; 559, 8804; 136; 3068 or 3069
      "<u>This is what Lord Yahweh said</u>:"

          2416; 589   518; 3808   (834)...
    "<u>I live on</u>, <u>whether or not</u> (yours live on). Those [followers of the imposter Jesus]

      cont.   871.1; 2723   they; 5307, 8799; 2719 sing.   (below)
    <u>who</u> are <u>within (Israel's) desolate areas</u>, <u>shall fall by a destructive weapon</u>, <u>and so</u>

      2050.1; 834   5921; 6440 (face)   1886.1; 7704   (3807.1; 2416; 1886.3; I; 5414, 8804; 2050.2)
    <u>shall those who</u> are <u>upon the surface</u> of <u>the cultivated land</u>. <u>I shall have given them</u>

32

<pre>   cont.   398, 8800; 2050.1   834   871.1; 4679 plur.   (below)</pre>
to its living creatures to devour. Then, those who are within the fortifications and

<pre>2050.1; 871.1; 4631 plur.   871.1; 1698; they; 4191, 8799</pre>
cave-like holes [bomb shelters and reinforced buildings] (N:6) shall die by pestilence."

<pre>   2050.1; I; 5414, 8804; 853   1886.1; 776   8077   2050.1; 4923   (below)</pre>
33:28   "When I (Yahweh) have made the country desolate and devastated, and the pride

<pre>   2050.1; 7673, 8738; 1347; 5797; 1886.3   2050.1; they; 8074, 8804; 2022; 3478</pre>
of its power has been ceased; and when the mountains of Israel have become deso-

<pre>   cont.   4480; 369; 5674; 8802</pre>
lated, of which none shall be passing through –"

<pre>   2050.1; 3045, 8799 or 8804   3588   589; 3068 or 3069   871.1; I; 5414, 8800 or 8804   853; 1886.1; 776</pre>
33:29   "Then they shall know that I am Yahweh; in that I shall have made the country

<pre>   8077   2050.1; 4923   5921   3605; 8441; 3963.1   834   (they; 6213, 8804)...</pre>
desolate and devastated because of all their abominations, which they shall have

<pre> cont.</pre>
committed."

(N:6) According to Ezekiel 33:27-29, after the prophesied areas of Israel are destroyed, many of the temporary survivors of Israel's catastrophic destruction, who shall have been taking cover within their bomb shelters, shall eventually die of pestilence from the aftermath. This prophesy is even more plausible during today's generation than it would have been during ancient times. In 1951, Israel's Civil Defense Law made it mandatory for all homes, residential buildings, businesses, government buildings, schools, and industries to have bomb shelters or to be constructed with reinforced concrete walls and blast-proof windows aimed at minimizing casualties from enemy attacks or defensive counter-attacks.[39] The homes or residential buildings that could not solely meet this requirement could jointly utilize a bomb shelter made available for their residents. Israel's exiled Arab neighbors, on the other hand, have no bomb shelters and no reinforced buildings to take cover in when Israel launches hundreds of airstrikes at a time upon the civilians of Gaza, the West Bank, and the other Arab territories that Israel has brutally attacked or retaliated against throughout the 20th and 21st centuries. [40]

<pre>   2050.1; 859   1121 sing.   120   1121 plur.   5971; 3509.2</pre>
33:30   [Jesus:] "Since you are a descendant of Adam, the descendants of your people

                they;1696, 8737   871.1; 3509.2   681 1886.1; 7023 plur.; 2050.1; 871.1; 6607 plur.; 1886.1;1004 plur.

<u>have been spoken to by you</u> <u>nearby</u> <u>the walls and doors of the houses</u> [of worship]."

            2050.1; he; 1696, 8765; 2297; 853 or 854; 259; 376 (Iyesh, Jesus)   854; 251; 2050.2

<u>Indeed, the one and only (actual) Jesus shall have spoken</u> <u>amongst his brethren</u>,

559, 8800   935, 8798; 4994   8085, 8798   4100   1886.1; 1697   (below)

<u>saying</u>: "<u>Come now, and intelligently listen to</u> <u>what</u> is <u>the Word</u> (of God)," <u>which he</u>

    he; 3318, 8802   4480; 853; 3068

<u>will be bringing forth</u> <u>from Yahweh</u>.

         2050.1; they; 935, 8799   413; 3509.2   3509.4; 3996; 5971   2050.1; they; 3427, 8799

33:31   "<u>When they shall come</u> <u>to you</u> [Jesus]; <u>as the people enter</u>, <u>they shall then sit</u>

   3807.1; 6440; 3509.2; 5971; 2967.1   2050.1; 8085, 8804   853; 1697; 3509.2   (below)

<u>before you (and) My people</u>, <u>but after they have heard</u> <u>your words</u>, <u>they, unfortun-</u>

2050.1; 853; 3963.1; 3808; 6213, 8799

<u>ately, shall not follow them</u>."

     3588   5690; 871.1; 6310; 1992; 1992; 6213, 8802   (310; 2967.1)...

<u>Although</u> <u>with their mouth, they will be showing much love</u>; <u>behind the back of</u>

cont.   (871.1; 1215; 3963.1; 3807.1; 3820; 3963.1; It; 1980, 8802)...

<u>Mine</u>, <u>their heart will be following after their ill-gotten gain(s)</u>.

       2050.1; 2009; 3509.2   413; 1992 (3509.4; 7892; 5690; 3303; 6963; 2050.1; 2895; 5059; 8763)...

33:32   "<u>When beholding you</u> [Jesus], <u>to them</u>, <u>the beautiful sound (of the recitation) that</u>

          cont.   (2050.1; they; 8085, 8804; 853; 1697; 3509.2)...

<u>is pleasantly melodic will be like lovely singing</u>. <u>Unfortunately, they shall have</u>

    cont.   2050.1; 6213, 8802; 369; 3963.1; 853; 3963.1

<u>heard your words</u>, <u>but shall not be obeying them</u>."

      2050.1; 871.1; his or it; 935, 8800   2009   (it; 935, 8802 or 8804; 2050.1; they; 3045, 8799 or 8804)...

33:33   <u>So during his (second) coming</u>; <u>behold</u>! <u>It will be coming to pass, and then they</u>

    cont.   3588   5030 sing.   1961, 8804 871.1; 8432; 3963.1

<u>shall realize</u> <u>that</u> <u>a prophet</u> [of God] <u>has been</u> <u>in their midst</u>.

Ezekiel 34

34:1   _{2050.1; 1697   3068   1961, 8799   413; 2967.1   559, 8800}
Furthermore, the Word of Yahweh shall come to Mine, saying:

34:2   _{1121   120   it; 5012, 8734 or 8803   (5921; my; 7462, 8802)…}
"Son of Man [Jesus], let this (that follows) be prophesied against those who are

_{cont.   3478   5012, 8803 or 8734   2050.1; you; 559, 8804   (below)}
tending to My flock in Israel. Let it be prophesied what you had relayed regarding

_{413; 1992; 3807.1; 7462, 8802}
those that are tending to them."

_{3541; he; 559, 8804; 136; 3068 or 3069}
"This is what Lord Yahweh said:"

_{1945   7462, 8802   3478   834   they; 1961, 8804; 7462, 8802   (below)}
"Woe to those that are tending to Israel, who shall have been tending to them-

34:3*   _{853; 3963.1   1886.1; 3808; 1886.1; 6629; 7462, 8799   853; 2459; yours; 398, 8799}
selves, but shall not tend to the migrating flock (exiled). *Yours shall eat the choicest

_{2050.1; 854; 6785; yours; 3847, 8799; yourselves   1886.1; 2077; you; 2076, 8799}
(sheep meat), clothe yourselves in the wool; and you would butcher the plumpest."

34:4*   _{1886.1; 6629; 3808; you; 7462, 8799   (853; 1886.1; 2470; 8737; 3808; you; 2388, 8765)…}
"You shall not tend to the migrating flock (exiled), *whose weak you had not helped

_{cont.   2050.1; 853; 2470, 8802   3808; you; 7495, 8765   (2050.1; 3807.1; you; 7665, 8737; 3808; 2280, 8804)…}
strengthen, and whose sick, you had not cured; nor have you bandaged up (those

_{cont.   2050.1; 853; 5080, 8737; 3808; 7725, 8689)…}
whom) you, yourselves, have been injuring. You, also, have not allowed those driven

_{cont.   (2050.1; 6, 8802; 3808; you; 1245, 8765; 2050.1; 871.1; 2394; you; 7287, 8804; 853 or 854; 3963.1)…}
away to return, and you never searched for those that were being destroyed when

_{cont.   2050.1; 871.1; 6531}
you ruled them with violence, and with cruelty."

34:5   _{2050.1; they; 6327, 8799   (4480; 3605; 7642, 8802; 2050.1; they; 1961, 8799)…}
"Since they shall be scattered abroad, then all of those that were tending the flock

_{cont.   3807.1; 402; 3807.1; 3605; 2416   7704 sing.   (below)}
shall become the food for all the living creatures of the cultivated land. My flock

35

34:6*   ^{2050.1; they; 6327, 8799; *7686, 8799; 6629; 2967.1}   ^{(871.1; 3605; 2022)...}
shall, indeed, be scattered abroad. *They shall (safely) migrate throughout all of

^{cont.   2050.1; 5921; 3605; 1389; 7311, 8802   2050.1; 5921; 3605; 6440   (below)}
the mountains, upon each hill that's high, and upon all the (other) surfaces of the

^{1886.1;776   (6327, 8738; 6629; 2967.1; 2050.1; 369; 1875, 8802; 2050.1; 369; 1245, 8764)...}
earth. Yet no one (in Israel) will be inquiring or researching about My flock who

^{cont.}
shall have been scattered abroad."

        ^{3807.1;3651; 7462, 8802}   ^{8085, 8798 or 8804}   ^{853; 1697; 3068}
34:7   This is to those who are tending the flock; intelligently listen to the Word of God:

     ^{2416; 589}   ^{it; 5002, 8803}   ¹³⁶   ^{3068 or 3069}
34:8   "As I live (eternally), it was (clearly) stated in the Oracles, 'The Lord is Yahweh;'

^{518; 3808   per Ez. 33:30 & 34:7   3282   1961, 8804; 6629; 2967.1   3807.1; 957   (below)}
whether or not (you listen). Since My flock has been taken (over) for the spoil, and

      ^{2050.1; 1961, 8804; 6629; 2967.1; 3807.1; 402; 3807.1; 3605; 2416   1886.1; 7704}
(others of) My flock have become food for each living creature of the cultivated land

           ^{4480; 369; 7462, 8802}   ^(2050.1; 3808; 1875, 8804; 7462, 8802)
because of the rulers that were not caring for (all) the flock, and who had not even

^{cont.   853; 6629; 2967.1   2050.1; 7462, 8799; 7462, 8802   853; 3963.1   (below)}
inquired about My flock; and since the rulers are tending to their own, but will not

^{2050.1; 853; 6629; 2967.1; 3808; 7462, 8804}
have tended to My flock –"

    ^{3807.1; 3651}   ^{7462, 8802}   ^{8085, 8798 (or 8804); 853; 1697}   ³⁰⁶⁸
34:9   "Thus, to the rulers tending to the flock; heed the (following) Word of God:"

      ^{3541; 559, 8804; 136; 3068 or 3069}
34:10   "This is what Lord Yahweh said:"

     ^{2009; 2967.1}   ⁴¹³   ^{1886.1; 7462, 8802}   ^{2050.1; I; 1875, 8804}
"Behold Me being against the rulers tending the flock! I, therefore, have required

^{853; 6629; 2967.1   4480   3027; 3963.1   2050.1; I; 7673, 8689; 3963.1   4480   7462, 8800}
My flock to be away from their control, when I cause them to cease from tending to

<small>6629 sing.</small> <small>2050.1; 3808; they; 7462, 8799; 5750; 7462, 8802; 853; 3963.1</small> <small>(below)</small>
the flock. Hence, the rulers shall never again be tending to their flock after I have

<small>2050.1; I; 5337, 8689; 6629; 2967.1</small> <small>(4480; 6310; 1992; 2050.1; 3808; they; 1961, 8799; 3807.1; 1992; 3807.1; 402)</small>
snatched My flock away from their (creatures') mouths, so that they will not be food

<small>cont.</small>
for them."

          <small>3588</small> <small>(3541; he; 559, 8804)...</small> <small>cont.</small> <small>136</small> <small>3068 or 3069</small>
34:11 "Assuredly, this is what he [Jesus] had relayed: '*The Lord* is *Yahweh*.'"

<small>2009; 2967.1</small> <small>589</small> <small>2050.1; I; 1875, 8804</small> <small>853; 6629; 2967.1</small> <small>(2050.1; I; 1239, 8765; 3963.1)</small>
"Behold Me! I, indeed I, have demanded (back) My flock! For I have repeatedly

       <small>cont.</small> <small>3509.3; 1243, 8802; 7462, 8802</small> <small>5739; 2050.2</small> <small>871.1; 3117</small> <small>(below)</small>
34:12* looked after them *like a shepherd tending to his sheep. At the time this has taken

<small>it or this; 1961, 8804; 2050.2; 871.1; 8432; 6629; 2050.2</small> <small>6566, 8737</small>
place, his flock will be amongst (the ones) that were scattered abroad."

<small>3651; I; 1239, 8762</small> <small>853; 6629; 2967.1</small> <small>2050.1; 5337, 8689; 853; 1992</small> <small>4480</small>
"I shall properly look after My flock, once I have caused them to be rescued from

<small>3605</small> <small>1886.1; 4725</small> <small>834</small> <small>they; 6327, 8738; 8033</small> <small>(871.1; 3117; 6051; 2050.1; 6205)...</small>
all of the locations where they had been scattered during the day of the smoke cloud

       <small>cont.</small> <small>2050.1; I; 3318, 8689; 3963.1</small> <small>4480</small> <small>1886.1; 5971</small> <small>(below)</small>
34:13* and darkness. *After I had caused them to be brought away from those people, and

<small>2050.1; I; 6908, 8765</small> <small>3963.1</small> <small>4480</small> <small>1886.1; 776 plur.</small> <small>(2050.1; 935, 8689; 3963.1)...</small>
had then gathered them out of the (other) countries, and had helped them to enter

   <small>cont.</small> <small>413</small> <small>127; 3963.1</small> <small>2050.1; I; 7462, 8804; 3963.1</small> <small>413</small> <small>2022</small>
back into their own land; I then shall have tended to them upon the hilly country of

      <small>3478</small> <small>871.1; 650 plur.</small> <small>2050.1; 3605</small> <small>4186 plur.; 1886.1; 776</small> <small>(below)</small>
34:14* Israel, by the ravines and all of the country's inhabitable dwelling places. *I shall

<small>871.1; 2896; 4829; I; 7462, 8799; 853; 3963.1</small> <small>2050.1; 871.1; 2022; 4791</small> <small>3478</small>
tend to them by the desirable pastureland, and on the elevated, hilly terrain of Israel,

<small>1961, 8799; 5116; 1992; 8033</small> <small>they; 7257, 8799</small> <small>871.1; 5116; 2896</small> <small>(below)</small>
where their home will be. They shall recline in a pleasant house, and shall tend to

      <small>2050.1; 4829; 8082; they; 7462, 8799; 413; 2022 sing.; 3478</small> <small>589; I; 7462, 8799</small> <small>6629; 2967.1 (below)</small>
34:15* a rich pasture within Israel's hilly country. *I, Myself, shall tend to My flock, and I,

_{2050.1; 589; I; 7257, 8686; 3963.1}   _{it; 5002, 8803}
Myself, shall cause them to (finally) be at rest, as was stated in the Oracles of the

_{136   3069}
Lord God."

_{853; 6, 8802; I; 1245, 8762}   _(below)
34:16   "I shall repeatedly require (a punishment for) those who will be perishing, and

_{2050.1; 853; 5080, 8737; 7725, 8686}   _{per Ez. 34:13}   _(below)
shall return those that were driven away (back to their homeland). Moreover, I shall

_{2050.1; 3807.1; 7665, 8737; I; 2280, 8799}   _{2050.1; 853; 1886.1; 2470; 2388, 8762}   _(below)
(provide) bandaging for the injured and shall strengthen the sick, but shall cause the

_{2050.1; 853; 1886.1, 8082; 2050.1; 853; 1886.1; 2389; I; 8045, 8686}   _(I; 7462, 8799; 871.1; 4941; 2050.1; 859; 1886.3; 6629; 2967.1)
34:17* destruction of the (greedy) rich and powerful. (For) I shall rule*My flock and yours

_{cont.}
with justice."

_{3541; 559, 8804; 136; 3068 or 3069}
"This is what Lord Yahweh said:"

_{2009; 2967.1; 8199, 8802}   _{(996; 7716 (one of a flock); 2050.1; 3807.1; 7716, 3807.1; 352; 2050.1; 3807.1; 6260)}
"Behold! I will be judging between each individual of (My) flock and (your) flock,

_{cont.}   _{1886.1; 4592}   _{4480 or 4481; 3641}
34:18* (and between) the rulers and the leaders.   *It will be a small matter to yours that

_{1886.1; 4829; 1886.1; 2896; you; 7462, 8799}   _{per Ez. 34:2-4}   _{2050.1; 3499}   _{4829 plur.; 3641.1}
you shall rule the desirable pasture (for yourselves), but the rest of your pastures

_{per Ez. 34:19}   _{you; 7429, 8799}   _{871.1; 7272; 3641.1}   _(below)
(that the exiled flock utilize), you shall trample by your feet. Furthermore, yours

_{2050.1; 4950; 8354; you; 8354, 8799}   _{2050.1; 853; 1886.1; 3498, 8738}
shall drink clear water, but the rest (of the water) that shall have been the left over,

_{871.1; 7272; 3641.1; you; 7515, 8799}   _{2050.1; 6629; 2967.1; 4823; 7272; 3641.1; you; 7462, 8799}
34:19* yours shall muddy up with your feet. *Thus, you shall feed My flock what was trod-

_{cont.}   _{2050.1; 4833; 7272; 3641.1; they; 8354, 8799}
den (by) your feet, and they shall also drink (the water) muddied up (by) your feet."

34:20   3651   (3541; he; 559, 8804; 136; 3068 or 3069; 413; 1992)...   cont.

"Assuredly, this is what he [Jesus] had relayed to theirs; 'The Lord is Yahweh.'"

         2009; 2967.1   589   2050.1; I; 8199, 8804   996; 7716; 1277 (or 1279 or 1274)   (below)

"Behold Me! I, indeed I, shall have judged between the healthy, well fed flock and

        2050.1; 996; 7716; 7330   3282   871.1; 6654; 2050.1; 871.1; 3802; 1920, 8799

34:21* the underfed flock. *Because yours shall drive out those on the side(s) and slope(s)

           2050.1; 871.1; 7161; 3641.1   you; 5055, 8762   (below)

[of Israel], and with your strength, yours shall repeatedly wage war (against) all of

        3605; 1886.1; 2470, 8737; 5704   834   you; 6327, 8689; 3963.1; 853; 413   (below)

those being afflicted, until when yours had caused theirs to scatter abroad or to its

    1886.1; 2351; 1886.3; 2050.1; I; 3467, 8689; 3807.1; 6629 (8800); 2967.1   (2050.1; 3808; they; 1961, 8799; 5750; 3807.1; 957)

34:22* outskirts; * I, thus, shall have rescued My flock, and never again shall they be taken

           cont.

(over) for the spoil."

           2050.1; I; 8199, 8804   996; 7716; 3807.1; 7716

I, indeed, have been the judge between each individual amongst flock to flock,

        2050.1; I; 6965, 8689   (5921; 1992; 7462, 8802; 259; 2050.1; 7462, 8804; 853; 1992; 853; 5650; 2967.1; 1732; 1931)...

34:23* *and I have appointed him, My beloved servant (Jesus, to be) the one that will be

               cont.   (he; 7462, 8799; 853; 3963.1; 2050.1; 1931; 1961, 8799)

ruling among them, who had (formerly) ruled theirs.   He shall rule them after he

          cont.   3807.1; 1992; 3807.1; 7462, 8802   2050.1; 589; 3068; I; 1961, 8799; 3807.1; 1992

34:24* becomes the caring ruler of theirs (remaining). *Then I, Yahweh, shall exist for these,

    3807.1; 430; 3963.1   2050.1; 5650; 2967.1; 1732   5387   871.1; 8432; 3963.1   589; 3068   (below)

as their God, once My beloved servant is the ruler in their midst; as I, Yahweh, had

         I; 1696, 8765

repeatedly promised.

          2050.1; I; 3772, 8804   3807.1; 1992; 1285

34:25   Thus, after I have cut off the covenant with these [who had followed the imposter

          2050.1; I; 7673, 8689; 2416; 7451   4480; 776

Jesus], and I have caused the evil beasts to cease existence from the (Holy) Land,

	they or theirs; 3427, 8799 or 8804	871.1; 4057; 3807.1; 983	(2050.1; 3462, 8799; 871.1; 3293 plur.)

theirs (remaining) shall dwell in the wasteland for security, or shall sleep in the

cont.
woods.

            2050.1; I; 5414, 8804   853; 3963.1   2050.1; 5439   1389; 2967.1   1293 (below)

34:26   For I had (once) given them and (its) neighbors My hilly (land) as a blessing; and

        2050.1; 3381, 8689; 1886.1; 1653   871.1; 6256; 2025.2   (1653 plur.; poss.; 1293; they; 1961, 8799)...

I had caused the rain to come down during its season. Showers of blessing(s) would

    cont.   2050.1; 5414, 8804; 6086   1886.1; 7704; 853; 6529; 2050.2   2050.1; 1886.1; 776

34:27* exist * when the tree(s) had yielded its fruit (in) the cultivated field, and the ground

        5414, 8799 2981; 1886.3   2050.1; they; 1961, 8804   5921; 127; 3963.1; 3807.1; 983 (below)

would yield its produce. Theirs had, indeed, existed upon their land, in safety, when

        2050.1; they; 3045, 8804   3588 589   3068 or 3069

they had acknowledged that I (Yahweh) am God.

        871.1; 7665, 8800 or (I; 7665, 8804); 853; 4133 sing.; 5921 w/o marks (or 5923); 3963.1 (below)

After Mine have destroyed the oppression amongst theirs, and I have caused

        2050.1; I; 5337, 8689; 3963.1   4480; 3027 (below)

theirs (who were being persecuted) to be rescued from the hand of the ones who

        5647, 8802; 3963.1; 871.1; 1992   2050.1; 3808; they; 1961, 8799; 5750   957 (below)

34:28* were (just) serving those of their own, *then never again shall they be the prey of

    3807.1; 1471   2050.1; 2416 plur.; 1886.1; 776   (3808; they; 398, 8799; 3963.1)...

the gentiles that were also the country's beasts. Never (again) shall they destroy

    cont.   2050.1; they; 3427, 8799 or 8804; 3807.1; 983; 2050.1; 369   2729, 8688

theirs. For they shall dwell in safety, and no one will be causing (them anymore)

cont.
fear.

        2050.1; I; 6965, 8689; 3807.1; 1992; 4302 (below)

34:29   Furthermore, I shall have also caused a garden to grow for these, so they shall

    2050.1; 3808; 1961, 8799; 5750; 622, 8803   7458   871.1; 776 (2050.1; 3808; they; 5375, 8799; 5750; 3639)

never again be victimized with hunger in the (Holy) Land; nor shall they ever again

        cont.   1886.1; 1471 plur.   2050.1; they; 3045, 8804 3588 589 3068

34:30* bear the insults of the (other) nations. *For they have known that I, Yahweh, am

430; 1992   854; 1992   2050.1; 1992   5971; 2967.1

their God that's with them, and that they are My people.

1004 sing.   3478   it; 5002, 8803   136   3068 or 3069

To the House of Israel, it was (clearly) stated; '*The Lord is Yahweh*.'

2050.1; 859   6629; 2967.1   6629   (below)

34:31   [Jesus]: "When yours are also My flock; the (rectified) flock (shall reside in) My

4830; 2967.1   120; 859   589   430; 3641.1   it or that; 5002, 8803

pasture. You are a human being. I am your God. That (is what) was stated in the

cont.   136   3069

Oracles of the Lord God."

Ezekiel 35

2050.1; it; 1961, 8799; 1697; 3068   413; 2967.1   559, 8800

35:1   Moreover, the Word of God shall come to Mine, saying:

1121   120   7760, 8798; 6440; 3509.2   5921; 2022; 8165

35:2   "Son of Man [Jesus], set your face towards Mount Seir [41] [the mountain range in

the West Bank and on the west side of Jordan between the northern tip of the Dead

2050.1; it; 5012, 8734   5921; 2050.2   (2050.1; you; 559, 8804)

35:3*   Sea and the Gulf of Aqaba], and let it be prophesied concerning it * what you had

cont.   3807.1; 2050.2

relayed to his [i.e., to the false Messiah's followers occupying the Mt. Seir region]."

3541; he; 559, 8804; 136; 3068 or 3069

"This is what Lord Yahweh said:"

2009; 2967.1   413; 3509.2   2022   8165   (I; 5186, 8804; 3027; 2967.1; 5921; 3509.2)…

"Behold, I am against yours at Mount Seir! I shall have stretched out My hand

cont.   2050.1; 5414, 8804; 3509.2; 8077   2050.1; 4923   5892; 3509.2; 2723; I; 7760, 8799

35:4*   against you and made you desolate and an object of horror. *I shall lay your guarded

cont.   2050.1; 859   8077; 1961, 8799   2050.1; you; 3045, 8799 or 8804; 3588; 589; 3068 or 3069

cities in ruin. After you are ruined, then you shall realize that I am God."

35:5   3282   you; 1961, 8804; 3807.1; 3509.2   342; 5769   per Ez. 13:5-6; 33:25-26; 30:4-5; 33:2; 38:13

"Because (many of) yours have had a perpetual hatred [for the Arab Muslims],

              2050.1; 5064, 8686; 853; 1121; 3478   (5921; 3027; 2719 sing.)...

that shall cause the descendants of Israel to pour out a powerful destructive weapon

       cont.   871.1; 6256; 343; 3963.1   871.1; 6256   5771

from above, oppressing theirs over time, then in due time, (this) punishable iniquity

            per 35:5   7093

(of hating and oppressing one's neighbors) shall have an end."

35:6   3807.1; 3651   2416; 589   it; 5002, 8803   136

"For certain, as I live (eternally), it was (always) stated in the Oracles; '*The Lord*

   3068 or 3069   3588   3807.1; 1818   I; 6213, 8799; 3509.2   2050.1; 1818

is Yahweh.' Because of the bloodshed, I shall commit yours to bloodshed, as well.

    it; 7291, 8799; 3509.2   518; 3808   1818; you; 8130, 8804   (below)

It shall pursue yours; whether or not you hated the bloodshed.   After bloodshed

35:7*   2050.1; 1818; 7291, 8799; 3509.2   2050.1; I; 5414, 8804   853; 2022; 8165 3807.1; 8077 (below)

shall pursue yours, *I, consequently, shall have made Mount Seir into a desolate and

   2050.1; 8077

wasted land."

             2050.1; I; 3772, 8689; 4480; 2050.2; 5674, 8802; 2050.1; 7725, 8802

"When I have caused its (residents) to be cut off from transgressing and reverting

                         2050.1; 4390, 8765   853; 2022; 2050.2

35:8* [to worshipping a lord other than God], *unfortunately, I shall have filled its mountains

   2491; 2050.2   1389; 3509.2; 2050.1; 1516; 3509.2   2050.1; 3605; 650 plur.; 3509.2 (below)

with its slain. Upon your hills and valleys, and by all of your watercourses, the slain

     2491; 2719 sing.; they; 5307, 8799   8077 plur.; 5769; I; 5414, 8799; 3509.2

35:9* shall fall by a destructive weapon. *I shall make yours be in utter ruins for a long

     cont.   2050.1; 5892; 3509.2; 3808; you; 3427, 8799   (2050.1; you; 3045, 8804)...

time, and you won't reside in your guarded cities (anymore). For yours had (once)

     cont.   3588; 589   3068 or 3069   3282   (he; 559, 8804; 3509.2)...   cont.

35:10* known that I (Yahweh) am God, *since (before) he [the imposter Jesus] shall have

     cont.   853; 8147; 1886.1; 1471   (2050.1; 853; 8147; 1886.1; 776 plur.)

told your two gentiles [i.e., the Christian and Muslim gentiles], that (their) two coun-

_{cont.}   _{per Ez. 25, Ez. 30, & 35:1-2}   _{3807.1; 2967.1; they; 1961, 8799}

tries [Palestine and Jordan, and then later, Egypt] '*are for Mine*' [the Israelites],

_{2050.1; they; 3423, 8804; 1886.3}   _{2050.1; 3068 or 3069; 8033; he; 1961, 8804}

since they had occupied them when he, (as) 'God,' had previously been there."

_{3807.1; 3651   2416; 589   it; 5002, 8803   136}

35:11   "For certain, as I live (eternally), it was (always) stated in the Oracles; '*The Lord*

_{3968 or 3069   2050.1; I; 6213, 8804   (3509.4; 639, 3509.2; 2050.1; 3509.4; 7068; 3509.2)}

is Yahweh.'   Therefore, I shall have reacted having a similar anger and passion as

_{cont.   834   you; 6213, 8804; 1886.3   4480; 8135; 3509.2   871.1; 3963.1}

yours, (and shall have done to you) what yours had done out of your hatred of them

_{2050.1; I; 3045, 8738   871.1; 3963.1   3509.4; 834   I; 8199, 8799 or 8804; 3509.2}

because I was acknowledged by theirs.   When I (and not him) shall judge yours,

_{2050.1; you; 3045, 8799   3588; 589   3068 or 3069}

35:12*   *then you shall realize that I (Yahweh) am God."

_{I; 8085, 8804; 853; 3605   5007 plur.; 3509.2   834   you; 559, 8804   5921   2022; 3478}

"I have heard all of your blasphemies that yours have said upon Israel's hilly

_{cont.   559, 8800 (below)   Ref. 41}

terrain, saying; '*It* [the Mount Seir region in the West Bank and on the west side of

_{it; 8074, 8804   (below)   per Ez. 35:1-2 & 9-10, Ez. 25 & 26}

Jordan] *had (already) been made desolate*.   *They* [Palestine and Jordan, and then

_{3807.1; us; they; 5414, 8738; 3807.1; 402}

later, Egypt] *were given to us for (our) consumption*.' "

_{2050.1; you; 1431, 8686   5921; 2967.1   871.1; 6310; 3641.1   (below)}

35:13   "Yours shall also arrogantly (speak) against Mine in your speeches, which shall

_{2050.1; you; 6280, 8689   per Ez. 35:5 & 35:11   5921; 2967.1   (1697; 3641.1; 589; I; 8085, 8804)...}

have caused yours to multiply (in hatred) against Mine.   I, Myself, shall have heard

_{cont.   3541   559, 8804; 136; 3068 or 3069   (3509.4; 8055, 8800; 3605; 1886.1; 776; 8077; I; 6213, 8799)}

35:14*   your words.   * Thus, said the Lord, Yahweh, as the whole country celebrates, I

_{cont.   3807.1; 3509.2   3509.4; 8057, 8804, 3509.2   (below)}

35:15*   shall make (it) utterly desolate amongst yours; *similar to when yours rejoiced over

_{3807.1; 5159; 1004; 3478; 5921   834   you; 8074, 8804}

the family of Israel's inherited property, which yours had made desolate [after invad-

43

                                                   3651; I; 6213, 8799   3807.1; 3509.2 (below)

ing their Arab neighbors' lands]. <u>(N:7)</u> <u>I, therefore, shall do (the same)</u> <u>to yours</u>. <u>Your</u>

(your; 8077; 1961, 8799; 2022; 8165; 2050.1; 3605; 123)…   Ref. 41   cont.
<u>Mount Seir region</u> [in the West Bank and on the west side of Jordan], <u>and all of Edom</u>

                                          Ref. 35
[in the southern region of Jordan and Israel that's south of the Dead Sea to the Gulf

              cont.   3605; 1886.3; 2050.1; 3045, 8804 or 8799   3588; 589   3068 or 3069
of Aqaba] <u>will become desolate</u>. <u>For all of theirs have known</u> <u>that I</u> am <u>God</u>."

^(N:7) The "rejoicing over the family of Israel's inherited property" mentioned in Ezekiel 35:15, is in reference to the celebrations that have continued throughout the years, marking the day of Israel's statehood on May 14, 1948, which followed the 1948 Palestinian exodus, when an estimated 750,000 Palestinians were either expelled from or had terrifyingly fled from their homes in Palestine that afterwards became modern day Israel. [42] Although these Palestinians lost loved ones, their land, homes, and possessions during that time, Israel celebrated its 50th year anniversary ceremony on May 14, 1998 to rejoice this event. Due to the lack of sensitivity for the Arab exiles, Palestinians protested the Israeli celebration by throwing stones. As a result, Israeli soldiers opened fire with rubber coated steel bullets on the angered Palestinians during the anniversary festivities, leading to the death of nine Palestinians, among which were two eight year old boys. [43]

    The Palestinians continue to view May 14, 1948 as their "catastrophe" ("Nakba" in Arabic), and in recent times petitioned the United Nations General Assembly for international recognition of their losses by establishing Nakba Day. [44] As a result, on December 1, 2022 the U.N. passed the resolution recognizing May 15, 2023 as Nakba Day; to be a day of commemoration for the Palestinians. [45]

    Based on the prophesies in Ezekiel 25 through 35, and then later in Ezekiel chapters 36, 38 and 39, Israel will continue to capture and occupy Arab territories, and the bloodshed, oppressive takeovers, and cruel treatment of its refugees will continue and escalate after many of the Israelis accept the imposter Jesus as their awaited Messiah. In Ezekiel 35:9-10, God (Yahweh) reveals that although the Israeli Jews had beforehand worshiped only Him, because of their hatred for the one congregation of Arab gentiles that will <u>not</u> accept Israel's false Messiah, as soon as the imposter Jesus Christ tells the Israelis that the two prophesied gentile countries (Palestine and Jordan, and then later, Egypt) are for "His" people (i.e., for the Israelis), and not for the opposing hated Muslim Arabs, many of them will then welcome him as their Messiah, and will accept his blasphemous claim of being God in the body of Christ. However, throughout all of the chapters of Ezekiel, it is very clear that Jesus is not God and that the Lord, Yahweh, will instruct His prophet, Jesus (the Son of Man; Iyesh), on what to do and convey to the people. According to Ezekiel 34:31, God shall say to Jesus; "You are a human being. I am your God. That's what was stated in the Oracles of the Lord God."

Ezekiel 36

36:1 "Since you are the Son of Man [Jesus]; let it be prophesied to the hilly country of Israel what you had relayed at Israel's hilly territory [in the West Bank, including Jerusalem, and in the northern portion of Israel] after theirs had heard God's Word."

36:2 "This is what Lord Yahweh said:"

"Because the enemy (ruling) over yours, shall have said; 'Ugh! The ancient worship shrines have existed as a heritage of ours.'" (N:8)

36:3a "Thus, regarding this, let it be prophesied what you (Jesus) had relayed."

(N:8) To better understand this portion of the prophesy, refer back to Ezekiel chapter 6 in the first book of *Preserved for the End of Time*. This statement that is to be made by the imposter Jesus is either his response to God's warning that Old City Jerusalem's "offensive" worship shrines will be demolished, and its crosses and crucifixes will be destroyed, or it's what shall have been expressed sometime after Prophet Jesus had seized Jerusalem. Recall from these previous chapters, that God, Himself, will be the one instructing Jesus and his militia to capture Jerusalem and then years later to invade all of Israel, including annexed Egypt and the other Israeli occupied, Arab territories. The following passages reveal the reasons why Jerusalem is to be overthrown by Prophet Jesus and his army.

36:3b   ^{3541; 559, 8804; 136; 3068 or 3069}
"This is what Lord Yahweh said:"

^{3282   871.1; 3282; 8074, 8800; 2050.1; 7602, 8800; 853; 3641.1   (below)}
"A reason for (it) is because of yours causing the desolation and trampling of

^{4480; 5439   3807.1; 1961, 8800; 4181   3807.1; 7611   (below)}
the surrounding (lands) in order for yours to gain possession of the remainder of the

^{1886.1; 1471 plur.   (2050.1; you; 5927, 8735)...}
(neighboring) foreign nations, and because you [i.e., Israel's and annexed Egypt's

^{cont.   5921; 8193 plur.; 3956   (2050.1; 1681; 5971)...}
imposter Jesus] would be exalted over the news announcements, but (My) people

^{cont.}
(would have) bad reporting."

36:4   ^{3807.1; 3651   2022   3478   they; 8085, 8804 or 8798   (1697; 136; 3068 or 3069)...}
"Assuredly, the hilly country of Israel shall have heard the (following) Word of

^{cont.   (3541; he; 559, 8804)...   cont.   136; 3068 or 3069   3807.1; 2022; 2050.1}
the Lord God. This is what he [Jesus] had conveyed of the Lord God's, at its moun-

^{cont. (3807.1; 1389; 3807.1; 650; 2050.1; 3807.1; 1516, 2050.1; 3807.1; 2723; 8076 or 8074, 8802; 2050.1; 3807.1; 5892; 5800, 8737)}
tains, hills, watercourses, and valleys; and also at the devastated ruins, and aban-

^{cont.   834   they; 1961, 8804; 3807.1; 957}
doned cities, which shall have been taken for spoil:"

^{2050.1; 3807.1; 3933   3807.1; 7611}
"(Another reason is) because of the scorn (expressed) towards the remainder of

36:5*   ^{1471   834   per Ez. 36:5 & 14   4480; 5439   (below)}
the gentile people who were (exiled) out of the surrounding area, (and because), *for

^{3807.1; 3651 (3541; he; 559, 8804)...   cont.   136   3068 or 3069   518; 3808}
certain, this is what he [Jesus] had relayed, '*The Lord* is *Yahweh*;' whether or not

^{per 33:30 & 34:7}
(you listened)."

^{871.1; 784; 7068; 2967.1   I; 1696, 8765   5921   (7611; 1886.1; 1471 plur.)...}
"In My blazing anger, I had repeatedly warned about the remainder of the gentile

     cont.   2050.1; 5921   3605; 123   Ref. 35

nations that will be against all of Edom [in southern Israel and southwest Jordan;

     834   they; 5414, 8804; 853; 776; 2967.1

south of the Dead Sea to the Gulf of Aqaba], that shall have given the land of Mine

   3807.1; 1992   3807.1; 4181   871.1; 8057; 3605; 3824   871.1; 7589   5315

to their own for possession; with each having a joyful heart, with a malicious soul,

   4616; 4480   1644; 1886.3   3807.1; 957

on account of driving them out for the booty."

     3807.1; 3651   it; 5012, 8734   5921   127   3478   (below)

36:6   "For certain, let it be prophesied against the country of Israel, what you [Jesus]

2050.1; you; 559, 8804 or 8798   3807.1; 2022; 2050.1; 3807.1; 1389; 3807.1; 650; 2050.1; 3807.1; 1516

shall have relayed nearby its mountains, hills, watercourses, and valleys."

     3541; he; 559, 8804; 136; 3068 or 3069

"This is what Lord Yahweh said:"

   2009; 2967.1   871.1; 7068; 2967.1; 2050.1; 871.1; 2534; 2967.1; I; 1696, 8765   3282   (below)

"Behold Me! I have spoken in My anger, and in My fury, because you [imposter

     3639; 1471 plur.; you; 5375, 8804

Jesus] shall have uplifted the disgraceful gentiles!"

    3807.1; 3651   (3541; he; 559, 8804)...   cont.   136   3068 or 3069

36:7   "Assuredly, this is what he [Jesus] had relayed; '*The Lord is Yahweh*.'"

     589; I; 5375, 8804   853; 3027; 2967.1   518; 3808   1886.1; 1471   834   (below)

"I, Myself, shall have uplifted My own ministry; but not the gentiles that are with

   3807.1; 3641.1; 4480; 5439   1992; 5375, 8799   3639; 3963.1   2050.1; 859

36:8*   yours from the surrounding area, who will bear their own disgrace, *along with you."

     2022; 3478; 6057; 3641.1   they; 5414, 8799; 2050.1; 6529; 3641.1; 5375, 8799

"The hilly country of Israel's branches shall shoot forth and bear yours fruit that

    3807.1; 5971; 2967.1   per Ez. 36:5 & 14   3478   3588   they or their; 7126, 8765; 935, 8800

shall soon be for My people (exiled from) Israel. For their return has approached,

   3588   2009; 2967.1   410 (w/o marks); 3641.1   2050.1; I; 6437, 8804   (413; 3641.1)

36:9*   *because, behold, I (Yahweh) was the Almighty of yours when I had turned towards

47

_{cont.} _{2050.1; you; 5647, 8738; 2050.1; you; 2232; 8738} _{per Ez. 8:1-18; 20:3-8; 20:39}
yours; yet now, you, who had been conceived, have been worshiped (as if you are

_{2050.1; I; 7235, 8689; 5921; 3509.2; 120} ₃₆₀₅
36:10* God). *But I (Yahweh) had caused the humans amongst you to multiply, and all of

₁₀₀₄ ₃₄₇₈ _{3605; 1886.3; they; 3427, 8738; 1886.1; 5892} _(below)
the House of Israel! The guarded cities have been inhabited (by) all of them, who

_{2050.1; 1886.1; 2723 plur.; 1129, 8735} _(below)
36:11* would (cause) the wastelands to be built up. *I (Yahweh) had, indeed, caused the

_{2050.1; I; 7235, 8689; 5921; 3641.1; 120; 2050.1; 929} _{2050.1; they; 7235, 8804} _{2050.1; they; 6509, 8804}
people and animals amongst you to multiply. As they multiplied, they also shall have

_{cont.} _{2050.1; I; 3427, 8689; 853; 3641.1} _{871.1; 6927; 3641.1} _(below)
flourished when I resettled yours in (their) former states, and I made (yours) more

_{2050.1; I; 2895, 8689; 4480; 7221; 3641.1} _{2050.1; you; 3045, 8804} _{3588; 589}
prosperous than (they were) at first, because yours had (once) known that I (Yahweh)

_{3068 or 3069}
am God."

_{2050.1; I; 1980, 8689; 5921; 3641.1; 120 plur.} _(853 or 8054; 5971; 3478; possv.)
36:12 "Thus, I shall have caused the humans amongst you to depart, along with the

_{cont.} _{2050.1; 3423, 8804; 3509.2} _(2050.1; you; 1961, 8804; 3807.1; 1992)
Israeli people of yours that shall have driven (Mine) out when you were against

_{cont.} _{3807.1; 5159} _{refer to Ez. 33:24 and (N:21) in Section 5 of this book}
theirs regarding the inheritance [to all of Abraham's descendants, including to Jacob

_{2050.1; you; 3808; 3254; 5750} _(below)
(one of Abraham's grandsons)]. Consequently, you shall never again continue to

_{7921, 8763; 3963.1}
bereave theirs."

_{(3541; he; 559, 8804)...} _{cont.} ₁₃₆ _{3068 or 3069}
36:13 "This is what he [Jesus] had relayed; '*The Lord* is *Yahweh*.'"

₃₂₈₂ _{they; 559, 8802} _{3807.1; 3641.1}
"Because theirs have been saying this to you [i.e., to the imposter Jesus that the

_{you; 398, 8804 or 8802} _{(120; 853 (not 859); 2967.1; 2050.1; you; 7921, 8802)...}
Lord is Yahweh], you have been destroying My people and have been causing the

	cont. 1471; 3509.2 you; 1961, 8804
	bereavement of <u>your (exiled) gentiles</u> that <u>yours (once) existed (with)</u>."

           3807.1; 3651   120; 3808; you; 398, 8799; 5750   (below)

36:14   "<u>For certain</u>, <u>you shall never again destroy (My) people</u>, and <u>you shall never again</u>

        2050.1; 1471; 3509.2; 7921, 8762, 3808; 5750

<u>cause the bereavement of your exiled gentiles</u>."

          it; 5002, 8803   136   3068 or 3069

"<u>It was (clearly) stated in the Oracles</u>; '*The Lord is <u>Yahweh</u>*.' "

    2050.1; 3808; I; 8085, 8799 (or 8686); 413; 3509.2; 5750   3639; 1886.1; 1471   (below)

36:15   "<u>I shall never again listen to yours</u> or to <u>the disgraceful gentiles</u>, and <u>you shall no</u>

   2050.1; 2781; 5971 plur.; 3808; you; 5375, 8799; 5750   per Ez. 3:18-21 (1st book)

<u>longer bear the peoples' disgrace</u>. [Each person is accountable for their own sins.]

          2050.1; 1471; 3509.2; 3808; you; 3782, 8686; 5750

<u>Furthermore, you will never again overthrow your (neighboring) gentiles</u>."

         it; 5002, 8803   136   3068 or 3069

"<u>It was (always) stated in the Oracles</u>; '*The Lord is <u>Yahweh</u>*!' "

       2050.1; it; 1961, 8799; 1697; 3068 or 3069   413; 2967.1   559, 8800

36:16   <u>The Word of God shall also come</u> to <u>Mine</u>, <u>saying</u>:

      1121   120   (1004; 3478; 3427, 8802; 5921; 127; 3963.1; 2050.1; they; 2930, 8762; 853; 1886.3)...

36:17   "<u>Son</u> of <u>Man</u> [Jesus], <u>the famil(ies) of Israel are dwelling upon their land that they</u>

        cont.   871.1; 1870 sing.; 3963.1; 2050.1; 871.1; 5949 plur.; 3963.1   (3509.4; 2932)...

<u>shall utterly defile</u> with <u>their way of life and their actions</u> that are <u>similar to the spirit-</u>

        cont.   1886.1; 5079   per Ez. 14:3-5, 20:7, 36:18   it; 1961, 8804   (1870; 3963.1)...

<u>ual uncleanliness</u> of <u>the religiously impure</u> (idolaters), <u>which had been their way of</u>

        cont.

<u>life</u>."

          6440; 2967.1   2050.1; I; 8210, 8799   (2534; 2967.1; 5921; 1992; 5921; 1886.1; 1818)

36:18*   "<u>In the presence of Mine</u>, * <u>I, therefore, will pour forth</u> <u>My fury upon them for the</u>

        cont.   834   they; 8210, 8804   (5921; 1886.1; 776; 2050.1; 871.1; 1544 plur.; 1992; they; 2930, 8762; 1886.3)

<u>blood</u> that <u>they shall have spilled</u> <u>upon the (Holy) Land, which they shall have defiled</u>

```
              cont.                  2050.1; I; 6327, 8686; 853; 3963.1                        (871.1; 1471)
36:19* with their crucifixes.   * I will then cause theirs to scatter abroad (to be) amongst

              cont.            2050.1; 2219, 8735; 871.1; 776 plur.                    (below)
       the gentiles that shall be scattered throughout the (other) countries.   I shall have

              3509.4; 1870; 3963.1; 2050.1; 3509.4; 5949; 3963.1; I; 8199; 8804; 3963.1
       punished them according to their way of life and their actions."


              (2050.1; he; 935, 8799)...         cont.        413        1471 plur.        834; 8033
36:20    "When he [the imposter Jesus] shall enter into the foreign nations where (many

              they or theirs; 935, 8804     (2050.1; they; 2490, 8762; 853; 8034; 6944; 2967.1; 871.1; him; 559, 8800)...
       of) theirs shall have gone, they then shall continually profane My Holy Name be-

              cont.           413; 1992      (5971; 3068 or 3069; 428)...        cont.        (below)
       cause of him saying, regarding theirs, 'These [Israelis] are Yahweh's people,' after

              2050.1; they; 3318, 8804; 4480; 776; 2050.2     2050.1; I; 2550, 8799    5921    (below)
36:21* they had exited from his country; *and that I would have mercy on his (people) that

              8034; 6944; 2967.1; 834; 2490, 8765; 1886.3; 2050.2         1004 sing.    3478    (below)
       shall have profaned My Holy Name; (his people being) the House of Israel with the

              871.1; 1471      834; 8033; 935, 8804
       gentiles that had gone there."


                  3651           559, 8798              3807.1; 1004       3478
36:22     "Therefore, [Jesus] say (this that follows) to the House of Israel [led by the false

       Messiah]:"



                      3541       559, 8804; 136; 3069
         "This is what Lord Yahweh said:"

                              3808; 3807.1; 4616; 3641.1    589     6213, 8802     1004
         [Imposter Jesus:] "It's not on account of you that I will be dealing with the House

              3478     3588; 518    3807.1; 8034; 6944; 2967.1    834     you or yours; 2490, 8765
       of Israel; but rather, because of My Holy Name that yours shall have repeatedly

              cont.       871.1; 1471         834    you; 935, 8804    8033
       profaned, along with the gentiles, when you arrived there."
```

36:23   2050.1; I or mine; 6942, 8765   (853; 8034; 2967.1; 1886.1; 1419; 1886.1; 2490, 8794)

36:23   "Mine, however, shall have continually sanctified My Great Name that was being

      cont.   871.1; 1471   834   you; 2490, 8804   871.1; 8432; 3963.1   (below)

defiled in the gentile nations that you shall have profaned in their midst. But (soon),

    2050.1, 3045, 8799 or 8804; 1886.1; 1471; 3588; 589; 3068 or 3069   it; 5002, 8803   136

the gentiles will also realize that I am Yahweh. It was (clearly) stated; '*The Lord*

   3068 or 3069

is Yahweh.'"

        871.1; I; 6942, 8736   871.1; 3641.1   3807.1; 5869; 1992   (below)

36:24*   "When I (Yahweh) was deemed Holy amongst yours, before their eyes, * I had,

   2050.1; I; 3947, 8804 853; 3641.1; 4480   1886.1; 1471   2050.1; I; 6908, 8765; 853; 3641.1   4480 (below)

indeed, taken yours out of the gentile nations when I regathered yours from all of

    3605; 776 plur.   2050.1; I; 935, 8689; 853, 413   413; 127; 3641.1   2050.1; I; 2236, 8804 (below)

36:25* the countries, and had caused yours to enter your soil. *I, also, had sprinkled pure

    5921; 3641.1; 4325; 2889   2050.1; you; 2891, 8804   4480; 3605 (below)

(rain) water upon yours; seeing that yours had cleansed (themselves) from all of your

      2932; 3641.1   2050.1; 4480; 3605; 1544; 3641.1   per Ez. 8:12 (1st book)

(same) religious impurities, and from all of the idols of yours. (But because of serving

    per Ez. 36:20-22, 39:7   I; 2891, 8762 853; 3651.1   2050.1; I; 5414, 8804; 3807.1; 3641.1

36:26* you and profaning My Name), I must repurify yours, *after I had (already) given yours

     see Ez. 36:37   3820; 2318 or 2319   2050.1; 7307; 2318 or 2319; 1886.1; I; 5414, 8799

[who worshiped Yahweh] a renewed heart. I, indeed, shall render a renewed spirit

  871.1; 7130; 3641.1   2050.1; I; 5493, 8689   853; 3820; 1886.1; 68   4480   1320; 3641.1

within yours, after I have removed the heart of stone from the body(ies) of yours,

      I; 5414, 8804; 3807.1; 3641.1; 3820; 1320

and have given yours (who mend themselves) a heart of flesh [that is softhearted

and spiritually righteous]."

    2050.1; 853; 7307; 2967.1; I; 5414, 8799; 871.1; 7130; 3641.1 (2050.1; I; 6213, 8804; 853; 834; 871.1; 2706; 2967.1; 1980, 8799)

36: 27   "I shall, indeed, deliver My spirit amongst yours that I have dealt with, who shall

     cont.   2050.1; 4941; 2967.1; 8104, 8799   (2050.1; 6213, 8804; 3963.1)

follow My Laws and shall observe My Ordinances (from now on); like when yours

51

| | | cont. | | 2050.1; you or yours; 3427, 8804 | 871.1; 776 | 834 | I; 5414, 8804 | (below) |

36:28* had (once) practiced them *when yours dwelt on the land that I had given to the

| | 3807.1; 1; 3641.1 | | 2050.1; you; 1961, 8804 | | 3807.1; 2967.1; 3807.1; 5971 |

forefathers of yours, and when yours had been amongst the people of Mine."

| | | 2050.1; 595; I; 1961, 8799 | 3807.1;3641.1 | 430;3963.1 | 2050.1; I; 3467, 8689; 853; 3641.1 |

36:29* "When I, Myself, will (again) be, to yours, their God,*after I have saved yours

| 4480; 3605 | 2932; 3641.1 | (2050.1; I;7121, 8804; 413;1886.1; 1715: 2050.1; I; 7235, 8689; 853; 2050.2) |

from all of your religious impurities, I then shall have called for grain(s), which I shall

| | cont. | | | 2050.1; 3808; I; 5414, 8799 | | (below) |

have multiplied, (to be provided for yours) so that I do not cause (further) famine

| 5921; 3641.1; 7458 | 2050.1; I; 7235, 8689 | 853; 6529 | 1883.1; 6086 | 2050.1; 8570 plur. |

36:30* amongst yours. *I also shall have multiplied the fruit on the tree(s), and the crops

| | 1886.1; 7704 | 4616; 834 | (3808; you; 3947, 8799; 5750; 2781; 7458; 871.1; 1471 plur.)... |

on the cultivated land so that yours, along with the gentiles, shall never again suffer

| | cont. |

the disgrace of famine."

| | | 2050.1; you; 2142, 8804 | (853; 1870; 1886.1; 7451; 3641.1; 2050.1; 4611; 3641.1) |

36:31   [Imposter Jesus:] "After yours have remembered the evil ways and actions of

| cont. | 834 | 3808 | 2896 | 2050.1; yours; 6962, 8738; 871.1; 6440; 3641.1 | 5921 |

yours that were not good, and after yours in your presence have been grieved over

| 5771 plur.; 3641.1; 2050.1; 5921; 8441 plur.; 3641.1 | 3808; 4616; 3641.1; 589; I; 6213, 8802 |

the iniquities and abominations of yours, it's not on account of you (that) I am doing

| | | it; 5002, 8803 | | 136 | 3068 or 3069 | (below) |

36:32* (this, but because)*it was (clearly) stated in the Oracles; 'The Lord is Yahweh,' which

| it; 3045, 8735 3807.1; 3641.1 | (they; 954, 8804 or 8798; 3637, 8738 or 8735; 4480; 1870; 3641.1; 1004; 3478) |

shall (again) be apparent to yours. For the family of Israel had (once) been ashamed

| | cont. |

of (and) humiliated by your (sinful) ways."

| | (3541; he; 559, 8804)... | | cont. | 136 | 3068 or 3069 |

36:33   "This is what he [Jesus] had relayed; 'The Lord is Yahweh.' "

| | 871.1; 3117 | I; 2891, 8804 (or 8763) | 853; 3641.1 | 4480; 3605; 5771; 3641.1 |

"At the time that I shall have repurified yours away from all your sinful practices,

2050.1; 3427; 8689; 853; 1886.1; 5892 plur.   2050.1; 1129, 8738; 1886.1; 2723 plur.

I then shall have caused the cities to be inhabited, after the ruins have been rebuilt.

2050.1; 1886.1; 776; 8074, 8737; 5647, 8735   8478   834   it; 1961, 8804   8077

36:34* *When the desolate land will be tilled beneath where it shall have been wasteland,

3807.1; 5869 plur.   3605; 5674, 8802   2050.1; they; 559, 8804   1886.1; 776; 1977; 8074, 8737

36:35* in the sights of every passerby, *they, indeed, shall have thought; 'This land that was

cont.   1961, 8804   3509.4; 1588; 5731   2050.1;1886.1; 5892;1886.1; 2720   (below)

desolate has become like the garden of Eden, and the ruined cities that were deso-

2050.1; 8074, 8737; 2040, 8737   it; 1219, 8803   3427, 8804

late and destroyed, which were inaccessible, have become inhabited.'"

2050.1; 3045, 8804; 1886.1; 1471 plur.; 834; 7604, 8735; 5439; 3641.1

36:36   "Because the gentiles that shall be remaining as your neighbors have known

3500; 509   3068 or 3069   I or mine; 1129, 8804; 2040, 8737; 2050.1; I or mine; 5193, 8804   (below)

that I (Yahweh) am God, Mine shall have rebuilt what was ruined, and replanted what

8074, 8737

was destroyed."

589; 3068 or 3069   I; 1696, 8765   (2050.1, I or mine; 6213, 8804)…

"'I am Yahweh' is what I have repeatedly declared, and (I am the one) that Mine

cont.   (3541; he; 559, 8804;136; 3068 or 3069; 5750)…   cont.

36:37* have followed.   * Thus, again, this is what he [Jesus] has relayed, 'The Lord is

cont.   2063   I; 1875, 8735

Yahweh.'   Therefore, I must be worshiped!"

3807.1; 1004   3478   3807.1; 6213, 8800; 3807.1; 1992   (I; 7235, 8686; 853; 3963.1; 3509.4; 6629; 120)…

To the House of Israel: For acting against theirs, I shall multiply their people like

cont.   3509.4; 6629; 6944; 3509.4; 6629; 3389   871.1; 4150; 1886.3   3651   (below)

36:38* sheep; * as Jerusalem's holy flock, along with its congregation. Thus, these ruined

these; 1961, 8799; 1886.1; 5892; 2720   4392   6629; 120   2050.1; they; 3045, 8804; 3588; 589

cities (rebuilt) will become filled with the flocks of people, who have known that I

3068 or 3069

(Yahweh) am God.

Ezekiel 38

2050.1; 1961, 8799; 1697; 3068 or 3069   413; 2967.1 559, 8800

38:1   Indeed, the Word of God shall come to Mine saying:

1121   120   7760, 8798; 6440; 3509.2 sing.; 413 1463   per Ez. 38:18

38:2   "Son of Man [Jesus], set your face towards Gog, (who will be sending allied

776 sing.   4031 sing.   per Ez. 38:8-9, 38:18 & 39:4   (5387; 7218; 4902)...

troops to) the land of Magog [i.e. to Zionist Israel], (and who is) the Chief Ruler of

cont.   2050.1; 8422 (or Tubal)   2050.1; 5012, 8734   5921; him

Meshech [Moscow, Russia] and Tbil [Tbilisi, Georgia]; then prophesy against him,

2050.1; you; 559, 8804

38:3*   *what you had (previously) relayed."

3541; 559, 8804; 136; 3068 or 3069

"This is what Lord Yahweh said:"

2009; 2967.1   413 sing.; 3509.2 sing.; 1463   7218 5387; 4902 (Meshech); 2050.1; 8422 (Tubal or Tbil)

"Behold Mine going against you, Gog, Chief Ruler of Moscow and Tbilisi!

2050.1; I; 7725, 8790; you   2050.1; I or mine; 5414, 8804; 2397 plur.

38:4*   *When I have returned you back (to Me), after Mine shall have put twisted wires

3895 plur.; 3509.2   (2050.1; I; 3318, 8689; you sing.)...

(tacked into) your jaws [during the burial prep], and then when I have brought you

cont. per Ez. 38:7-8   854 3605 (2428; 3509.2 sing.; 5483 plur.; 2050.1; 657 plur.)

forth [for judgment], it shall occur along with all of your army and drivers of swift

cont.

vehicles."

3847, 8803; 4358; 3605; 3963.1; 6951; 7227 sing.   (below)

"All of theirs; the Commander's modestly dressed congregation, shall have a

6793 sing.   2050.1; 4043 sing.; 8610, 8802   (2719 plur.)...

shield that is a defensive protector handling [the discharging of] the destructive

cont.   3650; 3963.1   6539   3568

38:5*   weapons. All of theirs from *Persia [47] [Iran], Cush [48] [Saudi Arabia, Ethiopia and

2050.1; 6316   854; 1992   per 38:4, 6, & 15

Sudan], <u>and Put</u> [49] [Libya and Egypt], who will be <u>against these</u> (soldiers of yours),

3605; them   4043 sing.   2050.1; 3553 (helmet)

shall <u>each</u> have <u>a defensive protector</u> <u>that is an overhead protection</u>."

38:6   "<u>Gomer</u> [50] [including Russia, Ukraine, Georgia, Moldova, and Romania] <u>and all</u> of

its or her; 102 sing.   1004 sing.   8425   3411 plur.; 6828 fem.   854; 3605; 1992

<u>its army</u> will, to the <u>family</u> of <u>Togarmah</u> at the <u>north borders</u>, be <u>against all of theirs</u>.

102 plur.; its   5971 possv. or plur.; 7227; 3963.1   854; you

Thus, <u>the troops</u> of <u>their people's Commander</u> will be <u>against you</u> (Gog)!" (N:9)

(N:9) The descendants of Gomer are those living north of the Black Sea, including those which are living in Russia, Ukraine, Moldova, Romania and Georgia. In the past centuries, the Russian Empire had seized and annexed lands from its neighboring countries, and more recently, the former Soviet Union, which included fifteen republics, had also been dominated by Russia. During this 21st century, following Soviet Union's collapse in 1991, [51] Russia's army is once again working on expanding its country. Since 2008, Russian military has captured and occupied 20% of Georgia, [52] and according to Ez. 38:2-4, at the time when Gog's army shall attempt to invade the northern region of the Togarmah family's property, Georgia's capital, Tbilisi (Tbil or Tubal), will also be ruled by Russia. Moreover, since February of 2022, Russia's military has also been working on seizing control of Ukraine. [53]

According to Ezekiel 38:6, these descendants of Gomer, led by the prophesied Russian, Gog ruler, who will be allies of Israel and its false Messiah, will be going against the family of Togarmah, in an attempt to seize and dominate their territory. The land of the Togarmah family includes the predominantly Muslim region north of the Euphrates River, up to the land towards the east side of the Euphrates in Iraq. [54] This above prophesy, therefore, is in regards to Russian Gog's <u>intention</u> to also conquer the northern sections of the Togarmah territory, including land from east Syria and western Iraq. Recall from the previous Ezekiel chapters that God's true messenger, Jesus (Iyesh), who will initially be ruling from Babylon (Iraq and Syria) prior to invading and eventually also ruling Jerusalem (Ezekiel 17:12-14), will be the Chief Commander of the Arab and Turkish militia that is to defend the family of Togarmah. Also recall that it was prophesied in Ezekiel 8:11 and 12:4 in the first book of *Preserved for the End of Time* that Prophet Jesus will be aided in his defensive conquests by an Arabic assistant, who will be a descendant of both Shāphan and Prophet Mohamed.

                            3559, 8734; 2050.1; 3559, 8734   3087.1; 3509.2; 3087.1; 859   (2050.1; 3605; 6951; 3509.2)…

38:7   [Gog:] "<u>Get ready and be prepared</u> <u>for (when) you, yourself,</u> <u>as well as all of your</u>

            cont.   6950, 8737; 5921; 3509.2 sing.   2050.1; you; 1961, 8804   3087.1 per 38:10-12

<u>assemblage,</u> <u>are gathered up above,</u> <u>and you have been</u> (dealt with) <u>for</u> (wanting)

        1992; 4929, 8800   4480 pref.; 3117 plur. 7227 plur.; 3963.1   per Ez. 38:6

38:8*   <u>to hold theirs captive.</u> *<u>After the days</u> of <u>their commanders</u> (who shall defend the

                                 you; 6485, 8799

Togarmah people), <u>you will be punished!</u>"

     871.1; 319; 8141 plur.   you; 935, 8799; 413; 776 sing.   7725, 8796

"<u>In the end times,</u> <u>yours shall head towards the</u> (Israeli annexed) <u>territory</u> <u>returned</u>

                      4480; 2719 sing.   (6908, 8794; 5971 plur.; their; 7227)…

(to the Arab refugees) <u>by way of a destructive weapon</u> of <u>their Commander's people</u>

        cont.   5921   2022 sing.   3478   834 (it; 1961, 8804; 2723; 8548)…

<u>that had been gathered</u> <u>upon</u> <u>the hilly region</u> of <u>Israel.</u> <u>Because</u> <u>it had continually</u>

      cont.   2050.1; 1931; 4480; its; 5971 plur.   3318, 8717   per Ez. 38:11-12

<u>been laid in ruins,</u> <u>and because its people</u> <u>were moved out</u> (of their Israeli occupied

                               2050.1; they; 3427, 8799   413; 983   (below)

lands, and were residing elsewhere), <u>they, therefore, shall dwell</u> <u>in safety;</u> <u>all of</u>

     3605; 3963.1   2050.1; you; 5927, 8804   3509.4; 7722 sing.

38:9* <u>them!</u> *<u>But because yours had risen up</u> (against theirs) <u>like a destructive storm,</u>

   you; 935, 8799   3509.4; 6051 sing.; 3680, 8763; 1886.1; 776; 1961, 8799

<u>you shall depart</u> this world (and) <u>shall become like an overwhelming cloud</u> (of doomed

      859; 2050.1; 3605   102 plur.; 3509.2 854; 3509.2

souls); <u>you and all</u> of <u>your troops</u> <u>with you!</u>"

      (3541; he; 559, 8804)…   cont.   136   3068 or 3069

38:10   "<u>This is what he</u> [Jesus] <u>has relayed;</u> '*The Lord* is *Yahweh!*'"

     (2050.1; it; 1961, 8804)…   cont.   871.1; 3117 sing.; 1886.1; 1931   (below)

"<u>Therefore, when it</u> [Gog's demise] <u>has occurred,</u> <u>at that same time,</u> <u>thoughts</u>

                          5927, 8799; 1697; 5921   3824 sing.; 3509.2   2050.1; you; 2803, 8804   7451   4284   (below)
38:11* shall enter into your (soul's) conscience that you had plotted an evil scheme! *For

                    2050.1; you; 559, 8804   I; 5927, 8799I   5921; 776 sing.   (6519 plur.)
you shall have (beforehand) thought; 'I will rise up against the region's unwalled

              cont.   I; 935, 8799   they; 8252, 8802   they; 3427, 8802   3087.1; 983   (3605; 1992)
38:12a* villages and shall invade theirs that are resting and are living in a refuge. *All of

               cont.   they; 3427, 8802   871.1; 369   2346 sing.   2050.1; 1280
these (refugees) are dwelling (in makeshift tents) with no protective wall or gate bar;

          2050.1; 1817 plur.; 369
nor are there any doors.'"

Also recall from Ezekiel 21:20 in the 1st book, that one of the destructive weapons that will be intercepted shall have been aimed towards the direction of Amman Jordan, where many of the refugees from Palestine and Syria have been residing.

                                                               3087.1; 1992   7997, 8800; 7998 sing.   (below)
38:12b   "(Thus, you all shall have headed) towards them in order to take spoil, to steal

         2050.1; 962, 8800; 957; 7725, 8687   3027 sing.; 3509.2   5921   2723 plur.   (3427, 8737)
plunder, (and) to recover the control of yours over the desolate places that were

              cont.   2050.1; 413; 5971   622, 8794   4480   1471 plur.
inhabited (by theirs) and, also, by the people gathered from the foreign nations

      6213, 8002   4735   2050.1; 7075   3427, 8802   5921; 2872   776 sing.
dealing in livestock and goods, who shall have been dwelling amidst the region."

             7614   2050.1; 1719   2050.1; 5503, 8802   8659   2050.1; 3605
38:13   "Sheba⁵⁵ [Yemen], Dedan⁵⁶ [Arabia], and the merchants of Tarshish⁵⁷ and all of

             its; 3715   559, 8799   3087.1; you
its villages [i.e., Tarsus Turkey and its neighboring cities], will say to you (Gog):"

                    7997; 7998; 559; you; 935, 8802; 962, 8800; 957   (below)
"Are you invading in order to take spoil and to steal the plunder? Your multitude

       6950, 8689; 6951 sing.; 3509.2; (soldiers per 38:15)   5375, 8800   3701   2050.1; 2091 (below)
(of soldiers) have begun to assemble in order to carry off the silver and gold; to

57

	3947, 8800	4735	7075 plur. 7997, 8800	1419	7998

obtain the livestock and *goods*; *to take* immense *booty*!"

		423 prefix; 3651		it; 5012, 8734	1121	120	(2050.1; you; 559, 8804)...

38:14 "Consequently, let it be prophesied, Son of Man [Jesus], what you shall have

cont. 413 prefix; 1463

relayed to Gog."

	3541	559, 8804; 136; 3069

"This is what Lord Yahweh said:"

1931; 871.1; 3117	5971; 2967.1	per Ez. 36:5 & 14	3478	3427, 8800; 3087.1; 983

"That same day, when My people (exiled out of) Israel are (still) living in safety,

you; 3045, 8799		2050.1; you; 935, 8804	(below)

38:15* you will (then) understand (you were in the wrong) *when you have departed, away

4480; 4725; 3509.2	4480 prefix; 3411; 6828	859	2050.1; 5971; 7227	(854; 3509.2; 7392, 8802)...

from your homeland in the farthest north; you and the numerous people with you

cont.	5483 plur.	3605; 3963.1		6951; 1419	2050.1; 2438; 7227 sing.

riding swift vehicles; all of whom were (part of) a huge community and mighty army."

	2050.1; you; 5927, 8804	5921	5971; 2967.1

38:16 "So, because you (Gog) shall have risen up against My people [in order to join

per Ez. 38:11-13	3478	(below)

Israel in seizing more of its Arab neighbors' lands], Israel shall have what is like

3509.4; 6051	3680, 8763	1886.1; 776	871.1; 319; 1886.1; 3117 plur.	it; 1961, 8799

a cloud of smoke covering the country. In the end times, it shall come to pass

2050.1; I; 935, 8689; you		5921	776; 2967.1	3087.1; 4616	(below)

that I shall have caused you to depart from upon My land, for the sake of the Gen-

3045, 8800; 1471 plur.	853; 2967.1		6942, 8736	871.1; 3509.2

tiles knowing, namely Me (Yahweh, as God); for them to be blessed when you are

per 39:11	3087.1; 5869; 3963.1	1463

(destroyed) before their eyes, Gog!"

(3541; he; 559, 8804)...	cont.	136	3068 or 3069	859	(below)

38:17 "This is what he [Jesus] had relayed; 'The Lord is Yahweh.' You [Gog] are the

58

```
                1931   834      l; 1696, 8765      871.1; 3117; 6931         871.1; 3027          5650; 2967.1
         one that I had spoken of, in ancient times, through the (helping) hand of My servant

                 5030 plur.    3478      1886.1; 5012, 8737   871.1; 3117; 1992              8141 plur.
         prophets of Israel, who had prophesied in those days, (regarding) the years when

                       935, 8687; 853; you    5921; 1992
         you shall instigate an invasion against theirs."


                              2050.1; it; 1961, 8804        871.1; 1931; 3117; 871.1; 3117   935, 8800; 1463
38:18    Therefore, (the following) shall have occurred at the same time as Gog entering

         5921   127 sing.     3478         5002, 8803            136        3069
         upon the land of Israel, as was stated in the Oracles of the Lord God:


                  5927, 8799; 2534; 2967.1; 871.1; 639; 2967.1   2050.1; 871.1; 7068; 2967.1; 784; 871.1; 5678; 2967.1
38:19    In My anger, My fury shall rise! And so shall My blazing wrath, because of My

             cont.    l; 1696, 8765; 3808.1      871; 3117; 1931       1961, 8799; 7494; 1419
         indignation! Had I not surely warned that on this day, a mighty tremor would occur

         5921   127 sing.    3478
         upon the country of Israel?


                                                         2050.1; they; 7493, 8804; it or this
38:20        (The tremor will be so powerful that) the following shall have also shaken, (far

                   4480; 6440; 2967.1        1709      1886.1; 3220    2050.1; 5775
         enough) away from the presence of Mine: The fish of the sea, the flying creatures

         1886.1; 8064    2050.1; 2416    1886.1; 7704      2050.1; 3605; 7431
         of the sky, and the living animals of the area; as well as all of the creeping creatures

         1886.1; 7430, 8802  5921; 1886.1; 127   2050.1; 3605; 1886.1; 120   834      5921; 6440; 1886.1; 127
         that move on the ground, and all of the people that are upon the country's surface.

                    2050.1; they; 2040, 8738; 1886.1; 2022 plur.           2050.1; they; 5307, 8804; 4095
         Even mountains shall have been demolished, and steep cliffs shall have toppled.

             2050.1; 3605; 2346 sing.   4480; 776       5307, 8799     2050.1; l; 7121, 8804   (5921; it)...
38:21*       Indeed, every wall of the region [in Israel] shall fall* after I have summoned against

             cont.          3087.1; 3605; 2022; 2967.1; 2719 sing.              (5002, 8803)...
         it, a destructive weapon (directed) towards each of My mountains, as was stated in
```

	cont.	136	3069		2719 sing.		(376; 1961, 8799; 871.1; 251 sing.)...

the Oracles of the Lord God. The destructive weapon of Jesus' will be against the

	cont.		2050.1; 8199, 8738; my; 853; his or him		871.1; 1698	871.1; 1818

38:22* brotherhood *and him [Gog], who will bear My punishment with pestilence, blood-

	cont.	2050.1; 1653; 7857, 8802	(2050.1; 68 plur.; 417; 4305; 784; 2050.1; 1614; I; 1614, 8686)...

shed, and an overflowing downpour! I shall also cause pearl-like stones of sulfur-

	cont.	5921; him; 2050.1; 5921; his; 102	2050.1; 2050; 5971; 7227 plur.	834

ous fire to pour down over him [Gog], his troops, and the numerous people who are

854; him

amongst him!

	2050.1; I; 1431, 8694; 2967.1	2050.1; 6942; 2967.1	(below)

38:23   Hence, I shall have magnified My greatness and My holiness. For I had (already)

2050.1; I; 3045, 8738	3087.1; 5869 plur.	1471 plur.	7227; 3963.1	(below)

made Myself known in the eyes of the foreign nations. Their Commander and theirs

2050.1; they; 3045, 8804   3588; 589; 3068 or 3069

have known that I (Yahweh) am God.

Ezekiel 39

2050.1; 859	1121	120	5012, 8734	5921	1463	(below)

39:1   [Jesus:] "You, who are a descendant of Adam; prophesy against Gog, what you

2050.1; you; 559, 8804

had (once) relayed."

3541; he; 559, 8804; 136; 3068 or 3069

"This is what Lord Yahweh said:"

2009; 2967.1	413; 3509.2	1463	7218	5387	4902 (Meshech)	8422 (Tubal or Tbil)	(below)

39:2*   "Behold, I am against you, Gog, Chief Ruler of Moscow and Tbilisi! *When I

2050.1; I; 7725, 8790; you		2050.1; I; 8338, 8765; you	(below)

have returned you back (to Me), it will be after I had led you along, and after I

2050.1; I; 5927, 8689; you	4480; 3411; 6828	2050.1; I; 935, 8689; you	5921

had caused you to ascend away from the far North, and had, then, led you towards

	2022 plur. 3478 2050.1; 5221, 8689; I or mine 7198; 3509.2 sing. (below)
39:3*	the mountains of Israel, *(where) Mine shall have struck your shooting weapon out

4480; 3027; 8040; 3509.2
of your left hand!"

(2050.1; 2671; your; 4480; 3027; 3225; 3509.2 sing.; I; 5307, 8686)...
"Thus, Mine will cause your (shooting weapon's) ammunition to fall from your

cont.   per Ez. 39:2-3 and Ez. 39:9
right hand! (Via your own destructive weapon targeted towards the Arab refugees,)

	5921; 2022; 3478; you; 5307, 8799 (859; 2050.1; 3605; 102; 3509.2)
39:4*	* yours, (instead of theirs), will fall upon the mountains of Israel; you, all of your

cont.   2050.1; 5971   834   854; 3059.2   (below)
troops, and the people who are amongst you! I shall have given yours to the birds

3087.1; 5861; 6833; 2050.1; 3605; 3671; 2050.1; 2416; 7704; I; 5414, 8804; 3509.2   3087.1; 402   (below)
of prey, each type of flying creature, and to the land animals as food! You (all) will

	5921; 6440; 7704; you; 5307, 8799 3588 589
39:5*	fall upon the land's surface on account of * Me!"

I or mine; 1696, 8765   5002, 8803   138   3068
Mine had (clearly) relayed, as was stated in the Oracles; '*The Lord is Yahweh*.'

	2050.1; I; 7971, 8765; 784 871.1; 4031
39:6	Consequently, I shall have sent a raging inferno against Magog [the Zionist

2050.1; 3427, 8802
Israelis and their gentile allies following the false Messiah], who were dwelling

871.1; 339; 983   2050.1; they; 3045, 8804   3588; 589   3068
securely in the desirable coastlands. For theirs had (once) known that I am Yahweh.

	2050.1; 853; 6944; 2967.1; I; 3045, 8686 871.1; 8432 5971 3478 (below)
39:7*	*Thus, I shall (again) make My Holy Name known amongst the people of Israel, and

2050.1; 3808; I; 2490, 8686; 853; 6944; 2967.1; 8034; 5750
never again shall I let My Holy Name be profaned!

(2050.1; 3045, 8804; 1471 plur.)...   cont.   3588; 589   3068
And because the foreign nations [bordering Israel] have known that I, Yahweh,

	6918; 871.1; 3478 2009 it; 935, 8804 2050.1; it; 1961, 8738 (below)
39:8*	am the Holy One of Israel, * behold; it has arrived and shall have happened as was

61

                    5002, 8803   136   3069   1931   3117 sing.   834   I; 1696, 8804   (below)
39:9*   stated in the Oracles of the Lord God. This is the day which I had promised; *when

                     2050.1; they or those; 3318, 8804; 3427, 8802; 5892; 3478   (2050.1; 1197, 8765; 784)...
        those that were dwelling in the cities of Israel have departed after the fire had set

          cont.   (taken from end of sentence: 2050.1; they; 1197, 8765; 871.1; 1992; 784)...   cont.   (below)
        ablaze.   Theirs [Jesus and his militia] shall have, indeed, set the fire that was

       2050.1; 5400, 8689; 871.1; 5402   2050.1; 4043; 2050.1; 6793 sing.   871.1; 7198 (bow); 2050.1; 871.1; 2671 (arrows)
        ignited by the weapon that is a defensive shield with a projectile and ammunition,

          2050.1; 871.1; 4731; 3027; 2050.1; 871.1; 7420 (spear); worded above- 2050.1; they; 1197, 8765; 871.1; 1992; 784
        and also by hand sticks and a hurled weapon [by dynamite and grenades].

                  7651   8141   2050.1; 3808; they; 5375, 8799   (6086; 4480; 1886.1; 7704)
39.10* (For) seven years*after that, theirs (surviving) shall not carry off wood from the

          cont.   2050.1; 3808; 2404, 8799; 4480   3293 plur.   3588   871.1; 5402   (they; 1197, 8762)
        area, nor cut down (trees) from the forests, since, because of the arsenal, they shall

          cont.   784   2050.1; they; 7997, 8804   853   (7997, 8802; 3963.1)...
        burn in the fire. They shall have also despoiled, namely (those) that were despoiling

          cont.   2050.1; 962, 8804   853   962, 8802; 3963.1   (below)
        them, and shall have plundered, namely (those) that were plundering them, as was

                    5002, 8803   136   3069
        stated in the Oracles of the Lord God.

                     2050.1; it; 1961, 8804   871.1; 3117; 1931   I; 5414, 8799   3087.1; 1463
39:11   Furthermore, once it has occurred, on that same day, I shall assign for Gog, a

            4725; 8033; 6913   871.1; 3478; 1516   them or those; 5674, 8802   (below)
        burial site there, in a valley of Israel, with those that are passing away east of the

             6926; 1886.1; 3220   2050.1; them or those; 2629, 8802   1931 irreg.   853; 5674, 8802
        (Mediterranean) Sea, and with those that were stopping him that will also be pass-

          cont.   2050.1; they or those; 6912, 8804   8033; 854; 1463; 2050.1; 853; 3605   1886.1; 1995
        ing away. Then, those who had buried these there with Gog and all of his multitude,

              2050.1; 7121, 8804; it   1516   1996 (or 1995; 1463)
        shall have afterwards named it, the Valley of Hamon Gog [Gog's Multitude].

                       ((From Ez. 39:14: 7651; 2320); 2050.1; they; 6912, 8804; 1004 sing.; 3478)...
39:12   Also, (it shall have taken) seven months for the House of Israel (survivors) to have

```
                         cont.    1992      4616; 2891, 8763    853; 1886.1; 776    2050.1; 6912, 8804; they; 3605; 5971; 1886.1; 776
```
39:13* buried theirs, in order to cleanse its country. *For all the (other) people of the region

```
                cont.                    2050.1; it; 1961, 8804        3087.1; 1992; 8034      3117 sing.
```
that shall have buried them, it, indeed, shall have been an honor for them, the day

```
                          I; 3513, 8736                       it; 5002, 8803             136
```
that I have (again) been glorified. It was (clearly) stated in the Oracles; "The Lord

```
         3068 or 3069
```
is Yahweh."

```
                 2050.1, 582 plur.; 8548; 914, 8686        (5674; 8802; 1992)...
```
39:14   Moreover, the (surviving) men shall separate out those that will be passing

```
   cont.          871.1; 776 sing.       (4480; 6912, 8764; 1992; 853; 5674; 8802, 199)...
```
away throughout the country; those that had passed away that they shall be burying,

```
   cont.     853; 3498, 8737; 1992    5921     6440; 776      per Ez. 32:3-6, 32:27, 34:5, & 39:17-20
```
from those that shall be left upon the ground's surface (as food for the creatures);

```
2891, 8763; fem. it
```
utterly cleansing it.

```
           4480; 7097    7651; 2320 plur.    they; 2713, 8799   (2050.1; 5674, 8804; 5674, 8802; 1992)
```
39:15* At the end of the seven months, they will search for *those that had also passed

```
         cont.         871.1; 776            2050.1; he; 7200, 8804; 6106; 120
```
away traveling into the country, when (someone) shall have spotted a human bone,

```
2050.1; he; 1129, 8804   681; masc. it; 6725 sing.   5704    (6912, 8804; it; 853; 6912, 8764; 1992)...
```
and had erected a marker next to it, until those that were burying, shall have buried

```
   cont.   413; 1516    1995; 1463    2050.1; 1571    8034; 5892    1997
```
39:16* it at the Valley of Hamon Gog; *which shall also have the city's name, Hamonah. (N:10)

(N:10) Hamonah (or Himonah) is most likely today's Dimonah, Israel, which lies west of the Dead Sea, within a large valley in the Negev region [58], and where the country's nuclear research facility and a nuclear reactor is located.[59] Recall from the prophesy revealed in Ezekiel 20:46-48 in the first book of *Preserved for the End of Time* that the Negev planted forest, located about 30 miles south of Dimonah, will eventually be destroyed by a raging fire. From the uncovered prophesies in Ezekiel 30-39, it now becomes more clear that the Negev forest burning and the inferno that God will send forth against the Israelis and the gentiles following

Israel's false Messiah (Ez. 39:6-9), is to occur when Russia's Gog, Israel's Magog leader (the imposter Jesus), many of the imposter Jesus' followers, and both of their massive armies are annihilated by a mass destructive weapon they launch against Prophet Jesus' followers in the Arab refugee regions. Instead, their own destructive weapon will backfire on them after a counter defense weapon knocks the destructive weapon off course. Once this occurs, and the world sees that the true Jesus is the one who prevails via Yahweh's intervention, God makes it clear in Ez. 39:7 that His Holy Name must never again be profaned. Later, towards the end of this section, it is revealed that Jesus' followers who "knew that the Lord is Yahweh (Eloah, Elah, Alaha, or Allah)," and any of Israel's survivors and gentile supporters who shall afterwards mend their lives, and shall, from then on, correctly obey God's Commandments and Ordinances, and shall pray only to God, in God's Name, shall all be God's people.

_{2050.1; 2891, 8765   1886.1; 776}
[Jesus:] "After having utterly wiped out the country [of Israel and its annexed

_{2050.1; 859   1121; 120   (3541; 559, 8798; 136; 3068 or 3069; 559, 8804)…}
39:17* lands]; *you, who are a descendant of Adam, relate the following that Lord Yahweh

_{cont.   3087.1; 6833; 3605; 3671   2050.1; 3087.1; 3605; 2416   1886.1; 7704}
said, in regards to each winged bird and each creature of the cultivated region(s):"

_{them; 6908, 8734; themselves   2050.1; they; 935, 8804}
"Let them be assembled together (by) themselves, after these have departed.

_{them; 622, 8734; themselves; 4480; 5439   5921   2077; 2967.1}
Let them gather themselves from all around (to feast) upon My sacrificial offering

_{834; 859   2076, 8802   3087.1; you plur.   2077; 1419}
that I am slaughtering. Because of yours, an enormous sacrificial offering will be

_{5921   2022 plur.   3478   (2050.1; 398, 8804; yours)…   cont.   1320   (below)}
upon the mountains of Israel because yours had [symbolically] eaten the flesh and

_{2050.1; 8354, 8804; yours; 1818   1320; 1368   see (N:17) in Section 4 of this book}
39:18* had drunk the blood of *the Mighty One's body [during the Eucharist]."

_{(you; (land and air creatures – Ez. 39:17); 398, 8799; 2050.1; 1818; 5387; 1886.1 776; you; 8354, 8799)…}
"Therefore, you (land and air creatures) may eat from and drink the blood of the

_{cont.   (from end of sentence: 3605; 1992)}
country's Exalted Ruler [i.e., Israel's imposter Jesus Christ], as well as all of their

(deceased, sacrificial) rams, lambs, goats, and fattened bulls of Bashan [60] [which

39:19* had been raised at the farms in east Palestine]. *When you have devoured the fatty portions to satiety, and have drunk the blood to intoxication from My sacrificial

39:20* offering that I shall have slaughtered for you, *you surely shall have had (more than) enough at My table!"

Thus, when the Mighty One's swift vehicle (goes against the Gog and Magog people during) each battle of Jesus', as was stated in the Oracles of the Lord God,

39:21* *I, then, shall have manifested My glory in the foreign nations (worldwide), when all of the foreign nations have beheld My sentence that I have executed, and also, My

39:22* power that I have set against these, *because the House of Israel should have known that I, Yahweh, am their God!

39:23* From that day forward, *when the foreign nations (worldwide) have realized that the House of Israel has been banished for their sinning, since they shall have transgressed against Me, I shall hide My face from them (thereafter). For I, indeed, shall deliver them into the hand of their enemy [the Muslim Arabs], and they shall fall by a

39:24* destructive weapon; all of them! *On account of their religious impurity and their

65

<small>2050.1; 3509.4; 6588; 3963.1   I; 6213, 8804   854; 3963.1   (2050.1; I; 5641, 8686)...</small>

<u>transgressions</u>, <u>I shall have dealt</u> <u>with them</u>, <u>and then</u>, <u>(from that moment on) I shall</u>

<small>6440; 2967.1   4480; 1992</small>

<u>hide My face</u> <u>from them</u>.

<small>   3087.1; 3651 (3541; he; 559, 8804)...   cont.   136   3068 or 3069</small>

39:25   <u>For certain</u>, <u>this is what he</u> [Jesus] <u>had relayed</u>; "*The Lord* is <u>Yahweh</u>."

<small>   6258   I; 7725, 8686; 853; your; 7622 quere   per Ez. 38:8, 11-12; 39:26-27</small>

[Jesus:] "<u>From this time forth</u>, <u>I shall turn (My face) towards your exiles</u> (cast out

<small>   3290   2050.1; I; 7355, 8765   3605   1004; 3478</small>

by) <u>Jacob's posterity</u>. <u>For I had repeatedly had mercy</u> upon <u>all</u> of <u>the House of Israel</u>

<small>   2050.1; I; 7065 (from zeal or jealous), 8765   3087.1; 8034; 6944; 2967.1 (2050.1; I; 5375, 8804)</small>

39:26* <u>when I had persistently been protective</u> <u>concerning My Holy Name</u>, *<u>and I had for-</u>

<small>cont.   853; 3639; 3963.1   2050.1; 853; 3605; 4604; 3963   834   (below)</small>

<u>given</u> <u>their shameful acts</u> <u>and all of their transgressions</u>. But <u>because</u> <u>they shall</u>

<small>   they; 4603, 8804   871.1; 2967.1   871.1; 3427, 8800; 5921; 127; 3963.1 3087.1; 983 (below)</small>

<u>have transgressed</u> <u>against Mine</u>, <u>by settling upon their land of refuge</u>, <u>even though</u>

<small>   2050.1; 3808; 2729, 8688   871.1; 7725, 8788; I or me; 853; 3963.1   4480 (below)</small>

39:27* <u>none (of these) had caused terror</u>; then*<u>because of Me turning them away</u> <u>from</u> these

<small>   1886.1; 5971   2050.1; 6908, 8765; I; 853; 3963.1   4480; 776 plur. (below)</small>

<u>(Arab) people</u>, <u>I, consequently, shall have gathered them</u> <u>off the lands</u> <u>that were</u>

<small> 341, 8802; 3963.1   2050.1; I; 6942, 8738   871.1; 3963.1</small>

<u>their enemies</u>. <u>For I had (already) been proclaimed, "the Holiest,"</u> <u>by theirs</u>, and

<small>   3087.1; 5869   1471 plur.; 7227 plur.   2050.1; 3045, 8804 3588; 589   3068</small>

39:28* <u>through the eyes</u> of <u>numerous foreign nations</u>*<u>that have also known</u> <u>that I</u>, <u>Yahweh</u>,

<small>   430; 3963.1</small>

am <u>their God</u>."

<small>   871.1; I; 1540, 8687; 853; 3963.1   413; 1886.1; 1471 plur.</small>

"<u>When I have caused these (in Israel) to be exposed</u> <u>before the foreign nations</u>,

<small>   2050.1; I; 3664, 8765; 3963.1; 5921   127; 3963.1 (2050.1; 3808; I; 3498, 8686; 5750; 4480; 3963.1; 8033)</small>

<u>and I have gathered them (from) upon</u> <u>their land</u>, <u>then never again shall I make (any)</u>

		cont.		2050.1; 3808; I; 5641, 8686; 5750	6440; 2967.1	4480; 3963.1	(below)

39:29* of theirs leave from there.   *Nor shall I ever again hide My face from those whom I

               834; I; 8210, 8804   853   7307; 2967.1

have poured forth, namely, My spirit."

     5921 1886.1; 1004   3478   it; 5002, 8803   136   3068

"To the House of Israel, it was (clearly) stated; 'The Lord is Yahweh.' "

SECTION 3

God Assures That the Dead Will Be Resurrected and Judged

Ezekiel 33:1-20

2050.1; 1697 sing.   3068 or 3069   1961, 8799   413; 2967.1   559, 8800

33:1   <u>Indeed, the Word</u> of <u>Yahweh</u> <u>shall come</u> <u>to Mine</u>, <u>saying</u>:

1121   120   1696, 8761; 413   1121   (below)

33:2   "<u>Son</u> of <u>Man</u> [Jesus], <u>relate (the following) to</u> <u>the offspring</u> of <u>your people, what</u>

5971; 3509.2; 2050.1; you; 559, 8804; 413; 1992

<u>you had (once) relayed to theirs</u>:"

776; 3588; I or mine; 935, 8686; 5921; fem. it; 2719 sing.

"<u>When Mine will cause the destructive weapon to enter over the (Holy) Land</u>

2050.1; 3947, 8804; 5971; 1886.1; 776; 259; 376 (Iyesh; Jesus)   (4480; 7097; 1992)...

<u>because the people of the other Jesus had captured the land(s)</u> <u>outside of their</u>

cont.   2050.1; they; 5414, 8804; 853; 2050.2; 3807.1; 3963.1; 6822, 8802   (below)

33:3*   <u>border; and when they shall have appointed him as their watchman,</u> * <u>and he shall</u>

2050.1; he; 7200, 8804   853; 2719 sing.   935, 8802   5921   1886.1; 776   2050.1; 8628, 8804

<u>have seen that</u> <u>the destructive weapon</u> <u>was entering</u> <u>over</u> <u>the country</u> <u>and sounded</u>

7782   2050.1; 2094, 8689 853; 1886; 5971   2050.1; he; 8085, 8804   8085, 8802   (below)

33:4*   <u>a horn</u> <u>that warned the people,</u> *<u>then because he had heard</u> <u>the sounding</u> of <u>the horn</u>

853; 6963; 1886.1; 7782; 2050.1; 3808; he; 2094, 8737   2050.1; 935, 8799; 2719

<u>noise, but had not heeded the warning</u> <u>that the destructive weapon would come,</u>

2050.1; it; 3947, 8799; 2050.2; 1818; 2050.2; 871.1; 7218; 2050.1; 1961, 8799

<u>then when it takes him out, his blood will be on his own head</u>."

(853; 6963; 1886.1; he or his; 7782; 8085, 8804; 2050.1; 3808; 2094, 8737)...

33:5   "<u>(If) his (people) shall have heard the sound of the horn, but had not heeded the</u>

cont.   1818; 2050.2   871.1; 2050.2; 1961, 8799   (2050.1; 1931; he; 2094, 8737)...

<u>(previous) warning, their blood will be upon themselves; but he that had heeded</u>

cont.   he; 4422, 8765   5315 (soul or life); 2050.2

<u>the warning shall have saved his own life (and soul)</u>."

33:6   2050.1; 6822, 8802; 3588; 7200, 8799   853; 1886.1; 2719 sing.   (935, 8802)...

"Furthermore, if the watchman shall see that the destructive weapon is approach-

cont. 2050.1; 3808; he; 8628, 8804 871.1; 7782 sing. 2050.1; 1886.1; 5971 3808; 2094, 8737 (below)

ing, but he had not switched on the horn, so the people will not be warned, then

      2050.1; 935, 8799; 2719 2050.1; it; 3947, 8799; 5315 4480; 1992 (1931; 871.1; 5771; 2050.1)

when the destructive weapon comes and takes the life out of them, because of his

cont. 3947, 8738 2050.1; 1818; 2050.2 (below)

evilness, his (life) will be taken also, and with his own blood. I will require (a reck-

4480; 3027 (hand) or 3028; 6822, 8802; I; 1875, 8799

oning) because of the watchman's action [of not warning the people]."

    2050.1; 859 sing. 1121 120 6822, 8802 I; 5414, 8804; 3509.2

33:7   "When you, Son of Man, were keeping watch when I had (in the past) sent you

3807.1; 1004 3478 2050.1; you; 8085, 8804 4480; 6310; 2967.1; 1697 (below)

to the House of Israel, you, indeed, had heard the Word from My mouth, and you

2050.1; you; 2094, 8804; 853; 3963.1 4480; 4480; 2967.1

gave them the warning that was from Me."

    871.1; I; 559, 8800 (or 8804) 3807.1; 7563 7563 4191, 8800 you; 4191, 8799 (below)

33:8   "When I have conveyed to the wicked guilty of killing, '*You shall perish*,' but if

2050.1; 3808; you; 1696, 8765 2094, 8687 7563 sing. 4480; 1870; 2050.2

you had not spoken up, warning the morally wrong (to refrain) from his way of life;

1931; 7563; 871.1; 5771; 2050.2 4191, 8799 2050.1; 1818; 2050.2 (below)

because of his evilness, the guilty one shall perish, and with his own blood; but be-

4480; 3027 or (3028; 3059.2) I; 1245, 8762

cause of your action [of not relaying God's message], I would require (a reckoning)."

    2050.1; 859; 3588 you; 2094, 8689 (7563 sing.; 4480; 1870; 2050.2; 7725, 8800; 4480; 1886.3)

33:9   "However, since you [Jesus] have warned the wicked to turn away from his way

cont. 2050.1; 3808; he; 7725, 8804 4480; 1870; 2050.2 1931; 871.1; 7563; 2050.2; he; 4191, 8799

of life, but he has not turned away from his ways, he shall perish with his sinfulness,

2050.1; 859 5315 (soul or life); 3509.2; you; 5337, 8689

but you shall have saved your own life (and soul)."

    2050.1; 859 1121 120 559, 8804 or 8798; 413 1004 sing. 3478

33:10   "After you, Son of Man [Jesus], had spoken to the House of Israel [about the

3651; yours; 559, 8804 559, 8800

afterlife], yours had replied, like this, saying:"

       3588   6588 plur.; our; 2050.1; 2403 plur.   5921; us   (2050.1; 871.1; 3963.1; 587; 4743, 8737)...

"<u>If</u> <u>our transgressions and sins</u> are <u>upon us</u>, <u>and after we shall have become</u>

                cont.   349   we; 2421, 8799

<u>decayed, along with these (sinful acts)</u>, <u>how then</u> <u>shall we live on</u> [in the hereafter]?"

         559, 8798; 413; 1992

33:11   "Convey to theirs:"

     589; 2416   5002, 8803   136   3069   (518; I; 2654, 8799)...

"As <u>I live</u> (eternally), <u>as was stated in the Oracles</u> of <u>the Lord</u> <u>God</u>, <u>I shall not take</u>

   cont.   871.1; 4194   1886.1; 7563   3588   518   7563 sing.   871.1; 7725, 8800

<u>pleasure</u> <u>in the perishment</u> of <u>the sinner</u>; <u>but rather, that</u> <u>the sinner</u>, <u>in turning away</u>

       4480; 1870; 2050.2   2050.1; 2421, 8804   (he; 7725, 8804; him)...

<u>from his (vile) way of life</u>, <u>shall have, indeed, lived on</u>, because <u>he had turned himself</u>

   cont.   they; 7725, 8804; 1886.1; 7451; 4480; 1870; 3509.2; 2050.1; 4100   (below)

<u>around</u>. <u>When they shall have turned away from the evil ways of yours</u>, <u>why shall</u>

          yours; 4191, 8799; 1004; 3478

<u>yours (choose to) perish, House of Israel</u>?" (N:11)

(N:11) Confirming this Ezekiel 33:7-11 prophesy, which is further stressed in Ezekiel 33:12-19, we located a conversation Jesus had with his disciples in passages 164 - 165 of the Gospel of Barnabas [61] (again, not to be confused with the Epistle of Barnabas or the Acts of Barnabas), where Jesus, during his first advent, explained how God wills for each sinner <u>to repent and mend their lives</u>; contrary to the belief of the Pharisees at the time that a 'reprobate' (sinner) cannot become one of God's elect, and is <u>predestined</u> to damnation. Jesus' argument recorded in the Gospel of Barnabas is as follows:

G. Barn. 164   *Jesus, sighing, said: "O brethren; in saying that God has predestined the reprobate in such a way that he cannot become God's elect, they blaspheme God as being impious and unjust. For God commands the sinner not to sin, and when he sins, to repent; such predestination takes away the power from the sinner not to sin, and entirely deprives him of repentance."*

G. Barn. 165   *"Now listen to what God said through the prophet, Joel:" As I live, as your God, I do not will the perishment of a sinner, but rather, I seek that he shall be converted to penitence.*

"Would God then predestinate that which He does not will? Compare what God said to what the Pharisees of this present time are saying."

"Furthermore, God said through the prophet, Isaiah:" I have spoken, but you shall not listen to Me! ... All the time, I have spread out My hand to a people who do not believe what I said, but contradict Me.

"When our Pharisees say that the sinner cannot become God's elect, they then are saying that God mocks mankind ...

Also consider what our God said through the prophet, Ezekiel, that God's elect can also become reprobated:" As I live, said God, if the righteous forsakes his righteousness, and shall commit abominations, he shall perish, and I will no longer remember any of his righteousness; trusting in (his righteous deeds) shall forsake him in My presence, and it shall not save him.

"God is Truthful, and cannot tell a lie. God being truthful, speaks the truth. But the Pharisees of this present time with their doctrine, contradict God, altogether."

33:12   2050.1; 859; 1121; 120; 559, 8804 (or 8798)   413   1121 plur.
"You, Son of Man, shall have, indeed, relayed (the following) to the descendants

5971; 3509.2
of your people:"

6666   1886.1; 6662   3808; 5337, 8686; him   871.1; 3117   (below)
"The righteousness of the upright shall not help to save him at the time of his

6588; 2050.2   2050.1; 7564
rebellion [against obeying God and His messengers]. And as for the sinfulness of

1886.1; 7563   3808; he; 3782, 8735; 871.1; 1886.3   871.1; 3117   (below)
the wrongdoer; he shall not be ruined when his (sins are forgiven) at the time of his

his; 7725, 8800   4480; 7562; 2050.2   2050.1; 6662   (below)
turning away from his wrongdoing. Furthermore, the (once) righteous (person) shall

3808; he; 3201, 8799; 2421, 8800   871.1; 1886.3   (871.1; 3117)
not be able to live on [in Heaven] when his (sins committed are not forgiven) at the

cont.   his or him; 2398, 8800
time of (his death, because of) him going astray."

33:13   871.1; I; 559, 8804; 3807.1; 6662   (2421, 8800; he; 2421, 8799)
"In regards to the (once) righteous (person); when I had said that he shall surely

      cont.   2050.1; 1931; he; 982, 8804   5921 or 5922; 6666; 2050.2   2050.1; he; 6213, 8804   5766
live on, but then he felt confident about his righteousness, and he committed iniquity

                    3605; 6666 plur.; 2050.2   3808; they; 2142, 8735   (below)
(just prior to his death); all of his righteous deeds shall not be remembered, and be-

   2050.1; 871.1; 5766; 2050.2   834   he; 6213, 8804   he; 4191, 8799
cause of his wrongdoing that he had committed, he shall perish."

           871.1; I; 559, 8804   3807.1; 7563   4191, 8800; you; 4191, 8799   2050.1; he; 7725; 8804
33:14   "When I had conveyed to the wicked, '*you shall surely perish*;' but then he turned

      4480; 2403; 2050.2   2050.1; he; 6213, 8804   4941   6666
away from his sinfulness, and (from then on) followed what is just and righteous –

             2258; he; 7725, 8686; 7563   (1500; he; 7999, 8762)...
33:15* (For example), * if the wrongdoer pays back a loan pledge; if he makes restitution of

      cont.   871.1; 2708; 1886.1; 2416 plur.; he; 1980, 8804   (3807.1; 1115; 6213, 8800)...
things stolen; if he followed by the statutes of those living, without (further) commit-

   cont.   5766   2421, 8800; he; 2421, 8799   3808; he; 4191, 8799   3605; 2403; 2050.2
33:16* ting iniquity; he shall surely live on [in Heaven]. He shall not perish. * All of his sins

   834; he; 2398, 8804   3808; 2142, 8735   3807.1; 2050.2   (below)
that he committed shall not be remembered against him. Since he shall have prac-

     4941; 2050.1; 6666; he; 6213, 8804   2421, 8800; he; 2421, 8799
ticed what is just and righteous, he shall surely live on [in the hereafter]."

          2050.1; they; 559, 8804; 1121; 5971; 3605.2   3808; it; 8505, 8735; 1870; 136
33:17   "Yet, the descendants of your people have said that the ways of the Lord are un-

      cont.   2050.1; 1992   1870; 3963.1; 3808; it; 8505, 8735
fair; but to these [who have mended their lives], their way is not fair."

         871.1; 6662   7725, 8800 (or 8804)   4480; 6666; 2050.2   (2050.1; 6213, 8804)...
33:18   "When the righteous has turned away from his righteousness, and he has com-

      cont.   5766   2050.1; he; 4191, 8804   871.1; 1992   (below)
33:19* mitted unrighteousness, then he shall have perished because of it. * But the wicked

2050.1; 871.1; 7725, 8800; 7563; 4480; 7564; 2050.2   2050.1; 6213, 8804   4941   (below)
turning away from his evilness; because he (from then on) practiced justice and

   2050.1; 6666   5921; 1992   1931; he; 2421, 8799
righteousness; on account of this, he shall live on [in Heaven]."

	2050.1; you, plur.; 559, 8804	3808; 8505, 8735; 1870; 136	(below)

33:20   [Israelis:] Since yours have said that the way of the Lord is unfair, I shall judge

376 (Iyesh, Jesus); 871.1; 1870; 2050.2; I; 8199, 8799; 853; 3509.2; 1004; 3478

yours, the House of Israel, by Jesus' (righteous) ways.

Ezekiel 37:1-10

Unfortunately, since the Israelis and gentiles serving the imposter Jesus will not be heeding God's numerous warnings, and will continue to obey and worship their Jesus as God, instead of the Lord, Yahweh, and will also keep oppressing the neighboring Arabs and seizing their lands, then all of the Ezekiel prophesies regarding Israel's and their gentile allies' destruction, and their hereafter punishment, will be occurring. The following prophesy, regarding a demonstration on how God will be resurrecting the dead, is to occur sometime after Jesus shall have taken control of Jerusalem.

it; 1961, 8804; 5921; 2967.1; 3027; 3068 or 3069   (3318, 8686; 2967.1)...

37:1   The (helping) hand of God that had come upon Mine, shall carry Mine [Jesus]

cont.   871.1; 7307 sing.; 3068 or 3069   2050.1; 5117, 8686; 2967.1   871.1; 8432

off. When with (him), God's spirit (N:12) shall then bring Mine down into the midst of

1886.1;1237; 2050.1;1931   4392; 1886.3; 6106 plur.   2050.1; he; 5674, 8689; 2967.1   (below)

37:2*   a valley that will be full of bones. *He then shall have helped Mine to pass over

5921; 1992   5439; 5439   2050.1; 2009   7227; 3966   5921; 6440   (1886.1;1237; 2050.1; 2009)

them around each side, and behold very many upon the surface of the valley that,

cont.   3002; 3966

behold, were exceedingly dry.

(2050.1; he; 559, 8799)...   cont.   413; 2967.1

37:3   Then he [God's messenger spirit] shall say for Me [Yahweh]:

1121   120   2421; 8799; 1886.1; 6106; 428

"Son of Man [Jesus]; these (decomposed) bodies shall (once again) have life.

2050.1; 559, 8798   136   3068 or 3069   859; you; 3045, 8804

Therefore say; 'Lord Yahweh, (only) you, yourself, have had the know-how (to

resurrect the dead).' " (N:12 cont.)

| | 2050.1; he; 559, 8799 | 413; me | it; 5012, 8734 | 5921 | (below) |

37:4   He shall also say for Me: "(Jesus,) let it be prophesied about these dried bones,

1886.1;6106; 1886.1;428; 2050.1; 559, 8804; 413; 1992; 3002; 6106
what you had (formerly) relayed to theirs."

     8085, 8798; 2050.2   1697   3068 or 3068   3541   559,8804;136;3068 or 3069   (below)

37:5*   "Attentively listen to the Word of God. *This is what Lord Yahweh said concerning

3807.1; 6106; 428
these (decomposed) bodies:"

   2009   589; I; 935, 8688; 3807.1; 3641.1; 7307   (2050.1; 2421, 8804)

"Behold! I, Myself, will be causing the soul(s) of yours to depart, after yours had

   cont.   per Ez. 37:3 & 37:7-10   (2050.1; I; 5414, 8804; 5921; 3641.1; 1517 (sinew))...

37:6*   life (and will again bring them back to life). *I, surely, had (once) provided tendon(s)

   cont.   2050.1; I; 5927, 8689; 5921; 3641.1; 1320   2050.1; I; 7159, 8804

and ligament(s) for you and had caused flesh to arise upon you, and then covered

5921; 3641.1; 5785   2050.1; I; 5414, 8804   7307   5921; 3641.1   2050.1; you; 2421, 8804   2050.1; you; 3045, 8804

skin over you. After that, I had put a soul into you, and you had life. So yours should

   cont.   3588; 589   3068 or 3069   (2050.1; I; 5012, 8738)...

37:7*   have known that I am Yahweh. *For I, indeed, had been revealed through prophesy;

3509.4; 834   (I or mine; 6680, 8795)...   cont.   2050.1; he; 1961, 8799   per 37:4

such as when Mine [Jesus] shall have been commanded what he must do (and say

   cont.
to you)." (N:12 cont.)

(6963; 3509.4; I or mine; 5012, 8736; 2050.1; 2009)...   cont.

Thus, behold! As My prophet [Jesus] was reciting the proclamation (that only

   per Ez. 37:3 & 37:9 – 37:10   7494   (below)

God has had the ability to resurrect the dead), a tremor shall have occurred and the

2050.1; they; 7126, 8799; 6106 plur.   6106; 413; 6106; 2050.2   2050.1; I or mine; 7200, 8804

37:8*   bones shall come together; each bone to its own body. *Then, Mine shall have seen

2050.1; 2009   5921; 1992   (1517; 3963.1; 2050.1; 1320; 5927, 8804; 2050.1; 7159, 8799; 5921; 1992; 5785)...

that, behold; upon them, their tendons, ligaments, and flesh arose, and skin shall cont.   4480; 3807.1; 4605; 1886.3   2050.1; 7307; 369   871.1; 1992

<u>cover</u> <u>over them from above</u>; <u>but without the soul</u> <u>in them</u>.

          (2050.1; he; 559, 8799)...   cont.   413; 2967.1   it; 5012, 8734   (below)

37:9   <u>So then, he</u> [God's spirit] <u>shall say</u> <u>for Me</u> [Yahweh]: "<u>Let it be prophesied</u> con-

        413; 7307   it; 5012, 8734   1121   120   (2050.1; you; 559, 8804)...

<u>cerning the soul</u>. <u>Let it be prophesied</u>, <u>Son</u> of <u>Man</u> [Jesus], <u>what you shall have</u>

      cont.   413   7307 sing.

<u>relayed</u> <u>about</u> <u>the soul</u>."

        3541   (he; 559, 8804)...   cont.

"<u>This is what</u> <u>he</u> [Jesus] <u>had relayed</u>:"

      136   3068 or 3069   4480; 702   7307 plur.   see (N:12)

"<u>The Lord</u>, <u>Yahweh</u>, <u>through four</u> (of God's) <u>spirits</u> [angels Gabriel, Michael, Uriel

Name in Arabic   935, 8798; 2967.1; 1886.1; 7307   2050.1; 5301, 8798

(Azrael), and Raphael (Israphil)], (<u>shall command</u>), '*Come, My spirit(s), and breathe*

    871.1; 2026, 8803; 428   2050.1; they; 2421, 8799   (2050.1; I; myself; 5012, 8694)...

37:10* *<u>into these slain</u>, <u>so they shall live</u>*;' as *<u>I, Myself, had also prophesied will occur in the</u>

     cont.   3509.4; 834   (below)

<u>future</u> [afterlife]; and <u>like when</u> [during Jesus' first advent] <u>he had requested that a</u>

    he; 6680, 8765; 2050.1; 935, 8799; 871.1; 1992; 1886.1; 7307   2050.1; they; 2421, 8799; 2050.1; they; 5975, 8799   (below)

<u>spirit</u> (of Mine) <u>come to theirs</u> (deceased), <u>so that they could live and stand</u> upon

5921; 7272; 1992   2428; 1419; 3066; 3966

<u>their feet</u> having <u>exceedingly great strength</u>." (N:12 cont.)

(N:12) In Ezekiel 37:9-10, and then later in 37:14, Yahweh explains how, upon His command, He will transport 'His breath of life' via any <u>four</u> of His subservient spirits (angels), who will transport God's breath of life within each individuals' soul back to the deceased person's renewed body, bringing them back to life. According to the Jewish faith, Gabriel, Michael, Uriel and Raphael are the four angels of God that surround God's Throne, indicating their superior ranking and status. [62] In ancient times, these four angelic spirits are specifically mentioned by name in one of the books of Enoch as having interceded on mankind's behalf against the deceitful spirits amongst the race of beings referred to as "the watchers." [63]

In Ezekiel 37:1-3, one of God's four spirits (the messenger spirit) that is also referred to throughout Ezekiel as His helping hand, shall take Jesus to the prophesied valley with many bones for a demonstration to today's people on how God will be resurrecting the dead. There, God's spirit (angel) will be commanded by God to instruct Jesus to recite; "*Lord Yahweh, (only) you, yourself, have had the know-how (to resurrect the dead),*" and upon saying this, Jesus (and other witnesses) will observe how the dead are to be brought back to life in the hereafter.

It is important to point out that the "hand of God," "God's spirit" that is His messenger, who is also referred to as the "Holy Spirit" in other passages of the Bible, is not God, as many Christians believe, nor a partner of God's, but instead, is in reference to His subservient messenger angel, Gabriel. Most Jews, Christians, and Muslims understand that God's messenger angel (a spirit) is Gabriel; this is common knowledge, but not all congregations realize that "God's spirit," the "Holy Spirit" (one of the four pious spirits of God mentioned in Ezekiel 37:9) is actually in reference to Gabriel, God's messenger angel/spirit.

From Ezekiel 37:7-10, after Prophet Jesus shall heed God's messenger spirit (Gabriel) and shall recite the proclamation that only Lord Yahweh has had the know how to resurrect the dead, he (and other viewers) will behold tendons, ligaments, flesh, and skin cover over each corpse's bones; after which God will command His messenger spirit accompanying Jesus to transport God's breath of life within each individual's souls back to their new bodies, so they can again live. It is made very clear in Ezekiel 37:10 that this same process that will be demonstrated during Jesus' second coming is how Yahweh will resurrect the dead on the Day of Judgment. Moreover, it's how Yahweh (not Jesus) had actually resurrected, for instance, Jairus' daughter (Matthew 9:18-26; Mark 5:21-43; Luke 8:40-56), Lazarus (John 11:35-43), and a young man from Nain (Luke 7:11-12), during Jesus' first advent. Although the canonical Gospels accredit these miraculous resurrections solely to Jesus, and many Christians have believed that Jesus is God because of the resurrections and miracles accredited to him, Ezekiel 37:10 clearly corrects this mistaken belief.

In support of Ezekiel 37:5-10, which clarifies that it is God, and not Jesus, that resurrects the dead, we also found evidence in the Gospel of Barnabas that Jesus was instructed by God's messenger spirit, Gabriel, to pray in the Name of God when asking God to heal or resurrect a person, and God would grant his request. The Barnabas accounts of the resurrections of the deceased man from Nain [64], and of Lazarus [65], are provided as follows.

The Resurrection of the Young Man from Nain

G.Barn.47   Jesus went down, in the second year of his prophetic ministry, from Jerusalem to Nain. Whereupon, as he drew near to the gate of the city, the citizens were bearing the only son of his widowed mother to the sepulcher, over whom everyone was weeping. When Jesus arrived, the men understood Jesus was a prophet of Galilee, and so they set themselves to beseech him for the dead man, that he being a prophet might raise him up…

Then Jesus feared greatly, and turning himself towards God, prayed, *"Take me away from this world, O Lord, for the world is mad, and they will call me God!"* And after having said this, he wept.

Then the angel <u>Gabriel</u> appeared, and he said: *"O Jesus, fear not, for God has given you power over every illness, insomuch that all that you shall request in the <u>Name of God</u> shall be entirely accomplished."*

Hereupon Jesus gave a sigh, praying, *"Thy will be done, almighty Lord God, the merciful."* And having said this, he drew near to the mother of the dead, and with pity, said to her; *"Woman, weep not."* And having taken the hand of the dead, he said; *"I shall pray for you, young man; in the Name of God, arise up healed!"*

Then the boy revived, whereupon everyone was filled with fear, saying; *"God has elevated a great prophet amongst us, and has visited his people."*

The Resurrection of Lazarus

G.Barn.193   Now there were assembled at the death of Lazarus a great number of Jews from Jerusalem, and many scribes and Pharisees. Martha, after hearing of the coming of Jesus from her sister Mary, arose in haste and ran outside (to find Jesus)… When she arrived at the place where Jesus had spoken to Mary, Martha weeping said, *"Master, I wish to God you were here (sooner); for then my brother would not have died!"*

Mary then walked up weeping; whereupon Jesus shed tears, and sighing said: *"Where have you laid him?"* They answered: *"Come and see."* … Jesus, having come to the sepulcher where everyone was weeping, said: *"Weep not; for Lazarus sleeps, and I have come to awaken him."* … *"Take away the stone from the sepulcher."*

Martha exclaimed: *"O lord! He stinks! He's been dead for four days!"*

Jesus replied: *"Why then did I come here, Martha? Don't you believe me, that I shall awaken him?"*

Martha answered: *"I know that you are the pious one of God, who has sent you to this world."*

Then Jesus lifted up his hands towards heaven, and prayed: *"Lord God of Abraham, God of Ishmael and Isaac, God of our forefathers; please have mercy upon the affliction of these women. Glory be to thy Holy Name."* And when everyone said *"Amen,"* Jesus said with a loud voice: *"Lazarus, come forth!"*

Whereupon he that was dead arose; and Jesus said to his disciples, *"Unloosen him."* For he was bound in the grave-clothes with a cloth over his face; just as our forefathers were accustomed to bury (the dead).

37:11   (2050.1; he; 559, 8799)…   cont. 413; 2967.1
Then he [the messenger spirit] shall relay for Me [Yahweh]:

1121; 120   1886.1; 6106; 1886.1; 428   3605; 1004   3478   1992; 2009
"Son of Man, these bodies are (proof) for all of the House of Israel. Theirs, behold,

559, 8802   they; 3001, 8804; our; 6106 plur.   2050.1; it; 6, 8804; 8615; our
were thinking; 'When our bones are dried up, then our hope (to live on) has vanished.

we; 1504, 8738; 3807.1; us
To us, we shall have been cut off (from existence).' " (N:13)

37:12   3807.1; 3651   it; 5012, 8734   (2050.1; you; 559, 8804)…   cont. 413; 1992
"Therefore, let it be prophesied what you [Jesus] had relayed to theirs."

^{3541} $^{he;\ 559,\ 8804}$
"This is what he had conveyed:"

$^{136;\ 3068\ or\ 3069;\ 2009;\ 589}$ $^{6605,\ 8802}$ $^{853;\ 6913;\ 3641.1}$ $^{(below)}$
"Behold! I, Lord Yahweh, will be opening up your graves, and shall have caused

$^{I;\ 5927,\ 8689;\ 853\ or\ 854;\ 3641.1;\ 4480;\ 6913;\ 3641.1;\ 5971;\ 2967.1}$ $^{2050.1;\ I;\ 935,\ 8804;\ 853;\ 3641.1}$
My people amongst yours to rise up away from your graves, after I had brought you

^{413} $^{127\ sing.}$
(all) upon the ground."

^{3478} $^{2050.1;\ you\ or\ yours;\ 3045,\ 8804}$ $^{3588;\ 589}$ $^{3068\ or\ 3069\ (871.1;\ 6605,\ 8800)...}$
37:13*   "Israel: *Yours, indeed, had (once) known that I (Yahweh) am God. After opening

$^{cont.\ 853;\ 6913;\ 3641.1}$ $^{2050.1;\ 871.1;\ I;\ 5927,\ 8687;\ 853;\ 3641.1;\ 4480;\ 6913;\ 3641.1}$
up your graves, and after I have lifted yours up away from the graves of yours who

$^{5971;\ 2967.1}$ $^{2050.1;\ I;\ 5414,\ 8804}$ $^{7307;\ 2967.1}$ $^{871.1;\ 3641.1}$ $^{(below)}$
37:14*   are My people, *I shall have then transferred My breath within you (all, like) when

$^{2050.1;\ you;\ 2421,\ 8804}$ $^{2050.1;\ I;\ 5117,\ 8686;\ 853;\ 3641.1;\ 5921;\ 127;\ 3641.1}$
yours had (formerly) lived, and I had settled yours upon your land." $^{(N:13\ cont.)}$

$^{2050.1;\ you\ or\ yours;\ 3045,\ 8804}$ $^{3588;\ 589}$ $^{3068\ or\ 3069}$
"When yours have acknowledged that I (Yahweh) am God, then everything that

$^{I;\ 1696,\ 8765}$ $^{I;\ 6213,\ 8804}$ $^{it;\ 5002,\ 8803}$ $^{3068\ or\ 3069}$
I had promised, I shall have carried out as it was stated in the Oracles of Yahweh."

$^{(N:13)}$ Thus, from the prophesies uncovered in Ezekiel 33:1-19 and 37:1-14, it is very clear that upon God's command, He will be raising the dead from their graves, providing each one with a new physical body that will come to life after 'His breath of life' that's within each individual's soul, is transported back into the renewed bodies via four of His obedient spirits. At that time, every individual shall stand before God to be judged and sentenced. Despite the clarity of these Ezekiel revelations uncovered in Ezekiel 33:10 and 37:11, God discloses that some of the people in Israel would be in doubt concerning the resurrection and judgment of the dead, and also regarding their eternal punishment or everlasting bliss, which is to be based upon one's righteousness and correct worship and devotion to the Supreme Lord, Yahweh (God, Eloah, Elah, Alaha, or Allah).

It is prophesied that some doubters will say:

Ez. 33:10 "If our transgressions and sins are upon us, and after we shall have become decayed, along with these (sinful acts), how then shall we live on [in the hereafter]?"

Ez. 37:11 "When our bones are dried up, then our hope (to live on) has vanished. To us, we shall have been cut off (from existence)."

But then God will instruct Jesus to convey His responses to the skeptics:

Ez. 37:5-7 "Behold! I, Myself, shall be causing the soul(s) of yours departing, after yours had life, (to again live). * For I had (once) provided tendon(s) and ligament(s) for you and had caused flesh to arise upon you and had also covered skin over you; and then I had put a soul into you, and you had life."

Ez.37:9-10 "The Lord, Yahweh, through four (of God's) spirits [i.e., Gabriel, Michael, Uriel, and Raphael], (shall command); 'Come, My spirit(s), and breathe into these slain, so they shall live, * as I, Myself, had also prophesied will occur in the future [afterlife]; and like when [during Jesus' first advent] he had requested that a spirit (of Mine) come to theirs (deceased), so that they could live and stand upon their feet having exceedingly great strength.' "

Ez. 33:11 "As I (Yahweh) live (eternally), as was stated in the Oracles of the Lord God, I shall not take pleasure in the perishment of the sinner; but rather, that the sinner, in turning away from his (vile) way of life, shall have, indeed, lived on, because he had turned himself around. When they shall have turned away from the evil ways of yours, why shall yours (choose to) perish, House of Israel?"

Other than these few clear-cut Ezekiel prophesies, there are only a couple other passages found in the Hebrew Bible that, to us, explicitly refer to the resurrection of the dead; one located in Daniel 12:2, and another one in Isaiah 26:19. Then, among the Qumran Dead Sea Scrolls, the Hebrew texts of Pseudo-Ezekiel (P.Ez.) [66] and Messianic Apocalypse (M.A.) [67] also contain fragments that speak about the Resurrection.

Dan. 12:2   Many of those that sleep in the dust of the earth will awaken; some to an eternal life; others to (one of) reproaches (and) eternal abhorrence.

Isa. 26:19   Your dead shall live! The corpses of Mine shall rise! Awaken and shout for joy; you who are dwelling in the dust! For your (soul's) mist is (like) a radiant mist. Indeed, the earth shall cast out the dead.

M.A.   For He heals the wounded and resurrects the dead ... (4Q521 Fr. 2)
(God) the Life-giver will resurrect the dead of His people. (4Q521 Fr. 7)

P.Ez. (4Q385)

And Mine shall have said: "I have seen many from Israel, who have loved your Name, and have followed in the ways of your heart. So these things (prophesied), when will they come to pass, and how will they be compensated for their piety?"

Yahweh shall have said to Mine: "I shall make (it) manifest to the children of Israel, and they shall know that I am Yahweh."

"Son of Man, you must prophesy about the bones, and you must say: 'May each bone approach to its bone, and a joint to its joint.'"

And it was so. Then He (God) shall have said a second time: "You must prophesy."

And sinews (and flesh) shall rise up over them; and they shall be covered with skin upon them.

And it was so. Then He shall have said again: "You must prophesy about the <u>four spirits</u> of the heavens; that the spirits of the heavens will blow upon them, and they will live."

Thus, a great crowd of men will be revived, and will bless the Lord of Hosts (who shall have caused them to live again).

In addition to these aforementioned Biblical and Dead Sea Scroll passages regarding the resurrection of the dead, the Koran (The Meaning of the Holy

Qur'an; ISBN 0-915957-11-6) also contains quite a few passages about the Resurrection and Judgment Day, many of which we found to be strikingly similar to the ones uncovered in this Ezekiel translation. A few of these Koranic verses are quoted as follows.

Kn. 3:185   Every soul will experience death, and you will be given your compensation on the Resurrection Day.

Kn. 4:87   God - There is no god other than Him. Of a surety, He will gather you together on the Judgment Day, about which there is no doubt; and who is more true in word than God?

Kn. 16:124   Your Lord will indeed judge between them on the Day of Resurrection concerning that over which they used to differ.

Kn. 16:38   They swear their strongest oath by God, that God will not raise up those who die. Nay! But it is a promise made by Him in truth, yet most among mankind do not realize it.

      39   They must be resurrected in order that He may manifest to them the truth of that wherein they had differed, and also so the rejecters of the truth may realize that they had indeed (surrendered to) falsehood.

Kn. 19:66   Mankind says: "What! When I am dead, shall I truly be raised, alive?" Doesn't mankind remember that We [God as the Supreme King] created him before, out of nothing?

Kn. 30:27   God - It is He who originates the creation, then reproduces it; and for Him, it is most easy. To Him belongs the loftiest similitude in the heavens and the earth; for He is Exalted in Might, full of wisdom.

Kn. 83:4   Do the doubters not think that they shall be called back to account (for their actions and beliefs) on a Mighty Day;

      5   The day on which mankind shall stand before the Lord of the worlds?

      6   Nay! Surely the record of the wicked is preserved in the Sijjin.

      7   And what will explain to you what Sijjin is?

      8   It is a Register fully inscribed.

      9   Woe, on that Day, to those that deny –

      10   Those that deny the Day of Judgment.

Kn. 22:5 O people! If you have a doubt about the Resurrection, consider that We [God as the Supreme King] created you out of dirt elements, then out of sperm, then out of a leech-like clot, then out of a morsel of flesh, partly formed and partly unformed, in order that We may manifest Our power to you; and We cause whomever We will to rest in the wombs for an appointed term. Then We bring you out as babes, and foster you so that you may reach your age of maturity; and some of you are called to die early, while some reach the feeblest old age so that after having knowledge, they don't remember anything. Furthermore, you see the earth barren and lifeless, but when We pour down rain upon it, it is stirred to life; it swells, and then puts forth every kind of beautiful growth.

Kn. 22:6 This is because God is truthful. It is He who gives life to the dead, and it is He who has power over all things.

7 Thus, verily the Hour will come. There can be no doubt about it, or about the fact that God will raise up all who are in the graves.

Kn. 84:6 Oh you mankind. Verily you are toiling on towards your Lord – Painfully toiling; but you will meet Him.
7 Then, he who is given his Record in his right hand –
8 Soon will his account be taken by an easy reckoning…
10 But he who is given his Record behind his back –
11 Soon he shall cry due to Perdition;
12 And he will enter a blazing fire.

SECTION 4

Jesus' Outings at Jerusalem's and Israel's Notable Sites

This section contains the Ezekiel prophesies describing when God's messenger spirit (Gabriel) shall take Jesus on an outing to the prominent sites of Jerusalem and Israel, including for instance, the Dome of the Rock Shrine and Al Aqsa Mosque situated upon Temple Mount, and also the Holy Sepulcher Church located behind and northward of the Dome of the Rock Shrine. At the time of this book's publication, Temple Mount, located as part of the Muslim Quarter within the walls of Jerusalem's Old City, has also been opened at set times, daily, for non-Muslim tourists. But according to the prophesies throughout this translation of Ezekiel, around the time that Israel's false Messiah emerges, the Muslim gentiles, who shall have been exiled out of Israel and the Israeli-occupied, Arab territories, and their pilgrims, will be forbidden to enter the Temple Mount area that is to be taken over by the Israelis. Only the Jews and Christians who accept the false Messiah shall have had access to the Temple Mount area designated for theirs.

Unfortunately, this prophesy where the Israelis will prohibit the Muslims from entering the reassigned Temple Mount area has already begun to unfold. In June of 2023, a draft bill was prepared by a legislator from Prime Minister Binyamin Netanyahu's Likud Party, proposing to divide Temple Mount (Al-Aqsa Compound) between the Muslims and Jews. According to the proposal, the southern portion of Temple Mount, where Al-Aqsa Mosque is situated, would be allotted to the Muslims, while the northern and central sections, including the Dome of the Rock Shrine, would be allocated to the Jews. [68] Needless to say, this proposed division of Temple Mount, preventing the Muslims from entering and praying inside of the Dome of the Rock Shrine, or even worse, which could potentially lead to the tearing down of the Muslim shrine for the rebuilding of a third Jewish Temple in its place, would cause tremendous anger amongst the Muslims, who revere it as the spot where they believe Prophet Mohamed was ascended into the heavens one night (where he reportedly prayed with and spoke to several of God's prophets, including Moses and Jesus; and was also shown visions of Heaven and Hell). [69]

The Jews also regard the spot where the Dome of the Rock Shrine sits, as sacred. They believe the "Rock," which the Muslim mosque was built on top of, is where creation began; referring to its massive rock as the "navel of the earth." [70] They also believe that this particular site is where Abraham attempted to sacrifice his son to God, [71] and it's where they believe God had instructed theirs to perform animal sacrifices for the atonement of their sins, and where they should carry out their offerings to God. [72]

Israeli Jewish activists have been planning and hoping to rebuild their temple where the Dome of the Rock Shrine is located, [73] and have recently built an altar that they eventually hope to place upon Temple Mount. [74] But after thoroughly studying all of the Ezekiel prophesies more correctly translated, although there is a prophesy revealing that the sacrificial altar shall once again exist upon the mount (possibly prior to, and) during the reign of the imposter Jesus, we found no prophesy revealing that the Jewish temple will actually be rebuilt upon Temple Mount; only a prophesy where God shall scold the Israelis for designing and making plans to rebuild their temple there (Ez. 43:10). Instead, we discovered in the following chapters that all of the "temple" measurements foretold in this section appear to be the prophesied dimensions of several of the sacred houses of worship (temples) currently existing on Temple Mount and within the walls of Jerusalem Old City. When the real Jesus is instructed by God to take these measurements of the gates and few sacred buildings within Old City Jerusalem, it will be proof for the people of Israel, that the prophesies within this section are prophesying the dimensions of already existing structures, and not the dimensions of a rebuilt Jewish temple.

According to Ezekiel 40:1, which follows this introduction, the uncovered prophesies in this section are to occur "by the fourteenth year after Jerusalem had been stricken" by Jesus and his army, who shall have been instructed by God "to bring the city to ruin" (Ezekiel 43:3). Thus, the prophesies in this section are to occur 14 years after Jesus shall have seized Jerusalem and made a treaty with the imposter Jesus (which shall eventually be broken when the Israelis invade Egypt); but sometime before Israel and its' annexed Arab territories are actually destroyed by the prophesied mass destructive weapon(s) that shall kill both the imposter Jesus and the Russian leader (Gog). Recall again from Ezekiel 17:12-14, 24:2, 26:7-12, and 29:18-20 in the first book of *Preserved for the End of Time* that prior to Jesus capturing Jerusalem, and prior to the time that the prophesies in this section are to be fulfilled, the real Jesus shall have been ruling from Babylon (Iraq and Syria), whose people are predominantly Muslim. Because the uncovered Ezekiel prophesies reveal that the real Jesus will be aiding the Arab "A'madians" (i.e., Muslims), including those from the "family of Togarmah," in counterattacking Israel, many of today's Christians and Jews will be rejecting the real Jesus' warnings and correct teachings, and will unfortunately not be taking the uncovered warnings in this translation of Ezekiel seriously, until after Israel's imposter Jesus is killed and the real Jesus Christ survives to complete his mission.

The reader might be able to understand the timings revealed in this section, as well as all the other timings provided throughout the Book of Ezekiel, as soon as the false Messiah and actual Jesus Christ appear. But again, because the earlier scribes had moved sentences, passages and chapters out of their proper places, the correctness of the timings revealed in this book, as well as the order of events to occur, are difficult to discern at this time. Although the prophesies uncovered will be occurring, the timings may be off because of this. Also, the sequence in which the prophesied structures are to be visited and measured by Jesus and God's messenger spirit, may be somewhat out of place, even after we made an attempt in several instances to relocate them to where they more correctly belonged. The timings and order of events revealed throughout this translation of Ezekiel, as well as the sequence in which the places described in this section are to be visited and measured, can only be verified after Prophet Jesus is returned.

Ezekiel 40:1-3

40:1   871.1; 6242; 2050.1; 2568   8141   3807.1; 1546; our   871.1; 7218   1886.1; 8141   (below)
In the twenty fifth year of the captivity of ours, at the beginning of the year, by the

         871.1; 6218; 3807.1; 2320   871.1; 702; 6218; 1886.3   8141   310; 834 (5221, 8717; 1886.3; 1886.1; 5892)...
tenth of the month, which is also in the fourteenth year after the guarded city [Jeru-

            cont.   871; 6106; 1886.1; 3117; 1886.1; 2088   (1961; 8804; 5921; 2967.1; 3027; 3068)...
salem] was stricken; in this time frame, the (helping) hand of God shall have come

40:2*   cont.   2050.1; he; 935, 8686   853; 2967.1; 8033   871.1; 4759   410; 3963.1   (below)
upon Mine, and shall bring Mine where, *through the visions of their God, he had

          he; 935, 8689; 2967.1   413; 776   3478   2050.1; 5117, 8686; 2967.1   (below)
(formerly) brought Mine to the land of Israel. He then shall set Mine down upon the

           413; 2022; 1364; 3966   deduced from the second half of this sentence
highest peak of a mountain [north of Jerusalem's Old City, where Mount Scopus is

          2050.1; 5921; 2050.2   3509.4; 4011 (frame); 5892; 4480; 5045
located], and upon it, (the view) on the southside shall (look) like the outline of the

40:3*   cont.   2050.1; he; 935, 8686; 853; 2967.1; 8033; 1886.3; 2050.1; 2009; 376 (Iyesh)   (below)
city where he shall then bring Mine, who behold, will be Jesus. *His [skin tone]

      4758; 2050.2   3509.4; 4758   5178   (below)
appearance will be similar to the appearance of copper, and in his hand will be

2050.1; 6616; 6593; 871.1; 3027; 2050.2; 2050.1; 7070; 1886.1; 4060
a fibrous ribbon that's a measuring device [i.e., a tape measure].

40:4-49   [Relocated after Ezekiel 46; dimensions of Temple Mount's gates and temples]

41:1-26   [Follows Ezekiel 40:4-49; continuation of the temples' measurements]

42:1-20   [Follows Ezekiel 41:1-26; continuation of the temples' measurements]

Ezekiel 43:1-3 & 4b

<blockquote>

(2050.1; he; 1980, 8686; 2967.1)...   cont.   413; 1886.1; 8179   (below)

43:1   Then, he [God's messenger spirit] shall bring Mine [Jesus] towards a gate, which

8179; 834; 6437 or 6440; 8802; 1870; 1886.1; 6921   2050.1; 2009; 3519; [(410; 1886.3; possv.) or 430]

43:2*   is the gate facing eastward, *as (the people there) behold the glory of the God of

3478   it; 935, 8804   4480; 1870   1886.1; 6921   per Ez. 1:27-28 (1st book)   (below)

Israel, who had approached from the direction of the east (in a metallic craft) that

2050.1; 6963; 2050.2; 3509.4; 6963   4325 plur.; 7227   2050.1; 776   (below)

has a sound like the roar of mighty oceans, and of which the ground shall have shined

it; 215, 8689; 4480; 3519; 2050.2   2050.2; 3509.4; 4758   1886.1; 4758   834 (below)

43:3*   bright from its splendor. *It shall have the same appearance as the sighting that Mine

I or mine; 7200, 8804   3509.4; 4758   834; I or mine; 7200, 8804   871.1; 935, 880 (below)

shall have (previously) seen that looks like what Mine had seen when coming to

7843, 8763; 853; 1886.1; 5892   per Ez. 5:5-12 (1st book)   2050.1; 4758 plur.; 3509.4, 4758 834 (below)

bring this city to ruin [because of becoming unholy], and like the sightings that Mine

per Ez. 1:1 (1st book)   I or mine; 7200, 8804; 413; 5104; 3529   refer back to Ez. 1:1 and Ez. 3:15 (1st book)

[exiled] shall have seen nearby the Khabur River [a tributary of the Euphrates River

(2050.1; I or mine; 5307, 8799: refer back to Ez. 1:24-28 in 1st book)...   cont.

in Syria] when Mine [Jesus and the four beings] shall fall prostrate in worship [within

per Ez. 1:28 (1st book) 413   6440; 2967.1   2050.1; I or mine; 7200, 8799   2050.1; 2009   (below)

44:4b*   their craft] towards My Face, *and then when Mine shall see and behold the glorious

(below)   refer back to Ez. 1:27-28 in 1st book

one of God [God's messenger spirit, who shall have also been praying within his

it; 4390, 8804; 3519; 3068 or 3069; 853; 1886.1; 1004; 3068   (2050.1; I or mine; 5307, 8799)...

craft], after the House of God (in Syria) had filled, and Mine (there) shall fall prostrate

cont.   413; 6440; 2967.1

in worship towards My Face.

</blockquote>

43:4a-27   [Relocated after Ez. 44:1-5, which follows]

Ezekiel 44:1-5

44:1   He [the messenger spirit] <u>shall, thus, return</u> Mine [Jesus] to <u>the pathway</u> of the
(2050.1; he; 7725, 8686)...   cont.   853; 2967.1   1870   (below)

[Temple Mount] <u>sanctuary's outer gate</u> <u>that is facing east, and which was closed up</u>;
8179; 1886.1; 4720; 1886.1; 2435   1886.1; 6437, 8802   6921   2050.1; 1931   it; 5462, 8803

44:2*   *<u>and he shall call out to Me</u> [Yahweh]:   "<u>Yahweh, this gate</u> [the Golden Gate] *is*
2050.1; he; 559, 8799; 413; 2967.1   3068; 1886.1; 8179; 1886.1; 2088   (below)

<u>closed up</u>. <u>It is not opened</u>, <u>so Jesus cannot enter through it</u>. (N:14) <u>Although</u> their
5462; it; 1961, 8799   3808; it; 6605, 8803   2050.1; 376 (Iyesh); 3808; 935, 8799   871.1; 2050.2   3588

'<u>Lord</u>,' <u>the 'god' of Israel</u> [i.e., the imposter Jesus posing as God], <u>had (previously)</u>
3069; 410 (or 430); 3478   (he; 935, 8804)...

44:3a*   <u>entered</u> <u>through it</u>, <u>it has since been closed up</u> * <u>by its chief leader</u>. <u>He</u> [the Prime
cont.   871.1; 2050.2   2050.1; it; 1961, 8804; 5462, 8803; *854 or 853; 1886.1; 5387; 5387   1931

Minister of Israel] <u>would sit amongst him</u> <u>in order to eat</u> <u>the (sacramental) bread</u>
3427, 8799; 871.1; 2050.2   3807.1; 398, 8800   3899

<u>before</u> his '<u>Lord</u>.'"
3807.1; 6440   3069

(N:14)   The Eastern gate leading into what has been a part of the Muslim Quarter on Temple Mount since 1193 CE, is the Golden Gate. It was sealed shut by the Muslims in 810 CE, reopened by the Crusaders in 1102 CE, and then resealed in 1187 CE by Sultan Saladin after repossessing Jerusalem.[75] This gate, which faces the Mount of Olives, is where Jews believe the Messiah will enter, and where Christians believe Jesus once entered on Palm Sunday.[76] It was rebuilt along with the city's bordering wall, and again sealed shut in the early 1540's by Ottoman Sultan Suleiman.[77] Muslims refer to Temple Mount as Al Haram Al Sharif, "The Noble Sanctuary," where two of the prophesied "temples" (the Dome of the Rock Shrine and Al Aqsa Mosque) are situated.[78] When the false Jesus Christ temporarily controls Israel, the Golden Gate will reopen for his entrance(s) into Temple Mount. And according to Ezekiel 46:1, which is later prophesied in this section, during the imposter Jesus' reign, this eastern gate which will be closed on the six working days, shall reopen for worshipers each Sabbath day and, also, each month on the day of the new moon.

44:3b So, from the pathway of the gate's portico that he shall enter, he shall then exit
_{4480; 1870}   _{(197; 1886.1; 8179; he; 935, 8799; 2050.1; 4480; 1870; 2050.2; he; 3318, 8799)…}

44:4a* out of its pathway, *and shall lead Mine northward of this gate facing towards the
_{cont.   2050.1; he; 935, 8686; 2967.1   1870; 8179; 1886.1; 6828; 413; 6440   (below)}

temple.
_{1886.1; 1004}

44:5 Then he [God's messenger spirit] shall say (the following) for Me, Yahweh:
_{(2050.1; he; 559, 8799)…   cont.   413; 2967.1; 3068}

"Son of Man [Jesus], put your heart (into it); observe closely with your eyes and
_{1121   120   7760, 8798; 3820; 3509.2   2050.1; 7200, 8798; 871.1; 5869; 3509.2   (below)}

listen carefully with your ears to everything that I am explaining to you regarding
_{2050.2; 871.1; 241; 3509.2; 8085, 8798; 853 or 854; 3605; 834; 589   1696, 8764; 853 or 854; 3509.2   (below)}

each of (his) ordinances at the House of God, and regarding each of his teachings.
_{3807.1; 3605; 2708 plur.   1004; 3068 or 3069   2050.1; 3807.1; 3605   8451; 2050.2}

Also put (in) your heart how to enter the temple at all of the exits of the sanctuary
_{2050.1; 7760, 8798; 3820; 3509.2   3807.1; 3996 1886.1; 1004 871.1; 3605   4161 plur.   1886.1; 4720}

[on top of Temple Mount]."

44:6-8 [Relocated after Ez. 42:20 to a later prophesy in this section about the priests ministering atop Temple Mount]

44:9-31 [Relocated towards the end of this section following Ez. 45:4b and 44:27 & 26b (also about the priests)]

Ezekiel 43:4-5

<small>2050.1; 3519   3068 or 3069   he; 935, 8804   413; 1886.1; 1004   (below)</small>
43:4   When the glory of God [Gabriel] shall have headed towards the temple nearby the

<small>1870; 8179; 834; 6440; 2050.2; 1870; 1886.1; 6921; 2050.1; he; 5375, 8799; 29671; 7307; 2050.1; 935, 8686; 2967.1</small>
43:5*   gate's path that faces eastward, * the spirit shall then lift Mine and shall bring Mine

<small>413; 1886.1; 2691; 1886.1; 6442   (2050.1; 2009; it; 4390, 8804; 3519; 3068; 1886.1; 1004)...</small>
to the inner courtyard. And after behold(ing) the glorious one of God, the temple

<small>cont.   per Ez. 40:4</small>
(site) shall have filled (with observers).

43:6-27   [Relocated following Ez. 40:4 below.]

Ezekiel 40:4

<small>2050.1; 1931 masc.; 5975, 8802   871.1; 8179   (below)   (below)</small>
40:4*   Then, when they are standing by the entrance, * he [God's messenger spirit] will

<small>2050.1; he; 1696, 8762; 413; 2967.1</small>
relay for Me [Yahweh]:

<small>1886.1; 376 (Iyesh)   1121   120   7200, 8798   871.1; 5869; 3509.2   per 34:31</small>
"*This Jesus is a descendant* of *Adam*. *Look with your own eyes* [see that he is

<small>2050.1; 871.1; 241; 3509.2; 8085, 8798   2050.1; 7760, 8798; 3820; 3509.2; 3807.1; 3605   834   589</small>
human] *and listen with your ears*. *Then set your mind towards everything that* Mine

<small>7200, 8688; 853; 3509.2</small>
will be showing yours."

<small>3588; 4616; 7200, 8687; them; 3509.4; 1886.3   you; 935, 8717</small>
[Jesus:] "The reason for showing them like this is because you were brought back

<small>2008   Ez. 12:11, 14:8 & 24:27   5046, 8685   853; 3606   834   859   7200, 8802   413; 1004</small>
here (as a sign), so announce everything that you will be observing to the House

<small>3478</small>
of Israel."

Ezekiel 43:6-27

43:6 _{(2050.1; 8085, 8799; him; 1696, 8693; 413; 2967.1; 4480; 1886.1; 1004; 2050.1; 376 (Iyesh); he; 1961, 8804; 5975, 8802; 681; 2967.1)}
Mine away from the temple that Jesus shall have been standing close to will

43:7* _{cont.} _{(2050.1; he; 559, 8799)...} _{cont.}
also hear him speaking for Me. *Thus, he [the messenger spirit] will relay (the

_{413; 2967.1}
following) for Me [Yahweh]:

_{1121 120 853 or 854; 4725 3678; 2967.1 2050.1; 853; 4725 (below)}
"Son of Man, [in the heavens] at the place of My throne, which is the place where

_{3709; 7272; 2967.1; 834 I; 7931, 8799; 8033 (871.1; 8432; 1121 plur.; 3478; 3807.1; 5769)}
the undersurfaces of My footings are, I shall dwell there for eternity, amidst the de-

_{cont. (2050.1; 3808, 2930, 8762; 5750; 1004; 3478)...}
scendants of Israel that are the family of Israel who would no longer continue to

_{cont. 8034; 6944; 2967.1}
defile My Holy Name."

_{1992 2050.2; 4428; 1992 871.1; 2184; 3963.1 (below)}
"These (here), however, and their ruler; because of their sexual immorality, and

_{2050.1; 871.1; 6297 plur. 4428; 1992 (below)}
because of the lifeless idols of their (Messianic) Ruler [i.e., crucifixes] (at) their wor-

43:8* _{1116 plur.; 3963.1 871.1; 5414, 8800; 3963.1 (5592; 3963.1; 854; 5592; 2967.1)...}
ship places; *because of putting them (at) their entrance(s), nearby the entrance(s)

_{cont. 2050.1; 4201; 3963.1; 681; 4201; 2967.1 (2050.1; 1886.1; 7023)...}
of Mine, and (by) their doorpost(s), nearby the doorpost(s) of Mine, which will be a

_{cont. 996; 2967.1; 2050.1; 996; 1992 2050.1; they; 2390, 8765; 853 or 854; 8034; 6944; 2967.1 (below)}
barrier between Me and them; because they shall have defiled My Holy Name with

_{871.1; 8441 plur.; 3963.1 834 they; 6213, 8804 I; 3615, 8762; 853 or 854; 3963.1; 871.1; 639; 2967.1}
their abominations that they had committed, I shall put an end to them, in My anger!

43:9* _{6258 (they; 7368, 8762; 853; 2184; 3963.1; 2050.1; 6297; 4428; 1992)...}
*From now on, their sexually immoral ones, and the lifeless idols of their (Messianic)

_{cont. 4480; 2967.1 2050.1; I or mine; 7931, 8804 (below)}
Ruler, must be removed far away from Mine. For Mine shall have dwelled in (their)

        871.1; 8432; 3807.1; 5769
midst for too long."

43:10   859   1121   120   5046, 8685 853; 1004   3478   853; 1886.1; 1004
"You [Jesus] are the Son of Man. Inform the House of Israel (about) the temple;

    2050.1; they; 8637, 8735 or 8799   4480; 5771; 1992   2050.1; 4058, 8804; 853; 8508
that they should be ashamed of their wickedness for even (having) considered a de-

    cont.   refer back to the introduction of this section
sign plan [to rebuild their Jewish Temple upon Temple Mount, where the Dome of

the Rock Shrine is located]."

43:11   2050.1; 518   they; 8637, 8738   4480; 3605; 834   they; 6213, 8804   (below)
"When they become ashamed of all that theirs had carried out regarding the de-

    6699; 1886.1; 1004; 2050.1; 8498; 2050.2   2050.1; 4161; 2050.2
sign and arrangement(s) (for) the temple of his, and for his (people) moving (Mine) out

      2050.1; 4126; 2050.2   (below)
(of this sacred area) and entering it, then make them understand the layout of each

 (2050.1; 3605; 6699; 2050.1; 853; 3605; 2708; 2050.2; 2050.1; 3605; 6699; 2967.1; 2050.1; 8451; 2050.2; 3045, 8685; 853; 3063.1)
of his (sacred areas) and each of his ordinances, and also of My layout and Laws.

    2050.1; 3789, 8798   3807.1; 5869 plur.; 1992   (2050.1; they; 8104, 8799; 853; 3605; 6699; 2050.2)
Also, write (it all) down before their eyes, so that they can observe its entire layout

    2050.1; 853; 3605; 2708; 2050.2; 2050.1; they; 6213, 8804; 853; 3963.1
and (can compare My ordinances to) all of his ordinances that theirs had practiced."

43.12   2063   8451 (Torah)   1886.1; 1004 5921   7218; 1886.1; 2022   (below)
This is the guide of the temple on top of (Temple) Mount, (and of) all the holy

    3605; 1366; 2050.2; 5439; 5439; 6944; 6944   2009; 2063; 8451 (Torah); 1886.1; 1004
places (and) sacred things round about its border. Behold this guide of the temple,

    per the following passages and chapters   (2050.1; 428; 4060 plur.)...
43:13* (altar, gates, and of the sacred holy places in its vicinity), *as well as the measure-

    cont.
ments of these. [Refer to Appendix 2 for the biblical measurement conversions.]

          1886.1; 4196
The altar (N:15) [that shall have again been used by the Jews for their sacrificial

        871.1; 520 plur   520   520   2050.1; 2948   (2050.1; 2436; 1886.1; 520)
offerings], in cubits, cubit(s) by cubit(s), and in handbreadth(s), thus, has a bottom

     cont.   2050.1; 520 7341   2050.1; 1366; 1886.3; 413; 8193; 1886.3; 5439   (below)
portion of a cubit (deep) and a cubit wide; and the border around its edge is one

       2239; 1886.1; 259   2050.1; 2088; 1354; 1886.1; 4196   2050.1; 4480; 2436   (below)
43:14* handbreadth (high), which is the altar's rim. *Then, the bottom portion, from the

 1886.1; 776 5704; 1886.1; 5835; 1886.1; 8481 8147 520   2050.1; 7341; 520; 259; 2050.1; 4480; 1886.1; 5835; 1886.1; 6996
ground, up to the lower ledge, is two cubits, and one cubit wide; while from the small

   cont.   5704; 1886.1; 5835; 1886.1; 1419   702   520   2050.1; 7341; 1886.1; 520
ledge up to the larger ledge is four cubits, and a cubit wide.

              2050.1; 1886.1; 741   702 520 plur.   2050.1; 4480; 1886.1; 741   (below)
43:15   Furthermore, the altar's hearth is four cubits (tall), and the part of the hearth at

            2050.1; 3807.1; 4605; 1886.3; 7161; 702 (per Ez. 43:20)   (below)
43:16* its upper portion (on the corners), also has four horn-like projections. *Also, the

 2050.1; 1886.1; 741; 8147 & 6247 = 12 or 20; 1886.3; 753; 871.1; 8147 & 6247 = 12 or 20; 1886.3; 7341; 7251; 8803; 413; 702 (below)
hearth's length (and) width is twelve by twelve (cubits) squared, for the four of its

     7253; 2050.2   2050.1; 1886.1; 5835; 702; 6240; 1886.3; 753   871.1; 702; 6240; 7341   (below)
43:17* four sides, *and its ledge is fourteen (cubits) long by fourteen (cubits) wide, for the

    413; 702; 7253; 1886.3   2050.1; 1886.1; 1366; 5439; 853; 1886.3 2677; 1886.1; 520; 2050.1; 1886.1; 2436; 3807.1; 1886.3
four of its four sides; while the border around it is a half cubit, and the bottom of it is

    520   5439   2050.1; 4609; 2050.2 6437, 8800 6921
a cubit, all (the way) around. It also has a ramp facing east.

         (2050.1; he; 559, 8799)…   cont.   413; 2967.1 1121   120   (3541)…
43:18   Then he [the messenger spirit] shall say for Me; "Son of Man [Jesus], this is

  cont.   559; 8804; 136; 3069
what Lord Yahweh said:"

        428   2708; 1886.1; 4196   871.1; 3117   they; 6213, 8736   3807.1; 5927, 8687
"These were the altar's ordinances at the time they were erecting it for lifting up

      5921; 2050.2; 5930   2236, 8800 5921; 2050.2; 1818 sing. (2050.1; you; 5414, 8804; 1886.3)…
43:19* the Ola burnt offering upon it and scattering the blood on it; *and for when yours had

93

　　　　　　cont.　　　　　　　　　　　　　　　(below)
　　　given a cow's young bull calf, as the chatat sin offering, to the Kohanim, the Levites'

(413; 1886.1; 3548; 1886.1; 3881; 834; 1992; 4480; 2233; 6659; 1886.1; 7138; 413; 2967.1; 5002; 8803; 136; 3069; 8334; 8763; 2967.1; 6499; 1121; 1241; 3807.1; 2403)…
　　　priests that were from the line of Zadok; those near to Me, devoutly serving Me as

　　　　　　　　cont.　　　　　　　　(2050.1; you or yours; 3947, 8804)…　　　　　　　cont.
43:20*　stated in the Lord God's Oracles.　*Yours [from the lineage of Jacob] shall have also

　　　　cont.　　4480; 1818; 2050.2　　2050.1; 5414, 8804; 1886.3; 5921; 702; 7161 plur.; 2050.2　　2050.1; 413
　　　taken some of its blood, and put it upon its four horn-like projections that were at

　　　702; 6438 plur.　　1886.1; 5835　　　2050.1; 413; 1886.1; 1366; 5439　　　(below)
　　　the four corners of the (altar's) ledge that's on the surrounding border.　Since yours

　　　2050.1; you; or yours; 2398, 8765　　854; 2050.2; 2050.2; 3722, 8765; 2050.2　　　(below)
43:21*　have repeatedly sinned, yours had also made atonement with it. (N:15 cont.)　*For yours

　　2050.1; yours; 3947, 8804　　853; 1886.1; 6499　　1886.1; 2403　　(2050.1; 8313, 8804; 2050.2; 871.1; 4662)
　　　shall have taken the young bull as the chatat sin offering, and then burned it in the

　　　　　　　cont.　　　　　　1886.1; 1004　(4480; 2351; 3807.1; 4720)…　　　　　cont.
　　　designated area of the temple, outside of the [Dome of the Rock] Sanctuary Shrine."

　　　　　　2050.2; 871.1; 3117; 1886.1; 8145　　you or yours; 7126, 8686　　8163; 5795; 8549　　(3807.1; 2403)…
43:22　　"Also, at another time, yours shall offer an unblemished he-goat for the chatat

　　　　cont.　　2050.1; they or theirs; 2398, 8765; 854 or 853; 1886.1; 4196　　3509.4; 834　　they; 2398, 8765
　　　sin offering upon the altar, because they had sinned; like when they had atoned for

　　　　cont.　　　871.1; 6499
　　　sinning with the young bull."

　　　　　　　　871.1; you or yours; 3615, 8763　　4480; 2398, 8763　　you or yours; 7126, 8686　　(6499; 1121; 1241; 8549)
43:23　　"When yours shall have ceased from sinning, yours would offer a cow's unblem-

　　　　　　cont.　　　2050.1; 352; 4480; 1886.1; 6629; 8549　　per Ez. 43:25　　(below)
43:24*　ished bull calf, an unblemished ram from its flock, (and/or a he-goat).　*After yours

　　2050.1; you; 7126, 8689; 3963.1; 3807.1; 6440; 3068　　2050.1; 7993, 8689; 1886.1; 3548　　5921; 1992; 4417　(below)
　　　had presented them before Yahweh, and the priests had thrown salt upon them, they

　　　　　　2050.1; 5927, 8689; 853; 3963.1; 5930　　3807.1; 3068　　(below)
43:25*　then would lift them up as an offering to Yahweh.　*Each day, for seven days, yours

94

        7651; 3117; you or yours; 6213, 8799; 8163; 2403; 3807.1; 3117; 2050.1; 6400; 1121; 1241   (below)

would prepare a he-goat as a chatat sin offering, a cows' young bull calf, as well as

      2050.1; 352; 4480; 1886.1; 6629; 8549; 6213, 8799   7651   3117 (they; 3722, 8762; 854 or 853; 1886.1; 4196)

43:26* an unblemished ram from its flock. *For seven days, they would make atonement

      cont.   2050.1; they; 2891; 8765; 854 or 853; 2050.2   (2050.1; 4390; 8765; 3027; 2050.2)...

at the altar that they had ceremonially cleansed with. After their ministry shall have

      cont.   2050.1; they; 3615, 8762   853; 1886.1; 3117 plur.   (below)

43:27* become consecrated *when they would complete these days (of atonement), then

      2050.1; 1961, 8804; 871.1; 3117; 1886.1; 8066; 2050.1; 1973 (6213, 8799; 1886.1; 3548)

(from) the eighth day onward, when it shall have been performed, the Kohanim

      cont.   (5921; 1886.1; 4196; 853; 5930; 3641.1; 2050.1; 8002, 3641.1)...

would prepare the burnt offerings of yours, as well as the offering of thanks, upon

    cont.

the altar." (N:15 cont.)

    2050.1; I; 7521, 8804; 853; 3641.1   it; 5002, 8803   136   3068 or 3069

"When I had (once) favored yours, it was (clearly) stated; '*The Lord* is Yahweh.' "

Ezekiel 45

      2050.1; 871.1; 5307, 8687; 3641.1   853 or 854; 1886.1; 776   871.1; 5159   (below)

45:1   "After yours (were) made to settle on this region as inheritance, yours would lift up

      yours; 7311, 8686; 8641; 3807.1; 3069; 6944; 4480; 1886.1; 776   753

an offering to God (for) the portion of sacred land [in Jerusalem] having a length of

      2568; 2050.1; 6242; 505   753   7341   6235   505   (6944; 1931)...

twenty-five thousand (cubits) long and a width of ten thousand (cubits). This sacred

    cont.   871.1; 3605; 1366; 1886.3; 5439   it; 1966, 8799   4480; 2088 (below)

45:2* region that includes its entire surrounding, *shall have as part of this, a five hundred

      413; 1886.1; 6944; 2568; 3967 plur.; 871.1; 2568; 3967; 7251; 8794; 5439   2050.1; 2572

by five hundred (cubits) square (section) for the enclosed sanctuary, as well as a

    cont.   520   4054   3807.1; 2050.2; 5439   2050.1; 4480; 1886.1; 4060; 1886.1; 2063

45:3* fifty cubit(s) open land area for all around it. *Moreover, this portion from the section

    you; 4058, 8799   753; 2568; 2050.1; 6242   505   2050.1; 7341

where you shall measure the length (as) twenty-five thousand (cubits) and the width

```
                6235    505              2050.1; 871.1; 2050.2; 1961, 8799          also see Ez. 41:1-4
```
as ten thousand (cubits), shall also have within it [the Dome of the Rock Shrine],

```
          1886.1; 4720; 6944; 6944    6944; 4480; 1886.1; 776
```
45:4a* the most sacred shrine *of the Holy Land."

45:4b   [Relocated towards the end of this section regarding the priests ministering to the imposter Jesus' followers]

```
          2050.1; 2568; 2050.1; 6242; 505; (also see Ez. 48:13)      753  2050.1; 6235   505
```
45:5   "Additionally, (another) twenty-five thousand cubits long and ten thousand cubits

```
       7341           (it; 1961, 8799; 3807.1; 3881 plur.; 4480; 8334, 8764; 1886.1; 1004; 3807.1; 1992; 3807.1; 272; 6242; 3957)...
```
wide area exists as a possession of the Levites that were to minister to their twenty

```
          cont.         2050.1; 272; 1886.1; 5892        yours; 5414, 8799   2568    505
```
45:6*   chambered temple. *Then for the city's property, yours shall allot five thousand cubits

```
      7341    2050.1; 753   2568; 2050.1; 6242   505        3807.1; 5980 or 5981 (ummah)    (below)
```
in width, and a length of twenty-five thousand cubits; for the community as a sacred

```
      8641; 1886.1; 6944; 3807.1; 3605; 1004; 3478; it or that; 1961, 8799
```
offering that will be for the entire House of Israel."

```
          2050.1; 3807.1; 5387          4480 or 4481; 2088; 2050.1; 2088; 3807.1; 8641; 1886.1; 6944    (below)
```
45:7   "Also, for the leader, there are portion(s) on both sides of the sacred offering that

```
      2050.1; 3807.1; 272; 1886.1; 5892     413; 6440   8641; 1886.1; 6944   2050.1; 413; 6440
```
are next to the city's property; (one) in front of the sacred offering that is also in front

```
      272; 1886.1; 5892      4480; 6285; 3220    3220; 1886.3    (2050.1; 4480; 6285; 6924; 1886.3)...
```
of the city's property in the westward direction, west of it, and (one) in the eastward

```
      cont.    6921; 1886.3    2050.1; 753; 3807.1; 5980; 259      1886.1; 2506 plur.  (4480; 1366; 3220)...
```
direction, east of it, which is the length alongside one of the sections on the western

```
      cont.       413; 1366; 6921; 1886.3
```
border, close(st) to its eastern border."

45:8-11a [Relocated to Section 5, since it relates to the Holy Land inheritance]

45:11b-12 [Relocated following Ez. 45:13-14, below]

| | | 2063 | 1886.1; 8641 | 834 | yours; 7311, 8686 | 8345 | (1886.1; 374)... |
45:13 "This is the (grain) offering that yours would offer: About a sixth of the dry meas-

cont.　　　　　　　　　　　　　　　　4480 or 4481; 2563　　　　　　　　　(below)
urement (would be added to) the homer portion. Thus, yours shall have added a

(1886.1; 2406; you or yours; 2050.1; 8341, 8765; 1886.1; 374; 4480; 2563; 1886.1; 8184)...
sixth of the (finely grounded) wheat or barley grains as the dry measurement (to) the

cont.　　2050.1; 2706　　1886.1; 8081　　　　1886.1; 1324　　(1886.1; 8081)
45:14* homer part * that's the portion with the olive oil. The bath measurement of the olive

cont.　　　　　　　　　　　　4643　　　1886.1; 1324; 4480; 1886.1; 3734
oil (would be measured out) setting aside a tenth part from the vessel for the bath.

6235　　1886.1; 1324　　　　2563; 3588; 6235; 1886.1; 1324　　　2563
Ten of these baths would make a homer, since ten baths is a homer."

　　　　　　　4643　　1886.1; 2563　　1886.1; 1324
45:11b "Using the tenth part of a homer, or bath [23 to 37 liters; around 6 to 10 gallons],

(2050.1; 6224; 1886.1; 2563; 1886.1; 374 (dry measurement of unspecified amounts))...
the measurement of dry ingredients would then (be added to) the tenth of a homer

cont.　　　　　　　　　　413; 1886.1; 2563; it; 1961, 8799; 4971; 2050.2
of the liquid part, or its formula would be (scaled up) to a homer of the liquid part."

2050.1; 1886.1; 8255　　6242　　1626　　(6242; 8255; 2568; 2050.1; 6242; 8255; 6235; 2050.1; 2568; 8255)
45:12 "Moreover, a shekel is twenty gerahs. Fifteen, twenty, twenty-five (and so on)

cont.　　　　　　　　　　　　　　　　1886.1; 4488; it; 1961, 8799
shekels [i.e., from 3/4 cup to 1 & 1/4 cups, or scaled up] would be the (dry) weight(s)

3807.1; 3641.1
(measured out) by yours (at home)."

2050.1; 7716; 259　　4480; 6629　　4480; 3967 or 3969　　(4480; 4945)...
45:15 "Also, one lamb from (each) flock of two hundred, (selected) from irrigated pas-

cont.　3478　　　　　　　3807.1; 4503　　5020.1; 3807.1; 5930　(below)
tures in Israel, (shall have been sacrificed) as a meat offering, a burnt offering, and as

2050.1; 3807.1; 8002; 3963.1　　3807.1; 3722, 8763; 5921; 1992　　(it; 5001 or 5002, 8803)...
their peace offering, in order for theirs to make atonement. As it was prophesied

cont.　　136　　3069　(3605; 1886.1; 5971; 1886.1; 776; 1961, 8799; 413; 1886.1; 8641; 1886.1; 2063)
45:16* in the Oracles of the Lord God, *(nearly) all of the country's people shall come to this

	cont.	3807.1; 5387	871.1; 3478		(below)

45:17* oblation for the exalted one in Israel [who will claim to be Jesus and God]. *Further-

        2050.1; 5921   1886.1; 5387   (it; 1961, 8799; 1886.1; 5930; 2050.1; 1886.1; 4503; 2050.1; 1886.1; 5262)…

more, according to the exalted one, the burnt offering, meat offering, and drink of-

    cont.   871.1; 2282 plur.   871.1; 2320 plur.   2050.1; 871.1; 7676 plur.

fering should occur during the religious feasts, at the new moons, and on the Sab-

    cont.   871.1; 3605; 4150 plur., possv.; 1004; 3478   1931 (6213, 8799; 853; 1886.1; 2403)…

baths. Also, at each of the House of Israel's assemblies, he would perform the sin

    cont.   2050.1; 853; 1886.1; 4503   2050.1; 853; 1886.1; 5930   2050.1; 853; 1886.1; 8002; 3963.1

offering, the meat offering, the burnt offering, and their (communal) peace offering

    3807.1; 3722   1157   1004 sing.; 3478

for atonement on behalf of the House of Israel." (N:15 cont.)

      3541 559, 8804 136   3069   871.1; 7223; 871.1; 259; 3807.1; 2320   you or yours; 3947, 8799 (below)

45:18   "Hence, said the Lord God: On the first of each month, yours would fetch a young

      6499; 1121; 1241   8549   2050.1; you or yours; 2398, 8765   853 or 854; 1886.1; 4720

bull of the herd without blemish, after yours had utterly sinned within the sanctuary,

        2050.1; 3947, 8804; 1886.1; 3548; 4480; 1818   1886.1; 2403 (2050.1; he; 5414, 8804)

45:19* *and the priest shall have taken some of the blood of the sin offering and shall have

    cont.   413   4201   1886.1; 1004   2050.1; 413; 702 6438 plur. 1886.1; 5835; 3807.1; 4196

applied it upon the doorpost of the temple, on the four corners of the altar's border,

      2050.1; 5921; 4201   8179; 1886.1; 2691; 1886.1; 6442   2050.1; 3651; you or yours; 6213, 8799 (below)

45:20* and upon the doorpost of the inner court's gate. * Yours would also do this on the

    871.1; 7651   871.1; 2320

seventh of the month."

      4480; 376 (Iyesh)   7686, 8802   2050.1; 4480; 6612 (below)

"Because of the Jesus who is deceiving, and because of naivety; yours shall

    2050.1; yours; 3722, 8765   853 or 854; 1886.1; 1004

have, thus, made the atonement(s) by the temple [on top of Temple Mount]."

      871.1; 7223   871.1; 702; 1886.3 or 1886.1; 6240; 3117; 3807.1; 2320 (below)

45:21   "During the first month [Nisan], on the fourteenth day of the month, the Passover

  it; 1961, 8799; 3807.1; 3641.1; 1886.1; 6453; 2282   7651   3117   4682 (below)

celebration would begin for yours, and for seven days unleavened bread would be

                398, 8735   2050.1; he; 6213, 8804; 1886.1; 5387; 871.1; 3117; 1886.1; 1931   (below)
45:22* eaten. *On that day, the exalted one shall have also provided a young bull as a sin

                     1157; 2050.2; 2050.1; 1157; 3605; 5871; 1886.1; 776; 6499; 2403   (below)
45:23* offering, on behalf of himself, and on behalf of all the country's people. *Then, dur-

        (2050.1; 7651; 3117; 1886.1; 2282; he; 6213, 8799; 5930; 3807.1; 3069; 7651; 6499; 2050.1; 7651; 352; 8549; 3807.1; 3117;
        7651; 1886.1; 3117)...
        ing the seven days of the holiday, each day, for seven days, he would prepare the

                                        cont.   (2050.1; 2403)...
        burnt offering of seven unblemished bulls and seven rams to God, and the sin of-

         cont.   8163; 5795   3807.1; 3117   (2050.1; 4503; 374; 3807.1; 6499; 2050.1; 374; 3807.1; 352; he; 6213, 8799)
45:24* fering of kid goats; one for each day. *Also, as a meat offering, he would prepare a

                                        cont.   (below)
        measured amount of the bull and a measured amount of the ram, which would also

           2050.1; 8081; 1969   3807.1; 374
        have a hin of olive oil per measured amount(s)."

                   871.1; 7637   871.1; 2568; 6240   3117   3807.1; 2320   (below)
45:25   "During the seventh (month) [Tishrei], on the fifteenth day of the month, at the

            871.1; 2282   he; 6213, 8799   3509.4; 428   7651; 1886.1; 3117
        (Sukkot) festival, he would do the same as these other seven days, (and would pre-

                 (3509.4; 2403; 3509.4; 5930; 2050.1; 3509.4; 4503; 2050.1; 3509.4; 8081)...
        pare) in the same manner, the sin offering, burnt offering, and the meat offering

            cont.
        with the olive oil." (N:15 cont.)

(N:15) Although the Jews have believed that burnt offerings and animal sacrifices on the altar described in this section were required by God to be carried out atop Temple Mount for the penitence of their sins, and Christians have believed that Jesus was their sacrificial lamb replacement, who was crucified for the atonement of their sins, God makes it very clear throughout the Book of Ezekiel that salvation and the forgiveness of sins are only guaranteed through one's repentance, the mending of their life by, from then on, strictly obeying God's Commandments and actual Ordinances, and by praying only in the Name of God to the Lord, Yahweh (Eloah, Elah, Alaha, or Allah); not through animal sacrifices and offerings to God; nor through the sacrificial crucifixion of Jesus. In the Old Testament (Tanakh),

God had also made it very clear to His prophets- Isaiah, Jeremiah, and Amos, that animal sacrifices and burnt offerings were <u>not</u> a requirement prescribed by Him for the atonement of sins, and that this religious observance intended for the removal of sins has actually been disliked by Him. According to Isaiah 1:11-13, Jeremiah 6:20 & 7:21-22, and Amos 5:21-23, provided as follows, God had instead insisted that His people stop making animal sacrifices and offerings to Him because "they do <u>not</u> do away with sinning."

Isa. 1:11 "For what purpose are your multitude of sacrifices to Me?" said the Lord. "I've had enough of the burnt offerings of rams, and the fat of the fed animals; and I do not delight in the bloodshed of bullocks, lambs or he-goats!"

1:12 "When you come to appear before Me, who required this from your hand; trampling My courtyards?"

1:13 "Do not bring any more futile offerings! Its odor is offensive to Me. Calling the communities together (on) the new moons and Sabbaths (to make the offerings) does not do away with sinning!"

Jer. 6:20 "Your burnt offerings are not acceptable; nor are your sacrifices pleasing to Me."

Jer. 7:21 Thus, said the Lord of Hosts, the God of Israel: "Take away your burnt offerings; (I am) against your sacrifice offerings; so (just) eat the meat."

Jer. 7:22 "For I never spoke to your forefathers, nor commanded them, regarding the burnt offerings or sacrifices, when I had brought them out of the land of Egypt."

Am. 5:21 I loathingly reject your religious festivities and am not appeased by your solemn assemblies.

Am. 5:22 When you offer Me burnt offerings, or your meat offerings, I do not accept them, nor do I pay heed to your peace offerings of your fattened sacrificial animals.

Ezekiel 46

46:1   ³⁵⁴¹   ^{559, 8804; 136; 3069}
"This is what Lord Yahweh said:"

⁸¹⁷⁹   ^{1886.1;2691;1886.1;6442;1886.1;6437,8802;6921} ^{1961,8799;5462,8803}   ^(8337;3117;1886.1;4639)
"The gate of the inner court that's facing east will be closed on the six working

    ^{cont.}   ^{2050.1; 871.1; 3117; 1886.1; 7676}   ^{it; 6605, 8799}   ^{2050.1; 871.1; 3117}   ^{1886.1; 2320}
days; then, on the Sabbath day it would (re)open, and on the day of the new moon,

46:8*   ^{it; 6605, 8799}   ^{2050.1; 871.1; 935, 8800; 1886.1; 5387}   ^{1870; 197; 1886.1; 8179}
it would open. * Whenever the exalted one (was) to enter by way of the gate's

    ^{cont.}   ^{he; 935, 8799; 2050.1; 871.1; 1870; 2050.2; he; 3318, 8799}
portico that he would enter through, he would also exit out the same way."

46:2a   ^{(2050.1;935,8804;1886.1;5387)...}   ^{cont.}   ¹⁸⁷⁰
"So, the exalted one [posing as God in the flesh] shall have entered by way of the

  ¹⁹⁷   ^{1886.1; 8179; 4480; 2351}   ^{2050.1; he; 5975, 8804; 5921; 4201; 1886.1}   ^{8179; 2050.1; 6213, 8804; 1886.1; 3548}
portico outside of the gate, and stood by the gate's post as the priests prepared

    ^{853; 5930; 2050.2}   ^{2050.1; 853; 8002; 2050.2}   ^{2050.1; he; 7812, 8694}
his burnt offering and peace offering. (With his followers,) he then shall have prayed

46:10* ^{5921; 4670; 1886.1; 8179}   ^{2050.1; 1886.1; 5438}   ^{871.1; 8432; 3963.1}
above the gate's threshold. *After the exalted one was in the midst of these (wor-

        ^{871.1; he; 935, 8800 or 8804; 3963.1}   ^(he; 935, 8799; 2050.1; yours; 3318, 8804)
shipers), and after he had (allegedly) 'delivered' them, he would depart as yours

    ^{cont.}   ^{they; 3318, 8799}
exited; they would exit out (simultaneously)."

46:2b ^{2050.1; he; 3318, 8804 or 8799}   ^{2050.1; 8179}   ^{(3808; 5462, 8799 (not 8735); 5704; 1886.1; 6153)}
"Even after he shall have left, the gate, however, would not close until that eve-

46:3* ^{cont.}   ^{2050.1; 7812, 8694; 5971; 1886.1; 776}
ning, * so the country's people (who came later) shall have prayed (by) themselves

    ^{6607 sing.}   ^{1886.1; 8179; 1886.1; 1931; 871.1; 7676}   ^{2050.1; 871.1; 2320 plur.}
at the entrance of the gate, on the Sabbath and on (the days of) the new moons,

  ^{3807.1; 6440; 3068 or 3069}
facing towards Yahweh."

46:9   2050.1; 871.1; 935, 8800; 5971; 1886.1; 776   3807.1; 6440; 3068   (871.1; 4150; 1886.1; 935, 8800 or 8804)

"When the country's people arriving to face Yahweh during these appointed oc-

      cont.   1870   8179; 6828   3807.1; 7812, 8692   (below)

casions shall have entered by way of the north gate to pray by themselves, (they)

 he; 3318, 8799   1870   8179; 5045   2050.1; 1886.1; 935, 8800 or 8804   1870

would exit out by way of the south gate; and whoever shall have entered by way

  cont.   8179; 5045   3318, 8799   1870   8179; 6828; 1886.3   he; 3808; 7725, 8799

of the south gate would exit out by way of its north gate. (They) would not return

    1870   1886.1; 8179 834   he; 935, 8804   871.1; 2050.2   3588   (5226; 2050.2; 3318, 8799; 2050.2)

by way of the gate that (they) had entered through, but rather, would exit out the

      cont.

opposite side of it."

46:4   2050.1; 1886.1; 5930   834   (7126; 8686; 1886.1; 5387)...

"Additionally, the burnt offering that the exalted one would require (them) to pre-

  cont.   3807.1; 3069; 871.1; 3117; 1886.1; 7676   8337   3532 plur.; 8549   (below)

sent to God on the Sabbath day, would be six lambs without blemish, and an un-

  2050.1; 352; 8549   2050.1; 4503   374   3807.1; 352   (below)

46:5* blemished ram; *and as the meat offering, an unspecified amount of the ram and

  2050.1; 3807.1; 3532 plur.; 4503   4991   3027; 2050.2   2050.1; 8081; 1969

lambs' sacrificial meat would be (handed as) a gift into his hand, along with a hin of

    cont.   3807.1; 374   2050.1; 871.1; 3117   1886.1; 2320

46:6* olive oil for the unspecified amount (of meat). *Also, on the day of the new moon,

          (6499; 1121; 1241; 8549; 2050.1; 8337; 3532; 2050.1; 352; 8549; they; 1961, 8799)...

(the sacrificial offerings) would consist of a young bull (selected from) a herd without

        cont.   (2050.1; 374)...

46:7* blemish, six lambs, and an unblemished ram; *and (from) an unspecified quantity

  3807.1; 6499   2050.1; 374   3807.1; 352 sing.   (below)

of the bull, and an unspecified amount of the ram and lambs, he would also take

 (2050.1; he; 6213, 8799; 4503; 2050.1; 3532 plur.; 3509.4; 834; 5381, 8686; 3027; 2050.2; 2050.1; 8081; 1969; 3807.1; 374)...

(some of) the meat offering, as well as a hin of the oil for the unspecified amount;

      cont.

(taking) as much as his hand(s) could obtain."

46:11   ^{2050.1; 871.1; 2282}   ^{2050.1; 871.1; 4150}   ^(it; 1961, 8799; 1886.1; 4503)

"Likewise, at the religious festivals and at the fixed occasions, the meat offering

^{cont.}   ^{374; 3807.1; 6499; 2050.1; 374; 3807.1; 352; 2050.1; 3807.1; 3532}

would consist of an unspecified amount of the young bull, ram, and lambs (handed)

⁴⁹⁹¹   ^{3027; 2050.2}   ^{2050.1; 8081; 1969}   ^{3807.1; 374}

as a gift into his hand(s); as well as a hin of the oil for the unspecified amount (of

            ^{2050.1; 3588}   ^{he; 6213, 8799; 1886.1; 5387}   ^{5071; 5930}   ^(below)

46:12* meat). *And whenever the exalted one would prepare a voluntary burnt offering or

^{167; 8002}   ^(5071; 3807.1; 3068; 2050.1; it; 6605, 8804; 3807.1; 2050.2; 853; 1886.1; 8179; 1886.1; 6437; 6921)

peace offerings, voluntarily to Yahweh, then the gate that faces towards the east

            ^{cont.}   ^{2050.1; he; 6213, 8804}   ^{853; 5930; 2050.2}

shall have (been) opened for him. After he shall have performed his burnt offering

^{2050.1; 853; 8002; 2050.2}   ^{3509.4; 834; he; 6213, 8799}   ^{871.1; 3117; 1886.1; 7676}   ^{2050.1; he; (cont. below)}

and his peace offerings, just as he would do on the Sabbath day, he shall have then

^{3318, 8804; 2050.1; 5462, 8804; 853; 1886.1; 8179}

exited out and shut the gate."

         ^{310; 2967.1}   ^{they; 3318, 8804 or 8800}   ^(below)

46:13* "Sometime after Mine shall have left [this area], *yours would also prepare a

^{2050.1; 3532; 1121; 8141; 2050.2; 8549; you or yours; 6213, 8799; 5930; 3807.1; 3117; 3807.1; 3068}   ^(below)

burnt offering to Yahweh, daily, of an unblemished lamb (in) its first year. You(rs)

      ^{871.1; 1242; 871.1; 1242; you; 6213, 8799; 853; 2050.2}   ^(2050.1; 4503; you; 6213, 8799; 5921; 2050.2; 871.1; 1242; 871.1; 1242)

46:14* would offer it in the morning, each day. *Along with it, on each morning, you(rs)

            ^{cont.}   ⁸³⁴⁵   ³⁷⁴

would also prepare the grain offering of a sixth of the dry measure (of ingredients),

^{2050.1; 8081; 7992; 1886.1; 1969; 3807.1; 7450, 8800; 853; 1886.1; 5560}   ⁴⁵⁰³   ^(below)

and a third of a hin of the oil to moisten the flour. The meal offering (dedicated) to

^{3807.1; 3068}   ^{2708 plur.; 5769; 8548}   ^{2050.1}   ^(below)

46:15* Yahweh had regularly been (one of) the ancient ordinances. *And theirs had also

^(they; 6213, 8804; 853; 1886.1; 3532; 2050.1; 853; 1886.1; 4503; 2050.1; 853 or 854; 1886.1; 8081; 871.1; 1242; 871.1; 1242; 5930; 8548)

regularly prepared the lamb burnt offering and the meal offering with olive oil, in the

        ^{cont.}

mornings of each day."

46:16-18   [Relocated to Section 5, since they relate to the Holy Land Inheritance]

           (2050.1; he; 935, 8686; 2967.1)...   cont.   871.1; 3996   834   5921; 3802
46:19   He [the spirit] shall then lead Mine [Jesus] through an entrance that is on the side

       1886.1; 8179; 413; 1886.1; 3957; 1886.1; 6944; 413; 1886.1; 3548   1886.1; 6437, 8802   6828; 1886.3 (below)
of the gate to the priest's sacred chambers, which is facing towards its north, and

       2050.1; 2009; 8033; 4725; 871.1; 3411; 3220, 1886.3   2050.1; he; 559, 8799   413; 2967.1
46:20* there, west of it, will behold a site in a remote area.   *Thus, he shall relay to Mine:

   2088   1886.1; 4725 834; they; 1310, 8762; 8033; 1886.1; 3548; 853; 1886.1; 817; 2050.1; 853; 1886.1; 2403
"That's the place where the priests would cook the guilt and sin offering(s), and

   834   they; 644, 8799   853; 1886.1; 4503 3807.1; 1115; 3318, 8687; 413; 1886.1; 2691; 1886.1; 2435
where they would bake the meal offering(s) for (themselves, that were) not to go out

    cont.   6942, 8763; 853; 1886.1; 5971
into the outer court to sanctify the people."

    2050.1; he; 3318, 8686; 2967.1; 413; 1886.1; 2691; 1886.1; 2435   (2050.1; he; 5674, 8686; 2967.1)...
46:21   After that, he shall bring Mine to an outer court, and he shall have Mine cross

    cont.   413   702 4740 plur. 1886.1; 2691 2050.1; 2009 (1886.1; 2691; 871.1; 4740; 1886.1; 2691)...
over towards the four corners of the court, and behold the court at (each) corner of

    cont.   2691   871.1; 4740; 1886.1; 2691   871.1; 702; 4140
46:22* the court having an enclosure at (each) of the court's corner(s).   *At the four corners

   1886.1; 2691   2691 plur.; 7000, 8803   (705; 753; 2050.1; 7970; 7341; 4060)...
of the court, the areas that are enclosed have a measurement of forty (cubits) long

    cont.   259; 3807.1; 702; 3963.1   7106, 8716
and thirty (cubits) wide for each one of these four (enclosures) that are cornered.

    2050.1; 2905; 5439; 871.1; 1992   5439 (below)
46:23* *Also, inside them, a surrounding row (of masonry or a countertop) is all around in

   413; 702; 3963.1   2050.1; 4018   6213 (made); 8803; 2967.1; 4480; 8478; 2918; 5439
these four, which have hearths underneath the surrounding rows that were built

_{cont.}   _{per Ez. 46:13}
after Mine (had left).

_{(2050.1; he; 559, 8799)...}   _{cont.   413; 2967.1}
46:24   Thus, he [the messenger spirit] shall relay to Mine [Jesus]:

_{428   1004; 1886.1; 1310   834; they; 1310, 8762; 8033; 8334, 8764; 1886.1; 1004}
"This is the temple's cooking area where the attendants of the temple would cook

_{853; 2077; 1886.1; 5971}
the people's sacrificial offering(s)."

Ezekiel 40:5-49

_{2050.1; 2009   2346   4480   2351   3807.1; 1004   5439   (5439)...}
40:5   Next, behold the wall from outside of Temple (Mount) that is all around the sur-

_{cont.   2050.1; 871.1; 3027; 1886.1; 376 (Iyesh)   7070; 1886.1; 4060   8337   520   (below)}
rounding area; and in this Jesus' hand is the measuring device of six cubits and one

_{871.1; 520; 2050.1; 2948   (2050.1; he; 4058, 8799)}
handbreadth per cubit [i.e., a total of 10 to 12 feet in length, extended] that he shall

_{cont.   853 or 854; 7341; 1886.1; 1146; 7070; 259; 2050.1; 6967; 7070; 259}
measure the width and the height of (each) structure with; each reed (added to)

_{cont.}
each (subsequent) reed.

_{(2050.1; he; 935, 8799)...   cont.   413; 8178}
40:6   When he [Jesus, accompanied by God's messenger spirit] shall go to the gate

_{834   6440; 2050.2   1870; 1886.1; 6921; 1886.3   (below)}
[of Temple Mount] where its front is in the direction of the east, and he shall ascend

_{2050.1; he; 5927, 8799; 871.1; 4609; 2050.2; 2050.1; he; 4058, 8799; 853; 5592   1886.1; 8179   (below)}
up its stairs, he then (at that time) would measure (one) entrance of the gate as one

_{7070; 259; 7341   2050.1; 853; 5592; 259   7070; 259   7341   2050.1; 1886.1; 8372}
40:7*   reed wide, and the other entrance as one reed wide;*and (each) hall chamber as

_{7070; 259; 753   2050.1; 7070; 259   7341   2050.1; 996; 1886.1; 8372 plur.   2568   520 plur.}
one reed long by one reed wide, and between the chambers as five cubits.

	2050.1; 5592	1886.1; 8179	4480; 681	197; 1886.1; 8179	(below)

Then, the entrance of the gate from the (other) side of the gate's portico out

	4480; 1004	7070; 259	2050.1; he; 4058, 8799	853; 197; 1886.1; 8179	

40:8* from the temple is one reed; *and he shall also measure the (other) gate's portico

	4480; 1886.1; 1004	7070; 259

out from the temple as one reed.

	2050.1; he; 4058, 8799	853; 197; 1886.1; 8179	8083	520	(below)

40:9 Likewise, he shall measure the (interior) gate's portico as eight cubits, and its

	2050.1; 352; 2050.2; 8147; 520	2050.1; 197; 1886.1; 8179	4480; 1886.1; 1004	(below)

40:10* supports as two cubits. Then, at the gate's portico out from the temple, *which

	2050.1; 8372; possv.; 1886.1; 8179	1870; 1886.1; 6921	7969

will be (connected to) the chambers of the gate towards the east side having three

	4480; 6311	2050.1; 7969	4480; 6311

(entrances) on one side (of a chamber) and three on the other side, he shall take

	4060; 259	3807.1; 7969; 3963.1	2050.1; 4060; 259	3807.1; 352; 3963.1

a measurement for (each of) these three, and a measurement for their support(s)

	4480; 6311	2050.1; 4480; 6311	2050.1; he; 4058, 8799	(below)

40:11* that is on one side and then on the other side. *He shall also measure the (total)

853; 7341	6607; 1886.1; 8179	6235	520	753	1886.1; 8179	7969; 6240; 1886.3; 520

width of the gate entrance as ten cubits and the length of the gate as thirteen cubits.

	2050.1; 1366	3807.1; 6440	1886.1; 8372	520; 259

40:12* *Furthermore, a (walkway) space, at the front of the chambers, will be one cubit

	2050.1; 520; 259	1366	4480; 6311	(below)

(wide), and (there shall) also be a one cubit (wide) space on the other side of the

2050.1; 1886.1; 8372	8337	520	4480; 6311	2050.1; 8337; 520	4480; 6311

chamber that is six cubits (long) on one side, and six cubits (long) on the other side.

	2050.1; he; 4058, 8799	853 or 854; 1886.1; 8179; 4480; 1406	1886.1; 8372; 3807.1; 1406; 2050.1

40:13 He also shall measure from the roof of the gate to the roof of the chamber having

7341	6242; 2050.1; 2568	520	6607	5048	6607

a width of twenty five cubits at the entrance that's in front of the entrance (behind

	2050.1; he; 6213, 8799; 853; 352 plur.; 8346	(below)

40:14* it), *and then he shall do the sixty posts on the gate all around the surrounding area

40:15*   520 sing. ; 2050.1; 413; 352 sing.; 1886.1; 2691; 1886.1; 8179; 5439; 5439   2050.1; 5921   6449   (below)
of the enclosed courtyard; as a cubit for (each) post. *Then, above the front of the

          1886.1; 8179; 1886.1; 2978   5921; 3807.1; 6440   197   1886.1; 8179; 1886.1; 6442   2572 520 sing.
gate's entrance, to above the front portico of the interior gate, will be fifty cubit(s).

          2050.1; 2474 plur.; 331; 8801   413; 1886.1; 8372   (2050.1; 413; 352; 1992; 1886.3)...
40:16* *Moreover, (there are) narrow openings within the chambers, as well as within these

        cont.   413; 6441   3807.1; 8179   5439   5439   (2050.1; 3651; 3807.1; 361)...
posts on the interior of the gate around the surrounding area; and also near the

        cont.   2050.1; 2474   5439   5439   3807.1; 6441
porches and windows. And all through the surrounding area of inside (the court-

        2050.1; 413; 352   8561 plur.
yard), and by the (outer) wall, there are palm trees.

        (2050.1; he; 935; 8686; 2967.1)...   cont.   413; 1886.1; 2691; 1886.1; 2435 (below)
40:17   He [the messenger spirit] shall also take Mine [Jesus] to the outer courtyard, and

2050.1; 2009   3957 plur.   2050.1; 7531 sing.   they; 6213; 8804; 2967.1   (3807.1; 2691)...
will behold the chambers that have a pavement they made (for) Mine in the court-

cont.   5439   5439   7970   3957 plur.   (2050.1; 1886.1; 7531)...
yard around the surrounding area. Thirty chambers shall thus (be close to) this

        cont.   413; 1886.1; 7531 sing.   413; 3802 sing.   (1886.1; 8179 plur.; 3807.1; 5980; 753; 1886.1; 8179)
40:18* pavement*that's by the pavement towards the side of the gates parallel to the longer

        cont.   1886.1; 7531; 1886.1; 8481   (2050.1; he; 4058, 8799; 7341; 4480; 3807.1; 6440; 1886.1; 8179; 1886.1; 8481; 1886.3)
40:19* gates of the lower pavement. *He also shall measure the width from the front of its

        cont.   3807.1; 6440   1886.1; 2691; 1886.1; 6442; 4480; 2351   3967   520
lower gate to the front of the inner courtyard, from the outside, as a hundred cubits,

        1886.1; 6921; 2050.1; 1886.1; 6828
(located on) the eastside, but northward.

        (2050.1; 1886.1; 8179; 834; 6440; 2050.2; 1870; 1886.1; 6828; 3807.1; 2691; 2435; 4058, 8804; 753; 2050.2; 2050.1; 7341; 2050.2)
40:20   Additionally, he shall have measured the length and width of the gate that's face

        cont.   2050.1; 8372; 2050.2
40:21* is (in) the direction of the north, nearby the outer courtyard, *as well as its chamber(s);

        7969   4480; 6311   2050.1; 7969   4480; 6311   (2050.1; 352; 2050.2; 2050.1; 361; 2050.2; it; 1961, 8804)
three on one side and three on the other side. And its porch with post(s) shall have

| | cont. | 3509.4; 6020 | 1886.1;8179;1886.1;7223 | 2572 | 520 | 753; 2050.2 | 2050.1;7341 |

had a similar measurement as the first gate of fifty cubit(s) for its length, and a width

| 2568;2050.1;6242;871.1;520 | 2050.1; 2474; 2050.2 | 2050.1; 361; 2050.2 | (below) |

40:22* of twenty-five cubit(s). *Furthermore, its opening(s) and its porch that (is near)

| 2050.1; 8561; 2050.2 | 3509.4; 4060 | 1886.1; 8179; 834; 6440; 2050.2 |

its palm tree(s) shall have a similar measurement as (those) of the gate whose face

| 1870 | 1886.1; 6921 | 2050.1; 871.1; 4609 plur.; 7651; they; 5927, 8799; 871.1; 2050.2 | (below) |

is (in) the direction of the east. They then shall ascend by way of its seven steps, and

| 2050.1;361;2050.2 | 3807.1; 6440; 1992 | 2050.1; 8179 | 3807.1; 2691; 1886.1; 6442 | (below) |

40:23* its porch will be facing towards them *and the gate of the inner courtyard that is in

| 5048 | 1886.1;8179 | 3807.1; 6828 | 2050.1; 3807.1; 6921 | 2050.1; he; 4058, 8799 | (below) |

front of the gate towards the north, but on the eastside; and he shall measure from

| 4480; 8179 | 413; 8179 | 3967 | 520 |

(one) gate to (the other) gate as a hundred cubit(s).

| | 2050.1; he; 1980, 8686; 2967.1 | 1870 | 1886.1; 1864 | 2050.1; 2009 |

40:24   After that, he shall lead Mine in the direction of the south and (they shall) behold

| 8179 | 1870 | 1886.1;1864 | 2050.1; he; 4058, 8804 | 352; 2050.2 | 2050.1; 361; 2050.2 |

a gate towards the south. He then shall have measured its post(s) and its porch

| | 3509.4; 4060; 1886.1; 428 | (below) |

40:25* having the same measurements as these (previously measured ones); *as well as

| 2050.1; 2474; 3807.1; 2050.2;2050.1; 3807.1; 361; 2050.2 | 5439; 5439 | (below) |

the window openings that (are on) the porch nearby it, circling around, having similar

| 3509.4; 1886.1; 2474 | per Ez. 40:21 | (2572;520; 753;2050.1;7341;2568;2050.1;6242;520) |

window openings as the other (porches) that are fifty cubit(s) long and twenty five

| cont. | 2050.1; 4609; 7651; 5930; 2050.2 | 2050.1; 361; 2050.2 | 3807.1; 6440; 1992 |

40:26* cubit(s) wide. *Its stairs also have seven steps, and its porch that is in front of them

| 2050.1; 8561 plur.; 3807.1; 2050.2 | 259 | 4480; 6311 | 2050.1; 259 | 4480; 6311 | (below) |

shall also have palm trees by it; one on one side and one on the other side of its

| 413;352;2050.2 | 2050.1; 8179; 3807.1; 2691; 1886.1; 6442; 1870; 1886.1; 1864; 2050.1; he; 4058, 8799; 4480; 8179 |

40:27* post(s). *Furthermore, he shall also measure from the gate of the inner courtyard

| cont. | 413; 1886.1; 8179 | 1870; 1886.1; 1864 | 3967 | 520 |

(in) the south direction, to this gate in the south direction, as a hundred cubits.

40:28 He shall then take Mine to the interior courtyard through this south gate, and he shall measure the (interior) south gate having similar measurements as the others.

40:29* *Also, its chamber(s), post(s), and porch have similar measurements (as the ones measured previously), as well as the openings in it that's on its wall(s) and on its

40:30* porch circling around that is fifty cubit(s) long and twenty five cubit(s) wide. *Also,

40:31* the halls round about will be twenty five cubit(s) long and five cubits wide. *Moreover, its hallway to the outer court also has palm tree(s) by its post(s), and its stairway has eight steps.

40:32 He also shall lead Mine to the interior courtyard towards the eastern side, and

40:33* he shall measure a gate having similar measurements as these (others), *as well as its chamber(s), post(s), and hallway(s) having similar measurements as these (other ones), and also (similar) openings in it and in its porch round about that's fifty

40:34* cubit(s) long and twenty five cubit(s) wide. *Furthermore, its hallway(s) to the outer courtyard also has a palm tree close to its post(s). To get from here and out the other side, its stairway also has eight steps.

109

	2050.1; he; 935, 8686; 2967.1; 413; 8179; 1886.1; 6828 (2050.1; he; 4058, 8804)...
40:35	He shall take Mine to (another) gate of the north, as well, (where) he shall have
	cont. 3509.4; 4060; 1886.1; 428 (8372; 2050.2; 352; 2050.2; 2050.1; 361; 2050.2)
40:36*	also measured similar measurements as these (others for) *its chamber(s), post(s),
	cont. 2050.1; 2474 plur.; 3807.1; 2050.2; 5439; 5439 753 2572 520 (below)
	and porch with the openings in it, roundabout, having a length of fifty cubit(s) and
	2050.1; 7341 2568; 2050.1; 6242 520 2050.1; 352; 2050.2 (3807.1; 2691; 1886.1; 2435)
40:37*	a width of twenty-five cubit(s). *Additionally, its post(s) will be close to the outer
	cont. 2050.1; 8561 413 352; 2050.2 4480; 6311 (below)
	courtyard, with a palm tree nearby its post(s). (To get) from here and out the other
	2050.1; 4480; 6311; 2050.1; 8083; 4609; 4608; 2050.2
	side, its stairway also has eight steps.
	2050.1; 3957 sing. 2050.1; 6607; 1886.3 871.1; 352 1886.1; 8179 8033 (below)
40:38	Then, (near) the hall that's its entrance, by the posts of the gates, is where they
	they; 1740, 8686 854 1886.1; 5930 or 5927 w/o marks
	shall make ablution [at an ablution fountain] by the ascension (site) [located in the vicinity of the Dome of the Rock, where Muslims believe Prophet Mohamed's night-time ascension into the heavens occurred].
	2050.1; 871.1; 197 1886.1; 8179 8147 7979 4480; 6311; 2050.1; 8147; 7979 (below)
40:39	Also by the portico of the gate, will be two tables on one side, and two tables on
	4480; 6311 (below)
	the other side for theirs [i.e., for the Jews and gentiles following the false Messiah]
	3807.1; 7819, 8800; 413; 1992; 1886.1; 5930 2050.1; 1886.1; 2403; 2050.1; 1886.1; 817
	to slaughter the sacrifice that is a purification from sin and atonement of trespasses.
	2050.1; 413; 1886.1; 3802 (4480; 2351; 1886.3; 3807.1; 5927, 8800 or 8802; 3807.1; 6607; 1886.1; 8179; 1886.1; 6828; 1886.3)
40:40*	*And nearby the ramp of its outside area for ascending up to this northern gate
	cont. 8147; 7979 2050.1; 413; 1886.1; 3802; 1886.1; 312 834 (below)
	entrance, will be two tables, and towards the other side, which is near the gate's

40:41* ^{3807.1; 197; 1886.1; 8179; 8147; 7979} portico, will be two tables. (Thus, there will be) * ⁷⁰² four ⁷⁹⁷⁹ tables ^{4480; 6311} on one side ^{2050.1; 702} and four

⁷⁹⁷⁹ tables ^{4480; 6311} on the other side ^{3807.1; 3802; 1886.1; 8179} of the gate's ramp; ⁸⁰⁸³ eight ⁷⁹⁷⁹ tables (total, which) ^{413; 1992; 7819, 8799} theirs would

^{cont.} slaughter on. ^(N:16)

^(N:16) These prophesied slaughter tables will be made available for the Israelis who will be following the imposter Jesus' ordinances foretold in this section. Although Muslims slay sheep, goats, or cows at the end of Hajj (pilgrimage to Mecca) and also in commemoration of Abraham's willingness to sacrifice his beloved son for his love of God, the animal sacrifices are performed as an act of thanks to God for the meat they would share with family, friends and the needy. Unlike the Jews, Muslim's do <u>not</u> perform animal sacrifices as a purification from sin, or atonement of trespasses. [79] This was a practice once performed by the Jews before the second Temple was destroyed by the Romans in 70 CE, [80] and which, according to this prophecy, will again be carried out by the Jews as soon as the Muslims are forbidden to enter the Temple Mount area that shall specifically be allocated for the Jews; many of whom shall eventually become followers of the imposter Jesus. The sacrificial altar and slaughter tables mentioned in these Ezekiel chapters will most likely be installed soon after the Muslims were prevented entry into this prophesied Temple Mount area.

40:42 ^{2050.1; 702} Furthermore, four ^{7979 plur.} of the tables ^{3807.1; 5930} for the Ola burnt sacrifice ^(below) will be (made of) cut

^{68; 1496} stone ⁷⁵³ having ^{520; 259; 2050.1; 2677} a length of one and a half cubit(s), ^{2050.1; 7341} a width ^{520; 259; 2050.1; 2677} of one and a half cubit(s),

^{2050.1; 1363} and a height ^{520; 259} of one cubit. ^{413; 1992} Upon these, ^{2050.1; they or theirs; 3240; 8686} theirs would also lay ^{853; 1886.1; 3627} the instruments ^{834 (below)} that they

40:43* ^{they; 7819, 8799} would slaughter ^{853; 1886.1; 5930; 871.1; 3963.1; 2050.1; 1886.1; 2077} the sacrifice with, when (it was time for) the sacrifice. ^(2050.1; 8240 plur.) *Also, the

^{cont.} hooks [for hanging the butchered animals], ^{2948; 259} each a handbreadth (in size), ^(below) will be

^{3559; 8716} attached ^{871.1; 1004; 5439} throughout the temple's surrounding area; ⁵⁴³⁹ round about, ^(2050.1; 413; 1886.1; 7979) and nearby the

111

<pre>   cont.   1320; 1886.1; 7133</pre>
tables (for cutting) the sacrificial Korban meat.

<pre>   2050.1; 4480; 2351; 1886.3; 3807.1; 8179; 1886.1; 6442; 3957   (7891, 8802; 871.1; 2691; 1886.1; 6442)…</pre>
40:44   Also, outside of the inner gate halls, is where theirs shall have been chanting in

<pre>   cont.   834   413; 3802   8179; 1886.1; 6828   2050.1; 6440; 1992   (1870; 1886.1; 1864)</pre>
the inner courtyard that is on the side of the north gate that faces theirs in the south

<pre>   cont.   259   413; 3802   8179; 1886.1; 6921   (below)</pre>
direction, and in another (courtyard) on the side of the eastern gate, facing toward

<pre>   6440; 1870; 1886.1; 6828</pre>
the north direction.

<pre>   (2050.1; he; 1696, 8762)…   cont.   413; 2967.1   2090; 1886.1; 3957</pre>
40:45   He [the messenger spirit] shall also say to Mine [Jesus]: "That chamber (there)

<pre>   834; 6440; 1886.3   1870; 1886.1; 1864   3807.1; 3548 plur.   8104, 8802; 4931</pre>
that faces the south direction was for the Kohen (priests) maintaining the safeguard

<pre>   1886.1; 1004   2050.1; 1886.1; 3957   834; 6440; 1886.3; 1870; 1886.1; 6828   3807.1; 3548 plur.</pre>
40:46* of this temple; *and the chamber that faces the north direction was for the Kohen

<pre>   8104, 8802; 4931   1886.1; 4196   1992   1121 plur.   6659   (below)</pre>
safeguarding the sacrificial altar (site). They are descendants of Zadok, from the

<pre>   1886.1; 7131; 4480; 1121; 3878; 413; 3068; 3807.1; 8334, 8763; 2050.2</pre>
offspring of Levi, who was near to God in serving Him."

<pre>   2050.1; he; 4058, 8799   853; 2691   753   3967; 520; 2050.1; 7341; 3967; 520   7251, 8794</pre>
40:47   After he shall measure the courtyard length and width as 100x100 cubits squared,

<pre>   per Ez. 40:6-37   2050.1; 1886.1; 4196   3807.1; 6440   1886.1; 1004   2050.1; he; 935, 8686; 2967.1</pre>
40:48* the gates, and the sacrificial altar in front of the temple, *he shall then lead Mine

<pre>   413; 197 sing.   1886.1; 1004   2050.1; he; 4058, 8799; 352 (or 413)   197 sing.</pre>
to a portico of the temple, and he shall measure a wall projection of the portico as

<pre>   2568   520   4480; 6311   2050.1; 2568   520   4480; 6311   2050.1; 7341   (below)</pre>
five cubits on one side, and five cubits on the other side; and then the width of the

<pre>   1886.1; 8179   7969   520   4480; 6311 2050.1; 7969   520   4480; 6311   (below)</pre>
40:49* entranceway as three cubits on one side and three cubits on the other end. *The

(753; 1886.1; 197; 6242; 520; 2050.1; 7341; 6249; 6240; 520; 2050.1; 871.1; 4609; 834; they; 5927; 8799; 413; 2050.2)…

<u>portico hall that's nearby the steps that they shall ascend upon is twenty cubit(s) long</u>

cont.   2050.1; 5982 plur.; 413; 1886.1; 352   259; 4480; 6311   (2050.1; 259; 4480; 6311)

<u>and eleven cubit(s) wide</u>, <u>and has posts near the wall</u> <u>on one side</u> <u>and on the other</u>

cont.

<u>side</u> (of the entranceway).

The portico of this temple being described in Ez. 40:48-49, is most likely in reference to a front portico of the Dome of the Rock sanctuary shrine, based on the following Ezekiel passages. From the architecture descriptions in these passages compared to the actual design of each described temple within today's Old City Jerusalem, the weight of evidence strongly suggests that Prophet Ezekiel was given a vision of how the most sacred temples upon Temple Mount and its vicinity would look like when the false Messiah appears, and Jesus returns for his second advent. These particular prophesies have clearly, previously been mistranslated to indicate that a new Jewish temple with the prophesied dimensions would be built by Ezekiel, of which he never built; disproving the earlier translations. There is no mistaking that the porticos, circular structures, arches, tiers, and galleries described in these passages are depicting the structures that are astonishingly similar to those of the houses of worship located today in the same east, north, and south sections of Old City. The described placements of the prophesied buildings are in the exact location of the domed temple, mosque, and galleried church located upon and nearby Temple Mount. To obtain a better visualization of how the following Ezekiel descriptions compare to today's layout, we recommend that the reader watch any of the available YouTube tours of the Dome of the Rock Shrine (the domed temple), the Al Aqsa Mosque, and the Holy Sepulcher Church (the galleried temple).

Ezekiel 41

(2050.1; he; 935, 8686; 2967.1)…   cont.   413; 1886.1; 1964

41:1   <u>When he</u> [the messenger spirit] <u>shall lead Mine</u> [Jesus] <u>to this sanctuary building</u>

2050.1; he; 4058, 8799   (below)

[i.e., to the Dome of the Rock Shrine], <u>he shall also measure</u> <u>the breadth (between)</u>

(853; 1886.1; 352; 8337; 520; 7341; 4480; 6311 or 6310; 2050.1; 8337; 520; 7341; 4480; 6311 or 6310; 7341; 1886.1; 168)…

<u>the posts of a prayer tent structure</u> [the Dome of the Chain] <u>as six cubits wide for</u>

113

cont.
an opening, and six cubits wide for the other(s).

     2050.1; 7341   1886.1; 6607   6235 520
41:2 Moreover, the width of an entranceway [of the sanctuary building] is ten cubits,

  2050.1; 3802   1886.1; 6607 2568 520 4480; 6311 2050.1; 2568 520 (4480; 6311)
and the sides of the entranceway are five cubits on one side and five cubits on the

 cont.   2050.1; he; 4058, 8799; 753; 2050.2   705 520 (5020.1; 7341)
other side. He then shall measure its (entrance wall) length as forty cubit(s), and the

  cont.   6242 520   2050.1; 1886.1; 1146 834
41:12* width [or possibly the height] as twenty cubit(s). *Furthermore, this building that is

 413; 6440 1886.1; 1508 6285; 1870; 1886.1; 3220
at the front of the courtyard on the westward side [of Temple Mount] shall have a

     7341 7657 520   2050.1; 7023   1886.1; 1146 2568
(front view) width of seventy cubit(s), and (each) wall section of the building is five

 520 7341 5439; 5439
cubits wide all (the way) around.

     2050.1; he; 935, 8804 3807.1; 6441 2050.1; he; 4058, 8799 352; 1886.1; 6607 8147
41:3 After he shall have gone inside, he then shall measure the entrance post as two

 520 plur. 2050.1; 1886.1; 6607   8337 520 plur. 2050.1; 7341 1886.1; 6607 7651
cubits, the entrance (length) as six cubits, and the width of the entrance as seven

 520 plur. 2050.1; he; 4058, 8799 853; 753; 2050.2   (below)
41:4* cubits. *Next, he shall measure its length towards the front of the sanctuary temple

           6242; 520; 2050.1; 7341; 6242; 520; 413; 6440; 1886.1; 1964
[the Dome of the Rock Shrine] (as) twenty cubit(s), and the width (as) twenty cubit(s).

 (2050.1; he; 559, 8799)...   cont. 413; 2967.1 (below)
And then he [the messenger spirit] shall say to Mine; "This is the most holy site of

 2088; 6944; 1886.1; 6944 plur.
the sacred places (here)."

     2050.1; he; 4058, 8799 7023 sing.; 1886.1; 1004 8337 520 plur. 2050.1; 7341
41.5 Afterwards, he shall measure a wall of this temple as six cubits, and then the width

  1886.1; 6763 702 520 5439   5439; 3807.1; 1004; 5439
of a support structure as four cubits. Surrounding all (the way) around the circle of the

41:6* temple *that (includes) the support structures, where each support structure is next to a support structure; are (a total of) thirty-three occurrences (of piers and support structures) that are occurring nearby the wall, which are for the temple as the supports existing around the circle (they) are attached to. Thus, they are not (actually connected) on the temple's wall.

41:7 Furthermore, it [i.e., each support structure] shall have also broadened the space that was walked around. In regards to its upper (arcade) portion, higher up on the supports, because of its upper part winding all around the temple, then its upward (arcade) portion circling around in the temple above [closest to the wall], shall therefore be broader within the temple (compared) to its upper portion [at the center] that is, thus, the lower part that ascends upwards to the center's highest point [at the dome].

41:8 Then Mine shall have taken a look at the temple's (dome) height circling around as part of the foundations laid, (consisting) of the support structures (and piers) as a full reed; i.e., six cubits (between each arched) shoulder.

41:9 The width of a wall that is connected to an outside support structure is five cubits;

| | 2050.1; 834; 3240, 8716 | 1004; 6763 | 834 | 3807.1; 1004 | (below) |

41:10* which was also laid (over) the inside support structures that are in the temple. *Also,

| | 2050.1; 996 | 1886.1; 3957 plur. | 7341 | 6242 | 520 | 5439 | 3807.1; 1004 | (below) |

between the hallways is a width of twenty cubit(s) circling around in the temple; all

5439; 5439

(the way) around.

| 2050.1; 6607 sing. | 1886.1; 6763 sing. | 3807.1; 3240, 8716 |

41:11   Again, the opening (between) each support structure is for opening up space. At

| 6607 sing.; 259; 1870 | 1886.1; 6828 | 2050.1; 6607 sing.; 259 | 3807.1; 1864 | (below) |

one entrance toward the northside and one entrance towards the south, the width

2050.1; 7341; 4725; 1886.1; 3240, 8716; 2568; 520; 5439; 5439 (Ez. 41:12 was relocated after Ez. 41:2)

(of each wall section) is also five cubits all around that is (at) the open space area.

Ez.41:12b (2050.1; 753; 2050.2; 8763; 520); Ez. 41:13 (2050.1; he; 4058, 8804; 853; 1886.1; 1004; 753; 3967; 520)...

41:12b-13 He shall have also measured the length of the (other) temple [Al Aqsa Mosque]

cont. (~268 ft. or 190 cubits is the reported length of this mosque, while the reported width is ~180.4 ft.) [81]   (below)

as being one hundred and ninety cubit(s) long [with a width of ~128 cubits]. Also,

| 2050.1; 1886.1; 1508 | 2050.1; 1886.1; 1140 | 2050.1; 7023; 1886.1 | 753 | 3967 |

there's a separate place that's a building, and its walls have a length of a hundred

| 520 | 2050.1; 7341 | 3967; 520 (from end of sentence) | 6440 |

41:14* cubit(s). *Furthermore, (there's) a width of a hundred cubit(s) between the front

| 1886.1; 1004 | 2050.1; 1886.1; 1508 | 3807.1; 6921 | 3967; 520 (worded above) |

(side) of this temple and this separate place to the north. [This separate building is

most likely in reference to the Islamic Museum, which is located beside the Al Aqsa

Mosque on its north side.]

| 2050.2; he; 4058, 8804 | 753 | 1886.1; 1146 | 834 | (below) |

41:15   Afterwards, he shall have measured the length of the building which is over (the

| 5921; 310; 1886.3 | 2050.2; 862; 1886.3 |

wall) behind it, that is (where) its (temple's) galleries are [i.e., at the Holy Sepulcher

| 4480; 6311 | 2050.1; 4480; 6311 | 3967 |

Church].   (The length) on one side, and also on another side will be a hundred

520   (2050.1;1886.1;1964;1886.1;6442;2050.1;1886.1;197)

cubit(s). (Measurements shall have also been taken of) the temple's interior (cham-

       cont.   1886.1; 2691   1886.1; 5592   (2050.1; 2474; 1886.1; 331; 8801)...

41:16* bers) and halls nearby the courtyard * of the entrances that have the shutting win-

     cont.   2050.1; 1886.1; 862   5439   (3807.1; 7969; 3963.1)

dows. Furthermore, (the art relics of) the gallery were all around within three of

     cont.   5048   1886.1; 5592   7824; 6086

them. In front of the entranceway is a ceiled structure (with) a cross [i.e., the Edicule]

           5439; 5439; 2050.1; 1886.1; 776   5704   1886.1; 2474 plur.   (below)

that is enclosed all around (from) the ground up towards the windows that shall have

       2050.1; 1886.1; 2474; 3680, 8794   5921

41:17* been the covered windows * above it.

        4480; 5921   1886.1; 6607   2050.1; 5704   1886.1; 1004; 1886.1; 6442; 2050.1; 3807.1; 2351

From above the entrance, and then up to the inner and outward (chambers) of the

     cont.   2050.1; 413; 3605; 1886.1; 7023   5439; 5439   871.1; 6442   2050.1; 871.1; 2435   4060

temple, there are also, on each wall all around on the interior and exterior, large size

            2050.1; they or theirs; 6213, 8804; 2967.1   3742 plur.   2050.1; 8561

41:18* (images) * that theirs shall have made of Mine [i.e., of Jesus] with cherubs and palms,

      2050.1; 8561   996   3742 sing.   3807.1; 3742   2050.1; 8147; 6440   (below)

and a palm tree amongst a cherub next to (another) cherub, with both facing towards

        3807.1; 3742   2050.1; 6440   120 sing.

41:19* the (other) cherub. * Also, (there will be an image of) the face of the (Son of) Man

       413; 1886.1; 8561; 4480; 6311   2050.1; 6440   3715   (413; 8561; 4480; 6311)...

on one side next to a palm tree and the face of a lion on the other side next to the

     cont.   they or theirs; 6213, 8804; 2967.1

palm tree that theirs shall have made of Mine, (along with the other art pieces)

        413; 3605; 1004   5439   5439   4480; 1886.1; 776; 5704; 4480; 5921   (below)

41:20* throughout all of the temple surrounding all around * from the ground up to above the

   1886.1; 6607   1886.1; 3742 plur.   2050.1; 8561 plur.   6213, 8804; 3963.1   2050.1; 7023; 1886.1; 1964

entrance with the cherubs and palm trees theirs had made for the temple's wall(s)

      1886.1; 1964   4201 plur.

41:21* and * the temple doorposts.

<small>7253 w/o marks; 2050.1; 6440   1886.1; 6944; 1886.1; 4758   (3509.4; 4758)</small>
(In) the quarter section, also facing this sacred sightseeing area, is a similar

<small>cont.   1886.1; 4196 sing.; 6086   7969; 520; 1364   2050.1; 753; 2050.2; 8147; 520</small>
41:22* sightseeing (area) with *an altar cross that is three cubits tall and two cubits long.

<small>2050.1; 4740; 2050.2; 3807.1; 2050.2; 2050.1; 753; 2050.2; 2050.1; 7023; 2050.2; 6086</small>
Moreover, along its altar's length, corners, and sides, is wood.

<small>(2050.1; he; 1696, 8762)...   cont.   413; 2967.1</small>
Then he [the messenger spirit] shall relay to Mine:

<small>2088   1886.1; 7979   834   3807.1; 6440   3068 or 3069   (2050.1; 8147; 1817)...</small>
41:23* "This is the table which has been for facing towards the Lord.   *And (over there

<small>cont.   3807.1; 1964; 2050.1; 3807.1; 6944   2050.1; 8147   1817 plur.   (below)</small>
41:24* are) the double doors of the temple and sacred site, * and two (other) doors next to

<small>3807.1; 1817; 8147   4142, 8716; 1817; 8147; 3807.1; 1817; 259   2050.1; 8147</small>
the double doors; two swing-open doors are (attached) as one door, and then two

<small>1817 plur.   3807.1; 312   (they; 6213, 8804; 1886.3; 413; 1992; 413; 1817; 1886.1; 1964; 3742; 2050.1; 8561)</small>
41:25* (separate) doors for the others.   * Theirs have made cherubs and palm trees nearby

<small>cont.   3509.4; 834   they or theirs; 6213, 8802   3807.1; 7023 plur.</small>
the doors of this temple, similar to what theirs were creating for the walls.   There is

<small>2050.1; 5646   6086   413; 6440   1886.1; 197; 4480; 1886.1; 2351   (2050.1; 2474; 331, 8801)</small>
41:26* also an overhanging cross towards the front of the outside portico, *as well as shut-

<small>cont.   (2050.1; 8561 plur.; 4480; 6311; 2050.1; 4480; 6311; 413; 3802; 1886.1; 197; 2050.1; 6763; 1886.1; 1004)...</small>
ting windows. Also, palm tree decorations are on each side of the temple's portico

<small>cont.   2050.1; 1886.1; 5646</small>
sides, and on the support beams and the overhangs."

Ezekiel 42

<small>(2050.1; he; 3318, 8686; 2967.1)...   cont.   413; 1886.1; 2691; 1886.1; 2435</small>
42:1   He [the messenger spirit] shall also bring Mine [Jesus] to the outer courtyard that

<small>1886.1; 1870; 1870; 1886.1; 6828   2050.1; he; 935, 8686; 2967.1   413; 1886.1; 3957   834   5048</small>
is towards the north direction, and he shall take Mine to a chamber that is in front of

42:2* the courtyard, which is also in the front of the northside of the building. *At the front

42:3* of the northward entrance, (it) is a hundred cubits long and fifty cubits wide. *In front of (another section) is twenty (cubits), which is next to the inner court and in front of the pavements that are for the exterior courtyard of the (temple's) gallery. At

42:4* the front of the gallery with three (tiers) *that are towards the front of the chambers, is a walkway of ten cubits wide. The pathway to the interior that is at their northward entrance is one cubit.

42:5 Furthermore, the upper chambers are shorter (in height) because of the galleries that prevail away from these that are at the lower section, which is the building's (lofty)

42:6* center. *Because of these (chambers) being separated throughout the three areas that do not have pillars like the pillars of the (central) court chamber, the above (tier) was therefore deprived (of space), because of the bottom that is part of the midsection at the ground (level).

42:7 Also, the wall in front of the chambers that are towards the outside, (and) alongside the chambers toward the exterior court chamber, has its length as fifty cubit(s).

42:8* *Since the length of the chambers that are towards the exterior of the court chamber

	2572	520	2050.1; 2009		5921; 6440; 1886.1; 1964		3967

are <u>fifty</u> <u>cubit(s)</u>, <u>then behold</u>: (The wall) <u>over the front of the temple</u> is <u>a hundred</u>

42:9*   <u>cubit(s)</u>, *<u>and so is the part beneath</u> <u>these chambers</u> <u>at the east entrance</u> <u>for theirs</u>
(numbers above: 520   2050.1; 4480 or 4481; 8478; 1886.3   3957 plur.; 1886.1; 428   1886.1; 3996; 4480; 1886.1; 6921   (below))

42:10*   <u>to enter from the exterior of the court chamber</u>, which is *<u>along the width</u> of <u>the wall</u>
(numbers above: 935, 8800; 3807.1; 2007; 4480; 1886.1; 2691; 1886.1; 2435   871.1; 7341   1444 sing.)

of <u>the court chamber</u> <u>towards</u> <u>the east</u>, <u>next to the front of</u> <u>the courtyard</u> <u>that is at the</u>
(numbers above: 1886.1; 2691   1870   1886.1; 6921   413; 6440   1886.1; 1508   2050.1; 413; 6440)

<u>front of</u> <u>the building</u>.
(numbers above: cont.   1886.1; 1146)

42:11*   <u>The chambers</u>*<u>that are towards their front</u> are <u>similar in appearance</u> to <u>the cham-</u>
(numbers above: 3957 plur.   2050.1; 1870; 3807.1; 6440; 1992   3509.4; 4758   (1886.1; 3957))

<u>bers</u> <u>that</u> are <u>northward</u>, (and have) <u>a similar length as them</u>. <u>Likewise, the width of</u>
(numbers above: cont.   834   1886.1; 1870; 1886.1; 6828   3509.4; 753; 2050.2   (3651; 7341; 2050.2)...)

<u>them</u> <u>and of all their exits</u> shall <u>also have their similar specifications</u>, <u>as well as their</u>
(numbers above: cont.   2050.1; 3605; 4161; 2007   2050.1; 3509.4; 4941; 2007   (2050.1; 3509.4; 6607 plur.; 2007))

42:12*   <u>similar doors</u> *<u>that are like the door</u> to <u>the chambers</u> <u>that</u> are <u>southward</u> <u>of the door</u>
(numbers above: cont.   2050.1; 3509.4; 6607 sing.   1886.1; 3957 plur.   834   1870; 1886.1; 1864   6607)

<u>at the main entranceway</u>, <u>directly in front of the wall</u> <u>towards</u> <u>the east</u>.
(numbers above: 871.1; 7218; 1870   1870; 871.1; 6440; 1886.1; 1448; 1903   1870   1886.1; 6921)

42:13*   <u>When entering</u> (the temple's central court chamber), *<u>he</u> [the messenger spirit]
(numbers above: 871.1; 935, 8800   (2050.1; he; 559, 8799)...)

<u>shall then relay</u> <u>to Mine</u> [Jesus] <u>regarding</u> <u>the chambers</u> on <u>the north side</u> and the
(numbers above: cont.   (413; 2967.1)...   cont.   3957 plur.   1886.1; 6828)

<u>chambers</u> on <u>the south side</u>, <u>which</u> are <u>nearby the front of</u> <u>the courtyard</u>:
(numbers above: 3957 plur.   1886.1; 1864   834   413; 6440   1886.1; 1508 sing.)

"<u>These are the sacred rooms</u> <u>where (their) holiest of the sacred priests that are</u>
(numbers above: 2007; 3957; 1886.1; 6944   (834; 398, 8799; 8033; 1886.1; 3548; 834; 7138; 3807.1; 3068 or 3069; 6944; 1886.1; 6944))

<u>'allies' of God</u>, <u>would consume</u> (the Eucharist); <u>where their holiest of the holy</u> would
(numbers above: cont.   per Ez. 39:17-18 & 44:7   8033; they; 3240, 8686; 6944; 1886.1; 6944)

         cont.   2050.1; 1886.1; 4503   (2050.1; 1886.1; 2403; 2050.1; 1886.1; 817)
         place (the wafer and wine during) the sacrificial tribute that's for the purification and

           cont.
         atoning of sin."

                 3588   1886.1; 4725   6918   871.1; 935, 8800; 3963.1   (1886.1; 3548 plur.; 2050.1; 3808; 3318; 8799)
42:14*   "Because this site is sacred,* after entering these (areas), the priests would then

                cont.   4480; 1886.1; 6944 sing.   413; 1886.1; 2691; 1886.1; 2435 (2050.1; 8033; they; 3240, 8686; 899; 1992)
         not exit out of this sacred place onto the exterior court, until after they would leave

              cont.   834; they; 8334, 8762; 871.1; 2007   3588   (6944; 2007)…
         their robes there that they would minister in. Because of being a sacred item of

             cont.   they; 3847, 8799   899 plur.; 312; 2050.1; 7126, 8799-Kethiv   413, 834; 3807.1; 5971
         theirs, they would put on other robes when they would approach to where the people

         were."

                       2050.1; he; 3615, 8765   853 or 854; 4060 plur.   1886.1; 1004; 1886.1; 6442 (below)
42:15   After he (and Jesus) finished with the measurements of this temple's interior, he

                          2050.1; he; 3318, 8689; 2967.1   1870   1886.1; 8179   834   6440; 2050.2
         [the messenger spirit] shall have then brought Mine towards a gate, of which its front

                1870; 1886.1; 6921   2050.1; he; 4058, 8804; 2050.2; 5439; 5439   per Ez. 42:20
         (faces) the east direction, and he shall have measured on every side (of the wall sur-

                                                    he; 4058, 8804; 7307 or 7308   (1886.1; 6921)
42:16*   rounding this temple area).   *The (messenger) spirit shall have measured the east

             cont.   871.1; 7070; 1886.1; 4060   2568 3967 (quere) 7070   871.1; 7070
         side with a measuring device as five hundred reeds, by way of a (special) measuring

            cont.   1886.1; 4060   5439
         device (for taking) the measurement of the surrounding(s).

                        he; 4058, 8804; 7307   1886.1; 6828   2568; 3967; 7070
42:17   The spirit shall have (also) measured the north side (wall as) five hundred reeds

                    871.1; 7070   1886.1; 4060 sing.   5439
42:18*   with the measuring device (for taking) the measurement of the surrounding(s). *Like-

                 853; 7307   1886.1; 1864; he; 4058, 8804   2568; 3967   7070
         wise, the spirit shall have measured the south side (wall as) five hundred reeds, as

                                                                                                     121

                871.1; 7070   1886.1; 4060 sing.

well, <u>with the measuring device</u> for (obtaining) <u>the measurement</u>.

                he; 5437, 8804; 853; 7307   1886.1; 3220

42:19   After that, <u>the spirit being shall have turned</u> (towards the wall on) <u>the west side</u>, of

             he; 4058, 8804   2568   3967   7070 plur.   (871.1; 7070 plur.; 1886.1;4060)...

which <u>he shall have measured</u> as <u>five</u> <u>hundred</u> <u>reeds</u> <u>with the measuring device</u>

          cont.   3807.1; 702; 7307 plur.   he; 4058, 8804; 2050.2   (below)

42:20* <u>(for taking) the measurement</u> * <u>of the four sides</u>. <u>He shall have measured them</u> for

    2346; 3807.1; 2050.2; 5439; 5439   753   2568   3967   2050.1; 7341   2568

<u>its wall circling around</u>, having <u>a length</u> of <u>five</u> <u>hundred</u> (reeds) <u>and a width</u> of <u>five</u>

    3967   3807.1; 914, 8687

<u>hundred</u> (reeds, that shall have been built) <u>for the purpose of having a separation</u>

  996   1886.1; 6944   3807.1; 2455

<u>from</u> <u>this sacred site</u> <u>for the unholy</u>.

Ezekiel 44:6-8

        (2050.1; you; 559, 8804)...   cont.   413; 4805; 413; 1004

44:6   "<u>You</u> [Jesus], <u>indeed, shall have relayed</u> (the following) <u>to the rebellious House</u>

      3478

of <u>Israel</u>."

          3541   559, 8804; 136; 3068 or 3069

"<u>This is what Lord Yahweh said</u>:"

      (7227; 3807.1; 3641.1)...   cont.   (4480; 3605; 8441 plur.; 3641.1)...

"<u>Your 'Master'</u> [the imposter Jesus] <u>is the reason for</u> <u>all of the abominations of</u>

     cont.   1004; 3478   871.1; yours; 935, 8687; 1121 plur.; 5236   6189; 3820; 2050.1; 6189; 1320

44:7* your <u>Israeli clan</u>. * <u>Yours are allowing foreigners to enter in</u>, <u>uncircumcised of flesh</u>

        cont.   3807.1; 1961; 871.1; 4720; 2967.1   (below)

<u>and/or spirit</u>, <u>to be at My sanctuary</u> [on top of Temple Mount], <u>in order to continually</u>

 3807.1;2490,8763;2050.2;853;1004;2967.1;871.1;7126,8687;853;3899;2967.1   2459; 2050.1; 1818

<u>defile My temple by offering bread</u> (to) <u>Mine</u>, <u>and the finest</u> (wine as) <u>blood</u> [during

also per Ez. 39:17-18 and 42:13   2050.1; they; 6565, 8686   (853; 1285 sing.; 2967.1; 413)...
the Eucharist ceremony]. <u>But unfortunately, they shall break</u> My Covenant because

cont.   3605; 8441 plur.; your
of <u>all your abominations</u>." (N:17)

(N:17)   From Ezekiel 44:7-8, the Eucharist ritual that will also be observed by the imposter Jesus' followers, according to God, is an <u>abominable</u> practice, which <u>breaks</u> His Covenant. Since the onset of Pauline Christianity, the Eucharist rite involving the receiving of a bread wafer and wine, representing Jesus' body and blood, has been observed by most Christian denominations, and based on Ezekiel 39:17-18, 44:7, and 44:29, it will also be observed by the Israelis and Kohanim that will eventually be serving the imposter Christ, as well. In 1 Corinthians 11:20-25 (believed to be written around 53 to 54 CE at Ephesus, Turkey; about 20 years after Jesus had ascended into the heavens), [82] Paul, who was not a prophet of God, nor one of Jesus' chosen disciples, wrote the following regarding the Lord's Supper (also referred to as the Last Supper and the Passover Supper), which was served to Jesus and his disciples prior to Judas' betrayal:

1 Cor. 11:20   When you come together, therefore, into one place, (this gathering) is not to eat the "Lord's" Supper ...
["Lord God"; Gk. Strong's #2960]

11:23   For I (Paul) have received by means of the "lord" that which I have also delivered unto you, that lord Jesus, (on) the night which he was betrayed, took bread.
["lord"; Gk. Strong's # 2962; also translated as "sir" or "master"]

11:24   And when he (Jesus) had given thanks (to the Lord), he broke (it), and said, *"Take, eat; this is my body that is (broken) for you: Do this in remembrance of me."*

11:25   In the same manner, (he) also (took) the cup, when he had supped, saying, *"This cup is the <u>New</u> <u>Covenant</u> in my blood. Do this as often as you drink (it), in remembrance of me."*

Notice from Paul's writing to the Corinthians about the Eucharist ritual, that he insinuated to have received Christ's body (bread) and blood (the drink in the cup) directly from Jesus. However, nowhere in any of the Gospels is Paul mentioned as being present with Jesus and his disciples during the Lord's Supper, or as having actually met Jesus at any time during Jesus' first advent. Paul also claimed in his letter that the ritual of symbolically ingesting Jesus' blood was a "New Covenant." This unfortunately contradicts what God revealed in Ezekiel 44:7-8, where He states that those observing this "abominable" ritual, which is clearly not one of God's Ordinances, have <u>broken</u> His Covenant. Thus, based on the Ezekiel 44:7-8 prophesy, it is not plausible that Jesus went against God and instructed his disciples and followers to partake in this supposed "New Covenant" ritual, in remembrance of him.

Some may presume that Paul derived his account of the Lord's Supper from the Gospel of Mark, since it contains a very similar version as Paul's account of the Lord's Supper and Eucharist ritual (Mark 14:22-24). But this is highly improbable, since the Gospel of Mark was composed approximately two decades after Paul wrote his first Corinthians letter.[83] Moreover, in Acts 13:4-5, John Mark (believed through tradition, to be the writer of the Gospel of Mark) is mentioned as being Paul's and Barnabas' assistant, who accompanied them on their first missionary trip. Thus, Mark most likely had received his misinformation regarding the Eucharist from Paul. Furthermore, there are two other Gospel writers, Matthew and Luke, whose versions of the Lord's Supper are also very similar to Mark's account. Both of these writers wrote their Gospels around two decades after Mark's Gospel, [84] and presumably obtained their information based on Paul's and Mark's writings.

The Gospel of John (written around 100 CE; after the other Gospels) also provides details of what was said by Jesus and his disciples during the Passover Supper (John 13:1-30), but unlike the other Gospels, there is <u>no</u> mention of Jesus instructing his disciples during the meal to partake in the ritual of metaphorically drinking his blood and eating his body. It is inconceivable to us that John would have simply forgotten to mention this traditionally significant practice from his account of the Last Supper, especially when, in John 6:53-59, like the other Gospel's, he supposedly wrote that Jesus taught that whoever eats his flesh and drinks his blood would have eternal life. Thus, portions of John's Gospel reflect the teachings of Paul and Mark, but his reporting of the Passover Supper surprisingly resembles the Passover Supper account recorded in the Gospel of Barnabas.

John's version of the Passover Supper is as follows:

John 13:1   Now before the Passover feast, when Jesus knew that his hour was come that he should depart out of this world unto the Father;

having loved his own who were in the world. For he loved them unto the end.

13:2 When supper took place, the devil, by now, had put into the heart of Judas Iscariot, Simon's son, to betray him.

13:3 Jesus, knowing that the Father had given everything into his hands, and that he came from God, and goes (back) to God –

13:4 Rose up from supper, and laid aside his (outer) garments, and then took a towel tied around him.

13:5 After that, he poured water into a basin, and began to wash the disciples' feet, and to wipe (them with) the towel which he had tied around (himself).

13:6 When he came to Simon Peter; Peter then said to him, *"Do you wash my feet, lord?"*

13:7 Jesus answered and said to him, *"What I do, you don't understand now, but you shall understand hereafter."*

13:8 Peter said to him, *"You shall never wash my feet!"* Jesus told him, *"If I don't wash you, you have no part with me."*

13:9 Simon Peter replied to him, *"Not only my feet, lord, but also my hands and head."*

13:10 Jesus said to him, *"He that is washed, needs neither to wash (his) feet, but is clean throughout; yet not all (of you are clean)."* (13:11) For he knew who would betray him; therefore he said, *"You are not all clean."*

13:12 So after he had washed their feet, had retrieved his (outer) garments, and had sat down again, he said to them, *"Do you understand what I have done to you?"*

13:13 *"You call me 'master' and 'lord,' and you say I am 'good,' so…* (13:14) *if I then, as a lord and master have washed your feet [as a servant], you also* ought to wash one another's feet [as a servant]. (13:15) *For I have given you an example, which you should do, as I have done to you."*

13:16 *"Verily, verily, I say to you; the servant is not greater than his lord; neither is he that is sent* [i.e., Jesus], *greater than He* [i.e., God] *that sent him."*

13:17 *"If you understand these (words), you are blessed if you do it.* (13:18) *"I speak not of you all: I know whom I have chosen (as disciples); but so that the Scripture may be fulfilled, one that eats bread with me has lifted up his heel against me."*

13:19 *"I tell you now, before it occurs, that when it comes to pass, you must believe that I (still) exist* [Gk. Strong's 1510].*"*

13:20 *"Verily, verily, I say to you, he that receives whomever I send, receives me; and he that receives me, receives Him that sent me."*

13:21 After Jesus had thus spoken, he was troubled in spirit, and testified, and said; *"Verily, verily, I say unto you, that one of you shall betray me."*

13:22 Then the disciples looked one to another, doubting of whom he spoke.

13:23 Now there was leaning on Jesus' chest, one of his disciples, whom Jesus loved. (13:24) Simon Peter therefore beckoned to him, that he should ask who it would be, of whom he spoke. (13:25) He then, leaning on Jesus' chest, said to him, *"Who is it, lord?"*

13:26 Jesus answered, *"He it is, to whom I shall give a piece of bread, after I have dipped (it)."* And when he dipped the piece of bread, he gave it to Judas Iscariot, (the son of) Simon. (13:27) And after (receiving) the piece of bread, Satan then entered into him. Then Jesus said to him, *"That which you shall do, do quickly."*

13:28 Now, no man at the table knew for what reason he said this to him.

13:29   For some (of them) thought, because Judas had a bag, that Jesus had said to him, "*Buy what we have need of, for the feast,*" or that he should give something to the poor.

13:30   He then, having received the piece of bread, immediately went out; and it was evening.

Again, if Jesus had actually instructed his disciples during the Last Supper to symbolically consume his flesh and blood, it seems that it would have been mentioned in John's detailed account of the Passover Supper. Very similar to John's version of the Last Supper, the Gospel of Barnabas also reports about Jesus' Passover supper with his disciples, prior to Judas' betrayal. In Barnabas' account, there is also <u>no</u> mention of Jesus instructing his disciples to symbolically ingest his blood and body. The Passover Supper according to Barnabas, is provided below:

G. Barn. 213   The day having come for eating the (Passover) lamb, Nicodemus sent the lamb secretly to the garden for Jesus and his disciples; announcing all that had been decreed by Herod, by the governor, and the high priest.

> Whereupon Jesus rejoiced in spirit, saying: "*Blessed be your Holy Name, O Lord, because you have not separated me from the number of your servants that have been persecuted by the world, and slain. I thank you, my God, because I have fulfilled your work.*" And turning to Judas, he said to him: "*Friend, for what reason are you tarrying? My time is near. Wherefore? Go and do that which you shall do.*"
>
> The disciples thought that Jesus was sending Judas to buy something for the day of the Passover, but Jesus knew that Judas was betraying him...
>
> Judas answered: "*Allow me to eat, master, and then I will go.*"
>
> "*Let us eat,*" said Jesus, "*for I have greatly desired to eat this lamb before I am parted from you.*" And having arisen, he took a towel that covered around his hip, and having put water in a basin, he set himself to wash his disciples' feet. Starting from Judas, Jesus then came to Peter. Peter said: "*Shall you wash my feet, master?*"

Jesus answered: *"That which I do, you do not understand now, but you will understand hereafter."*

Peter replied, *"You should not wash my feet."*

Then Jesus rose up, and said: *"Neither shall you come in my company on the Day of Judgment."*

Peter exclaimed: *"Wash not only my feet, lord, but also my hands and my head!"*

After the disciples were washed, and were seated at the table to eat, Jesus said, *"I have washed you, yet not all of you are clean. Forasmuch as all the water of the sea will not wash whoever doesn't believe me."*

Jesus said this because he knew who was betraying him. The disciples were sad at these words, when Jesus said again: *"Verily, I say unto you, that one of you shall betray me, insomuch that I shall be sold like a sheep, but woe unto him, for he shall fulfill all that our forefather David said of such a person, that ' he shall fall into the Pit, which he had prepared for others.' "*

Whereupon the disciples looked upon each other, saying with sorrow: *"Who shall the traitor be?"*

Then, Judas asked: *"Shall it be me, O master?"*

Jesus answered: *"You have told me who it will be that shall betray me."* But the eleven apostles didn't hear it.

After the lamb was eaten, the devil approached behind Judas when he went forth from the house; Jesus having said to him again: *"Quickly do that which you shall do."*

Contrary to Paul's and Mark's teaching of the Eucharist ritual involving the symbolic ingestion of Jesus' flesh and blood, the term "Eucharist" was recorded in the early Christian text, *The Didache* (ISBN 9781973279471), also referred to as "the teachings of the 12 apostles;" as having no resemblance to the Pauline concept of the Eucharist. It was regarded by the earlier Church to be a thanksgiving meal, where its people gathered together, giving thanks to God for the food (bread) and drink they were about to consume, and then after eating, again giving thanks for their sustenance, and also for their knowledge and faith preventing them from sinning, which was taught to them by God's servant, Jesus. [85] The Eucharist meal gathering disclosed in *The Didache* is as follows:

Dida. 9:1   Now concerning the Eucharist; hold the Eucharist as thus:

9:2   First, concerning the Cup; *"We give thanks to you, our Father, for the holy (lineage) vine of David, your <u>servant</u> [Gk. Strong's #3816], which you did make known to us through Jesus, your <u>servant</u>. Glory be to you, forever."*

9:3   And concerning the broken Bread; *"We give you thanks, our Lord, for the life and knowledge which you did make known to us through Jesus, your servant. Glory be to you, forever."*

9:4   *"Just as (the miracle when) the broken bread was scattered upon the mountains, and was brought (back) together and became one (loaf), likewise let your Church be gathered together from the ends of the earth into Your Kingdom; for yours is the glory and the power through Jesus Christ, forever."*

9:5   *"But let no one eat or drink of your Eucharist, except those who have been baptized in the Lord (God's) Name. For concerning this, the Lord did also say, 'Do not give that which is holy to the dogs.' "*

Dida. 10:1   But then after you are satisfied with the <u>food</u>, thus give thanks:

10:2   *"We give thanks to you, Holy Father, for your Holy Name, which you did make to tabernacle in our hearts, and for the knowledge and faith that (shuns) immorality, which you did make know to us through Jesus, your servant. Glory be to you, forever."*

10:3   *"You, Lord Almighty, did create all things for your Name's sake, and did give food and drink to mankind for their enjoyment, that they might give thanks to you; but also you have blessed us with spiritual*

> *food and drink, and eternal light through your servant* [Gk. Strong's #3816]."

10:4   "*Above all, we give thanks to you; for that you are mighty. Glory be to you, forever.*"

10:5   "*Lord, remember your Church, to deliver it from all evil, and to make it perfect with your love; and gather it together in its holiness through the <u>four spirits</u> of your Kingdom that you had prepared for it. For yours is the power and the glory forever.*"

10:6   "*Let grace come, and let this world pass away. Hosanna to the God of David. If any man is holy, let it come! If any man is not, let him repent. Our Lord (let it) come! Amen.*' "

10:7   "*And permit the prophets to hold Eucharist as often as they wish.*"

Hence, the Eucharist was originally a gathering of church members to give thanks to God for the meal they would enjoy together, and for the much appreciated guidance God had provided them through His servant messengers that descended from David. Again, it was not the partaking of a ritual symbolically consuming the blood and body of Christ, which God considers to be a repulsive practice. Rightly so, because according to God's Law, which Jesus and his disciples abided by, the eating of human flesh and the drinking of blood is prohibited. For instance, in Leviticus 23:29-30, God expressed His fury and warned of punishment for those that eat the flesh of their descendants, and in Leviticus 7:26-27 and 17:13-14, God forbade the drinking of blood and the eating of flesh that had not been properly drained of blood. Thus, it is understandable why, in Ezekiel 44: 7-8, God proclaims that the practice of eating Christ's flesh and drinking his blood is an unholy, abominable observance that breaks His Covenant. And we, therefore, can conclude that Jesus had not actually instructed his disciples or followers to partake in this symbolic ritual.

44:8   2050.1; 3808; yours; 8104, 8804; 4931   6944; 2967.1   (below)
"<u>Since yours had not responsibly observed</u> <u>the holy practice(s) of Mine</u>, <u>yours</u>,

2050.1; yours; 7760, 8799   3807.1; 8104, 8802; 4931; 2967.1; 871.1; 4720; 2967.1; 3807.1; 3641.1
<u>thus, shall reappoint</u> <u>the responsibility of Mine at My sanctuary to your own keepers</u>."

44:9-31   [Relocated following Ez. 45:4b and 44:27 & 26b, but not in KJV sequential order]

Ezekiel 45:4b

                1931   3807.1; 3548 plur.   8334, 8764   1886.1; 4720

45:4b   This is in regards to the priests ministering at the sanctuary [atop Temple Mount];

            it; 1961, 8799; 1886.1; 7131   3807.1; 8334   853   3068   (below)

    those approaching it should be there to serve namely Yahweh. And according to

      (2050.1; it; 1961, 8804; 3807.1; 1992)...   cont.   (4725; 3807.1; 1004 plur.; 3963.1; 2050.1; 4720; 3807.1; 4720)

    these [serving their Jesus], it should have been the site for their own temples and

      cont.

holy sanctuary.

Ezekiel 44:27 & 26b

        (2050.1; 871.1; 3117; they; 935, 8800 or 8804; 413; 1886.1; 6944; 413; 1886.1; 2691; 1886.1; 6442)...

44:27   On the day when they [the priests] shall have come to the interior court of the

      cont.   3807.1; 8334, 8763; 871.1; 6944   (he; 7126, 8686; 2403; 2050.2)...   cont.

    sanctuary to minister at the sanctuary, he [their Jesus] would present himself as

      cont.   (2893; 2050.2; 7651; 3117; they; 5608, 8799; 3807.1; 2050.2)...

44:26b* a sin offering. *(Then, for) seven days, (thereafter) they would report to him (about)

      cont.

the purification ritual of his (followers).

Ezekiel 44:26c & 44:9-31

            it; 5002, 8803   136   3068 or 3069

44:26c   It was (clearly) stated in the Oracles, "*The Lord is Yahweh*."

         3541   559, 8804; 136; 3068 or 3069   per Ez. 44:6

44:9   "This is what Lord Yahweh said [which Jesus shall have relayed to the Israelis]:"

```
                3605; 1121; 5236              6189; 3820; 2050.1; 6189; 1320      3808; 935, 8799      (below)
```
"Any foreigner that is uncircumcised of flesh and/or spirit must not come to My

```
        413;4720;2967.1   3807.1; 3605; 1121; 5236     834         (871.1; 8432; 1121 plur. ; 3478)...
```
sanctuary; that (includes) any foreigner that is (already) in the midst of Israel's de-

```
              cont.          3588; 518    1886.1;3881 plur.  834   7368,8804;4480;5921;2967.1    (below)
```
44:10* scendants. *For assuredly, the Levites who have strayed away from Me, during the

```
        871.1; 8582, 8800; 3478        834; they; 8582, 8804; 4480; 5921; 2967.1; 310      1544 plur.; 1992
```
going astray of Israel, who have strayed away from Me to follow 'the idols' of theirs

```
   refer back to Ez. 28:2-7 and Ez. 28:12-19 (1st book)   2050.1; 5375, 8804         (5771; 3963.1)...
```
[i.e., Jesus and the Holy Spirit], shall have, indeed, borne the punishment for their

```
              cont.
```
iniquity."


```
                             2050.1; they; 1961, 8804; 871.1; 4720; 2967.1; 8334, 8764
```
44:11   When they shall have become the ministers at My sanctuary [on Temple Mount],

```
          6486      413; 8179 plur.; 1886.1; 1004    2050.1; 8334, 8764   853;1886.1;1004   1992
```
in charge of the temple's gates and to attend to the temple, these [converted Levite

```
                          per Ez. 44:10                    they; 7819, 8799    (853; 1886.1; 5930)...
```
Priests, who will be serving 'Jesus,' as if he was God] shall slaughter the Ola burnt

```
          cont.     2050.1; 853; 1886.1; 2076 or 2077; refer to Ez. 44:7, 15, & 21  (3807.1; 5971; 2050.1; 1992; 5975, 8799)
```
offering (there), and shall offer the (Eucharist) offering to the people when they

```
          cont.       3807.1; 6440; 1992    3807.1; them; 8334, 8763    3282    834    they; 8334, 8762
```
44:12* shall stand in front of these ministering to them. *Because of what they shall serve

```
        853; 3963.1    3807.1;6440   1544 plur.; 1992    2050.1; they; 1961, 8804    (3807.1;1004; 3478)
```
these (followers) in front of their crucifixes, they, thus, shall have caused the House

```
          cont.    3807.1; 4383; 5771    5921; 3651; I; 5375, 8804    3027;2967.1    5921; 1992
```
of Israel to fall into iniquity. I, therefore, shall have lifted up My Hand against them!

```
                     it; 5002, 8803              136        3068 or 3069      (below)
```
It was (clearly) stated in the Oracles; "*The Lord* is *Yahweh*," hence, they shall

```
               2050.1; they; 5375, 8804; 5771; 3963.1
```
have borne the punishment for their own sin(s).

	2050.1; 3808; they; 5066, 8799; 413; 2967.1	(3547, 8763; 3807.1; 2967.1)...

44:13   Furthermore, they must never (again) approach Mine in order to serve as the

cont.   2050.1; 3807.1; 5066, 8800; 5921; 3605; 6944; 2967.1   (413; 6944; 2967.1; 1886.1; 6944)

priest(s) of Mine; or to even come near to any of My sacred places (that are) for the

cont.   2050.1; they; 5375, 8804   3639; 3963.1   (2050.1; 8441 plur.; 3963.1)

holiest of Mine. They shall have surely borne their own disgrace for their detestable

cont.   834   they; 6213, 8804

practices that they performed.

         2050.1; I; 5414, 8804   853; 3963.1   8104, 8802; 4931   (below)

44:14   I, indeed, had (once) given namely theirs the responsibility of watching over the

1886.1; 1004; 3807.1; 3605; 5656; 2050.2 2050.1; 3807.1; 3605   834   6213, 8735

temple for all of its service(s), and for all (the observances) that should be practiced

871.1; 2050.2 2050.1; 1886.1; 3548 plur. 1886.1; 3881 plur. 1121 plur. 6659 (below)

44:15* within it. *But the priests of the Levites; the descendants of Zadok, who had the

834; 8104, 8804; 853; 4931   4720; 2967.1   871.1; 8582, 8800   (below)

responsibility of watching over My sanctuary during the going astray of Israel's

1121; 3478; 4480; 5921; 2967.1   1992; 7126, 8799   (413; 2967.1; 3807.1; 8334)...

descendants (that strayed) away from Me, shall approach these, in order to minister

cont. 8763; 2967.1; 2050.1; they; 5975, 8804 3807.1; 2967.1; 3807.1; 7126, 8687; 3807.1; 2967.1; 2459; 2050.1; 1818 (below)

44:21* Mine, and shall have stood before Me to offer Mine the finest (wine) as blood. *But

2050.1; 3196; 3808; 8354, 8799; 3605; 3548   871.1; 935, 8800; 413   1886.1; 2691; 1886.1; 6442

a priest should never drink (or offer) wine when entering into the inner court [of

the sanctuary shrine on Temple Mount].

It; 5002, 8803   136   3068 or 3069

It was stated in the Oracles; "*The Lord is Yahweh*."

1992   (935, 8799; 413; 4720; 2967.1; 2050.1; 1992; 7126, 8799; 413; 7979; 2967.1)...

44:16   These [converted Kohanim] shall come to My sanctuary, and they shall approach

cont.   3807.1; 8334; 8763; mine   2050.1; they; 8104, 8804; 853; 4931; 2967.1

a table of Mine in order to serve Mine, who had (once) observed My Ordinance(s).

2050.1; it; 1961, 8804   871.1; 935, 8800; 3963.1; 413; 8179; possv.; 1886.1; 2691; 1886.1; 6442

44:17* *When it shall have occurred, at their arrival to the entrance of the inside court,

133

<small>899; 6593; they; 3847, 8799   deduced from Ez. 44:19, below</small>
<u>they would wear linen garments</u> (that were donned within a sacred chamber of

<small>   2050.1; it; 5927, 8799; 5921; 1992; 6785   871.1; 8334, 8763; 3963.1   (below)</small>
the shrine). <u>Moreover, wool could not go on them</u> while ministering (to) theirs at

<small>   871.1; 8179; possv.; 1886.1; 2691; 1886.1; 6442;2050.1; 1004; 1886.3   (6287; 6593 plur.; they; 1961, 8799)</small>
44:18* <u>the entrance of the inside court that is its temple's (interior).</u> *They would have

<small>   cont.   5921; 7218; 3963.1   2050.1; 4370; 6593   (1961, 8799; 5921; 4975 plur.; 1992)</small>
<u>linen headdresses</u> upon their head(s), <u>and linen underwear</u> would be (worn) upon

<small>   cont.   3808; they; 2296, 8799   871.1; 3154</small>
<u>their loins.</u> <u>They would not put on</u> (other materials) <u>because of the sweat.</u> ^(N:18)

<small>   2050.1; 871.1; 3318, 8800; 413   (1886.1; 2691; 1886.1; 2435; 413; 1886.1; 2691; 1886.1; 2435; 413; 1886.1; 5971)...</small>
44:19   <u>Then, when exiting out (to) the outer courtyard, towards the people at the outside</u>

<small>   cont.   they; 6584, 8799   853; 899; 1992   834; 1992; 8334, 8764; 871.1; 3963.1   (below)</small>
<u>court,</u> <u>they would (first) take off</u> <u>these clothes</u> <u>that they ministered in,</u> <u>and shall have</u>

<small>2050.1; they; 3240, 8689; 853; 3963.1; 871.1; 3957; 1886.1; 6944   2050.1; they; 3847, 8804   899; 312   (below)</small>
<u>set them down in the sacred chamber</u> <u>after they had put on</u> <u>other garments,</u> <u>since</u>

<small>   2050.1; 3808; they; 6942, 8762; 853; 1886.1; 5971   871.1; 899; 1992</small>
<u>they could not sanctify the people</u> <u>in their own clothing.</u>

^(N:18) The prophesied garments mentioned in Ezekiel 44:16-19, which will be worn by the Hebrew priests (Kohanim) that will convert and follow the commands and ordinances of the imposter Jesus, but shall also once again observe their ancient ordinances of performing animal sacrifices for the atonement of their sins, and presenting offerings to their "Lord," accurately describes the attire of Jerusalem's high priests when they once served in their tabernacle and temple. These high priests wore a "Kutonet" undergarment, robe, and headdress made of linen. The Talmud records show that the high priests were required to wear linen underwear in order to symbolize "the abolition of the distinction between the heavenly and the mortal part of man." [86] Also, as mentioned in the above prophesy, they would wear linen so as not to gird themselves with anything that caused sweat. Unlike wool and other fabrics, linen absorbs sweat away from the skin.

<small>   2050.1; 7218; 3963.1; 3808; they; 1548, 8762   2050.1; 6545; 3808; they; 7971, 8762</small>
44:20   <u>Furthermore, they would not shave their head(s);</u> <u>nor would they grow long hair.</u>

<small>3697, 8800; they; 3697, 8799; 853 or 854; 7218 plur.; 1992</small>

They would clip (it); trimming over their heads.

<small>(2050.1; 490 sing.; 2050.1; 1644, 8803; 1886.3; 3808; they; 3947, 8799; 3807.1;1992)...</small>

44:22 They also would not (typically) take for themselves, a widowed or divorced wo-

<small>cont. 3807.1; 802 plur.; 3588; 518   1330 sing.   4480; 2233   1004; 3478   (below)</small>

man as wives, but rather, a virgin from the offspring of the Israelite family.   They

<small>2050.1; 1886.1; 490; 834; 1961, 8799; 490; 4480; 3548 sing.; they; 3947, 8799</small>

would, however, take (as a wife), a widow who is the widow of a priest.

<small>(1886.1; 4503; 2050.1; 1886.1; 2403; 2050.1; 1886.1; 817; 1992; 398, 8799; 3963.1)...   cont.</small>

44:29 These [priests] shall consume the offering that was (both) a sin offering and a

<small>cont.   2050.1; 3605; 2764; 871.1; 3478</small>

guilt offering, since, in Israel, each dedicated thing [traditionally given over to God]

<small>3807.1; 1992; it; 1961, 8799</small>

would be for them.

<small>2050.1; 7225   3605; 1061 plur.   3605   2050.1; 3605; 8641   (below)</small>

44:30 Also, the first of all the firstfruits of each kind, and each contribution from all of

<small>3605; 4480; 3605; 8641 plur.; 3641.1   3807.1; 3548 plur.; 1961, 8799   (below)</small>

the offerings of yours of each type, would be for the Kohanim.   What's more, yours

<small>2050.1; 7225; 6182; 3641.1; yours; 5414, 8799   3807.1; 3548   (3807.1; 5117, 8687 (causing); 1293)...</small>

would give the first piece of a dough offering to a Kohen for bringing about a blessing

<small>cont.   413; 1004; 3509.2</small>

to remain in the home(s) of yours.

<small>3605; 5038 sing.; 2050.1; 2966; 4480; 1886.1; 5775 sing.; 2050.1; 1886.1; 4480; 929 sing.; 3808; 398, 8799; 1886.1; 3548 plur.</small>

44:31 The Kohanim would not eat any (creature's) carcass that died of itself, or that was

<small>cont.   refer back to Ez. 39:17-18, 42:13, 44:7-8, & 44:29</small>

torn from a bird or an animal. [Yet, after accepting Israel's imposter Jesus, they and

their converted congregation shall partake in the Pauline Eucharist ritual of eating

Jesus' torn flesh (broken bread/ wafer) and drinking his blood (wine)].

<small>2050.1; 413   4191; 8801   120   ** (834; 3808; 1961; 8804; 3807.1; 376 (Iyesh); 2390, 8691)...</small>

44:25 Moreover, for (any) deceased person that had not become (followers) of the Jesus

135

     cont.   (3808; he or his; 935, 8799)... cont.   3807.1; 2391; 1886.3
  (that) shall defile theirs, his [priests] would not approach it because of (being) defiled;

   3588; 518 3807.1; 1; 2050.1; 3807.1; 517; 2050.1; 3807.1; 1121; 2050.1; 3807.1; 1323; 3807.1; 251; 2050.1; 3807.1; 269
  whether or not (it was) regarding a father, a mother, a son, a daughter, a brother, or

    cont. **worded above;* 2050.1; 310; 2967.1
44:26a* a sister * that followed Me [Yahweh].

     2050.1; 1961, 8804; 3807.1; 1992   3807.1; 5159; 589   (below)
44:28 And what(ever) had existed of theirs for inheritance to Mine, yours would not

    (5159; 3963.1; 2050.1; 272; 3808; yours; 5414, 8799; 3807.1;1992; 871.1; 3478; 589; 272; 3963.1)...
  give Mine in Israel their inheritance and possession(s), (even though it was) their

   cont.
  possession.

     2050.1; 3808; 5971; 2967.1; they; 3384, 8686   996   6944
44:23 They also should not have allowed the casting out of My people amongst the holy

      3807.1; 2455   (below)
  [from Temple Mount] for the sake of the unholy! For they shall not make theirs

     2050.1; 996; 2931; 3807.1; 2889; they; 3045, 8686; 3963.1
  understand the difference between what is morally impure and what is pure.

    2050.1; 5921; 7379   1992; 5975, 8799   3807.1; 8199, 8800 (below)
44:24 Thus, over the dispute, these (priests) shall stand for judgment in accordance

    871.1; 4941; 2967.1   2050.1; they; 8199, 8799; 2050.2 (below)
  with My (actual) Ordinances, and they shall also face judgment (based on) My

  2050.1; 853; 8451; 2967.1; 2050.1; 853; 2708; 2967.1; 871.1; 3605; 4150; 2967.1 they; 8104, 8799; 2050.1; 853 or 854 (below)
  Laws and My Statutes that each appointee of Mine shall preserve, as well as My

  7676; 2967.1 they; 6942, 8762
  Sabbaths that they should observe.

Ezekiel 47

   (2050.1; he; 7725, 8686; 2967.1),,, cont.   cont. 413; 6607 sing. (below)
47:1 Afterwards, he [the spirit] shall return Mine [Jesus] back to the entrance of the

<small>1886.1;1004   2050.1; 2009   4325   it; 3318, 8802 (4480; 8478; 4670; 1886.1;1004; 6921; 1886.3)...</small>

<u>temple</u> <u>and (they shall) behold</u> that <u>water</u> <u>was issuing out</u> <u>from below, east of the</u>

<small>cont.   3588; 6440; 1886.1; 1004   6921   (2050.1; 1886.1; 4325; it; 3381, 8802)...</small>

<u>temple's threshold,</u> <u>since the temple faced</u> <u>eastward.</u> <u>The water was also issuing</u>

<small>cont.   4480; 8478   4480; 3802; 1886.1; 1004; 1886.1; 3233   4480; 5045   3807.1; 4196</small>

<u>out</u> <u>from below,</u> <u>on the right side of the temple,</u> and <u>on the southside</u> <u>of the altar</u>.

<small>   2050.1; he; 3318, 8686; 2967.1   1870   8179; 6828; 1886.3   (2050.1; he; 5437, 8686; 2967.1)</small>

47:2   <u>He shall then lead Mine out,</u> <u>by way of</u> <u>its northern gate,</u> <u>and shall lead Mine</u>

<small>cont.   1870; 2351   413; 8179; 1886.1; 2351   1886.1; 6437, 8802; 6921   (2050.1; 2009)...</small>

<u>around</u> <u>an outside path</u> <u>nearby the outer gate</u> <u>that faces eastward,</u> <u>and (they) shall</u>

<small>cont.   4325   6379, 8764   4480; 1886.1; 3802; 1886.1; 3233</small>

<u>behold</u> that <u>spring water</u> <u>was pouring</u> <u>out of the right side slope</u>. ^(N:19)

^(N:19) According to this and the following Ezekiel prophesies, the messenger spirit will be pointing out and explaining to Jesus about a water source for Temple Mount, and then later in the subsequent verses about other water resources for Jerusalem and Israel. The spring mentioned in Ezekiel 47:2 is in reference to Gihon Spring, which has also been referred to in the Old Testament as Shiloah and Siloam. Gihon Spring's water emerges from a cave on an eastern slope of the ancient City of David, and flows into the adjacent Kidron Valley. At one time, it was the main source of water for Temple Mount, the Pool of Siloam, and the ancient City of David. [87]

<small>   871.1; he; 3318, 8800 or 8804; 1886.1; 376 (Iyesh)   6921   (2050.1; 6957)...</small>

47:3   <u>After this (actual) Jesus shall have departed</u> <u>the east side,</u> <u>with a measuring</u>

<small>cont.   871.1; 3027; 2050.2   inferred per Ez. 47:3-8a</small>

<u>device</u> <u>in his hand,</u> (he will be transported to another water resource for Jeru-

salem), [which is today located in the region around Rosh Ha-Ayin, just 25 miles

<small>   2050.2; he; 4058, 8799   505   871.1; 520   (below)</small>

north west of Jerusalem] [88] <u>and he shall measure off</u> <u>a thousand,</u> <u>in cubit(s),</u> <u>which</u>

<small>   2050.1; he; 5674, 8686; 2967.1   871.1; 4325   4325   657 plur.</small>

<u>shall cause Mine to cross over</u> <u>into the water,</u> where <u>the water</u> is up to <u>the ankles</u>.

137

	2050.1; he; 4058, 8799 505 2050.1; it; 5674, 8686; 2967.1
47:4	He then shall measure off (another) thousand that would cause Mine to pass

        871.1; 4325   4325   1290   2050.1; he; 4058, 8799

through the water where the water was up to the knees. Again, he shall measure

  cont.   505   2050.1; he or it; 5674, 8686; 2967.1   4325

off a thousand (cubits), which would cause Mine to go where the water was at the

     4975   2050.1; he; 4058, 8799   505   (5158)…

47:5*   hips. *When he shall measure off yet (another) thousand, it will be the stream

  cont.   834   3808; 3201; 2967.1   3807.1; 5674, 8800   (3588; 1342, 8804; 1886.1; 4325; 4325)…

area that Mine would not be able to cross through, since the spring water shall have

    cont.   7813   (5158; 834; 3808; it; 5674, 8735)…

risen up (to) a water (level) deep enough to swim in, whereby the stream could not

    cont.   (2050.1; he; 559, 8799)…   cont.   413; 2967.1

47:6*   be walked through. *Thus, he [the messenger spirit] shall say for Me [Yahweh]:

   (1886.1; 7200, 8804; 1121; 120)…   cont.   deduced per Strong's # 7813 worded above

"*Son of Man* [Jesus], *did you realize* (it would be this deep)?"

     2050.1; he; 1980, 8686; 2967.1; 2050.1; he; 7725, 8686; 2967.1   8193; 1886.1; 5158

He shall then lead Mine back, and shall help Mine return to the stream's bank.

   871.1; he; 7725, 8800 or 8804; 2967.1   (2050.1; 2009; 413; 8193; 1886.1; 5158; 6086; 7227; 3966)…

47:7   After he shall have returned Mine, (they) then will behold very many trees near-

   cont.   (4480; 2088; 2050.1; 4480; 2088; 2050.1; he; 559, 8799; 413; 2967.1; 1886.1; 4325; 1886.1; 428; 3318, 8802)

47:8a*   by the stream's bank; on one side, and also on the other side; *and he shall tell Mine

   cont.   (413; 1886.1; 1552; 1886.1; 6930; 2050.1; it; 3381, 8799 or 8804; 4325; 5921; 1886.1; 6160)

that this water is issued out to the eastern region and goes down into the (Negev)

  cont.   2050.1; it; 935, 8804   1886.1; 3220; 1886.3

desert, although it had (once) ran into the (Mediterranean) Sea.

47:8b-11   [Relocated after Ez. 47:12 below]

   2050.1; 5921; 1886.1; 5158   (5927, 8799; 5921; 8193; 2050.2; 4480; 2088; 2050.1; 4480; 2088; 3605; 6086; 3978)

47:12   Furthermore, next to the stream, each tree (there) for food shall grow along both

<u>sides of its banks.</u> cont. (3808; it; 5034, 8799; 5929; 2050.2; 2050.1; 3808; 8552, 8799; 6529; 2050.2; 3807.1; 2320; 2050.2) <u>Throughout its (growing) month(s), its leaves would not wither,</u>

<u>and its fruit shall not stop producing</u>; cont. it; 1069, 8762 <u>it would bear fruit</u> 3588; 4325 plur.; 2050.2 <u>because of its water supplies.</u>

(The people) <u>at the sanctuary</u> 4480; 1886.1; 4720 [on Temple Mount], where <u>these</u> 1992 (streams) <u>are supply-</u> (3318, 8802)...

<u>ing,</u> cont. <u>shall have also had</u> 2050.1; it; 1961, 8804 (the benefit of) <u>its fruit for food</u> 6529; 2050.2; 3807.1; 3978 <u>and its leaves for healing.</u> 2050.1; 5929; 3807.1; 8644 (N:20)

(N:20) The prophesy uncovered in Ezekiel 47:7-8a and 47:12 has just now in modern times begun to fulfill. The Rosh Ha-Ayin Forest, which was planted between 1976 and 1980 by the Jewish National Fund, contains various fruit orchards, as well as carob, pine, cypress, almond, jujube, and other trees. [89] The forest lies along the northern portion of the Nahal Raba tributary. The fruit and leaves of the jujube [90] and carob [91] trees have been found to have antimicrobial properties and other medicinal uses.

[Since the early 2000's, Israel has been drawing and desalinating most of its

47:8b* drinking water from the Mediterranean Sea.] *<u>In regards to its sea water</u> 413; 1886.1; 3220; 1886.3 <u>that is</u> (below)

1886.1; 3318, 8716 <u>drawn out,</u> 2050.1; 7495, 8738; 1886.1; 4325 <u>after the water has been treated</u> [via Israel's reverse osmosis process], [92]

47:9* *<u>it then shall have become</u> 2050.1; it; 1961; 8804 (drinkable) for <u>each living creature</u> 3605; 5315; 2416; 834 <u>that shall swarm</u> 8317, 8799 <u>to</u> (below)

<u>wherever any of (its) streams there shall run.</u> 413; 3605; 834; it; 935, 8799; 5158 plur.

<u>The fish that live</u> it; 2421, 8799; 2050.1; 1961, 8804; 1886.1; 1710 (in these fresh and desalinated waters) <u>shall have also became</u>

<u>very abundant,</u> 7227; 3966 <u>since</u> 3588 <u>these waters shall have also ran</u> 935, 8804; 8033; 1886.1; 4325 plur; 1886.1; 428 where <u>they would again be</u> (2050.1; they; 7495, 8735)...

<u>treated.</u> cont. <u>Anything that lives where these stream(s) run has, indeed,</u> 2050.1; it; 2425, 8804; 3605; 834; it; 935, 8799; 8033; 1886.1; 5158 (thrived).

139

47:10   ^{(2050.1; it; 1961, 8804)...}   ^{cont.}   ^(they; 5975, 8799; 5921; 2050.2; 1728)
It [the country's streams] has also existed for the fishermen that would stand

^{cont.}   ^{4480; 5872; 2050.1; 5704; 5872 (Ain Jidi)}
beside them (to fish); all the way from Ein Gedi [which has four springs that flow

into two deep gorges, forming the Nahal Arugot and Nahal David Streams in the

^{2050.1; 5704; 5882 (unidentified)}   ^(below)
Judean Desert, on the west shore of the Dead Sea],[93] to as far as Ein Eglaim. They

^{4894; 3807.1; 2764; they; 1961; 8799; 3807.1; 4327; 1886.3}   ^(below)
(also) exist for their breed as a remote place to spread out (and explore). Their fish

^(it; 1961, 8799; 1710; 3963.1; 3509.4; 1710; 1886.1; 3220; 1886.1; 1419; 7227; 1886.3; 3966)
(at these freshwater locations) will be exceedingly abundant like the fish in the

^{cont.}
great (Mediterranean) Sea.

47:11   ^{1207; 2050.2}   ^{2050.1; 1360 plur.; 2050.2}
(The brine from) its waterlogged area(s) and its marshes [along the Dead Sea

^{2050.1; 3808; 7495; 8735}   ^{3807.1; 4417}   ^{they; 5414, 8804 (not 8738)}
shore] that would not be treated, is (collected) for the salt they shall have formed

[which has a high mineral content that has been found to improve skin health, and

to treat psoriasis and rheumatoid arthritis].[94]

47:13a, 15-23   [Relocated to Section 5 regarding the rightful owners of the Holy Land]

SECTION 5

God Affirms That the Holy Land Inheritance Also Belongs to Israel's Arabs

---

Ezekiel 33:23-24

33:23 <u>The Word of Yahweh shall also come to Mine, saying</u>:

33:24 "<u>Son of Man</u> [Jesus], <u>those who are inhabiting these desolate areas upon the land of Israel have been talking, saying</u>:"

"<u>Abraham was the first that shall occupy the (Holy) Land, so we are also the masters of the (Holy) Land; it was (also) given to us as inheritance</u>." (N:21)

(N:21) At the time when this Ezekiel 33:24 prophecy occurs, the inhabitants of Israel and the Israeli annexed Arab lands shall have predominately been the Messianic Jews and Arab Christians, who shall have been following the imposter Jesus as their Messiah and Lord. The Arab Muslims and any Jew or Arab Christian that shall oppose the imposter Jesus and follow the true Jesus upon his return, shall have been exiled away from the Israeli occupied, Arab territories. The above prophesied dispute is a reasonable argument for Israel's Arab refugees; provided their people are believers in the one true God and are correctly obeying God's Commandments and Ordinances. Abraham is the forefather of many of God's pious prophets, including, for instance, Jacob (Israel), Moses, David, Isaiah, Ezekiel, Jesus, and, according to Islamic tradition, Mohamed. [95] The Promised Land was initially given to Abraham and was passed on to all of his sons, including Isaac and Ishmael, and also to all of Abraham's future offspring (Genesis 12:1-7). The Israelites are descendants of both Isaac (Genesis 32:28) and the ancient Canaanites, [96] while Israel's neighboring Arabs are descendants of the Canaanites [97] and Ishmael (according to Islamic belief).⁹⁸ This is why Israel's Arab refugees insist that they should have a shared claim to the land occupied by the Israelis.

Nevertheless, regardless of whether or not this argument is valid, in the following passages, God sets the record straight. Towards the end of the ages, during the second advent of the true Jesus Christ, the inheritance, which is today referred to as the "Holy Land" or the "Promised Land," shall not only be for the Israelis, but will also be for their exiled, Arab neighbors, and for the few gentile survivors in Israel and the Israeli occupied territories, who shall, from then on, strictly obey God's Commandments and actual Ordinances, accept all of God's prophets and messengers, including the real Jesus and Mohamed (Ez. 24:16-21 and Ez. 24:25 in the 1st book); and most importantly, shall devoutly worship God, solely in the Name of God (not in Christ's name, nor in the name of the Holy Spirit).

The prophesies in this section are to occur sometime around the time Israel and its annexed lands, including parts of Egypt, shall have been destroyed by the prophesied mass destructive weapon(s), and the ruins have been rebuilt (Ez. 36:33-36; repeated below).

36:33   (3541; he; 559, 8804)...   cont.   136   3068 or 3069
"This is what he [Jesus] had relayed; 'The Lord is Yahweh.' "

    871.1; 3117   I; 2891, 8804 (or 8763)   853; 3641.1   4480; 3605; 5771; 3641.1
"At the time that I shall have repurified yours away from all of your sinful practices,

    2050.1; 3427; 8689; 853; 1886.1; 5892 plur.   2050.1; 1129, 8738; 1886.1; 2723 plur.
I then shall have caused the cities to be inhabited, after the ruins have been rebuilt.

36:34*   2050.1; 1886.1; 776; 8074, 8737; 5647, 8735   8478   834   it; 1961, 8804   8077
*When the desolate land is tilled beneath where it shall have been wasteland,

36:35*   3807.1; 5869 plur.   3605; 5674, 8802   2050.1; they; 559, 8804   1886.1; 776; 1977; 8074, 8737
in the sights of every passerby, *they, indeed, shall have thought; 'This land that was

    cont.   1961, 8804   3509.4; 1588; 5731   2050.1; 1886.1; 5892; 1886.1; 2720   (below)
desolate has become like the garden of Eden, and the ruined cities that were deso-

    2050.1; 8074, 8737; 2040, 8737   it; 1219, 8803   3427, 8804
late and destroyed, which were inaccessible, have become inhabited.'"

36:36   2050.1; 3045, 8804; 1886.1; 1471 plur.; 834; 7604, 8735; 5439; 3641.1
"Because the gentiles that will be remaining as your neighbors have known

    3588; 589   3068 or 3069   I or mine; 1129, 8804; 2040, 8737; 2050.1; I or mine; 5193, 8804   (below)
that I (Yahweh) am God, Mine shall have rebuilt what was ruined, and replanted what

                    8074, 8737
was destroyed."

Ezekiel 47:13a & 47:15-23

                                      3541   559, 8804; 136; 3069
47:13a   [Israelis:] "This (that follows) is what Lord Yahweh said:"

                        2050.1; 5307, 8804; 1886.1; 776; 1886.1; 2063   3807.1; 3641.1; 871.1; 5159   (below)
47:15*   "This is the land that shall have fallen into the possession of yours, *which (in-

          2050.1; 2088; 1366; 1886.1; 776
cluded) the following region(s):"

          3807.1; 6285; 6828; 1886.3   4480; 1886.1; 3220; 1886.1; 1419   (1886.1;1870)
"On the country's north side, from the great (Mediterranean) Sea (coast), heading

cont.   2855 (Hethlon)   3007.1; it; 935, 8800; 6657 (Sadadah)
towards Hethlon [probably Lebanon], it went to Sadad [63 miles NE of Damascus]

         2574 (Hamath); 1268 (Beruta)   5453   834; 996; 1366; 1834; 2050.1; 996; 1366; 2574 (Hamath)
47:16*   *(from) Beirut, (then to) Hamah, Sibraim, which is between the regions of Hamah

         cont.   2691; 1886.1; 8484
and Damascus, and then (down to) the settlement towards the middle (of Jordan)

  834   413   1366; 2362
that is next to the Hauran region.[99] [which spans parts of southern Syria and North-

ern Jordan and includes the land that is east of the Jordan River]."

                    2050.1; it; 1961, 8804; 1366   (4480; 1886.1; 3220; 2691; 2703 or 2704)...
47:17   "Hence, it is the territory that (once) existed as part of the seashore settlement

        cont.   1366   1834   (2050.1; 6828; 6828; 1886.3)...
of Enon [possibly Saida] to the border of Damascus, then northward (from) its north-

       cont.   2050.1; 1366; 2574   2050.1; 853; 6285; 6828; 2050.1; 6285; 6921   (below)
47:18*   side to that which is Hamah's border. It also includes the north *and east sides of

          4480; 996; 2362; 2050.1; 4480; 996; 1834
the part separate from Damascus that's the Hauran[100] [where the Ghouta Oasis, the

                                                                      (below)
Al-Safa field, the Golan Heights, and Jordan's desert steppe are located], as well as

<small>1886.1; 1568; 2050.1; 4480; 996; 776; 3478   1886.1; 3383; 4480; 1366   (below)</small>
the part between the land of Israel and the Gilead region, at the Jordanian border, on

<small>5921; 1886.1; 3220; 1886.1; 6931</small>
the eastside of the (Dead) Sea."

<small>(you plur.; 4058, 8799; 2050.1; 853)...   cont.   6285; 6921; 1886.3   (2050.1; 6285; 5045; 8486; 1886.3)</small>
47:19*   "You [Israelis] shall also stretch out towards its east side, *as well as south of its

<small>cont.   4480; 8559   5704</small>
southern side; from Tamar [101] [a southern region of Israeli occupied Palestine], up to

<small>4325 plur.   4808</small>
the waters of Meriba [believed by us to include Lake Kinneret (Sea of Galilee)], the

<small>6946; 5158   (below)</small>
holy stream [where Jesus preached, and several miracles occurred], [102] down to the

<small>413;1886.1;3220;1886.1;1419;2050.1;853or854;6285;8486;1886.3;5045;1886.3   (below)</small>
47:20*   large sea that is southward on its south side [i.e., down to the Dead Sea]; *and then

<small>2050.1; 6285; 3220   1886.1; 3220; 1886.1; 1419   4480; 1366</small>
to the west side to the great (Mediterranean) Sea at the (southern) border [of Israel

<small>5704; 5227   (below)</small>
that will eventually, also annex Egypt], up to the opposite end of the same sea

<small>3807.1; 935, 8800; 2574; 2063; 6285; 3220</small>
leading towards Hamah."

<small>2050.1; yours; 2505, 8765   853; 1886.1; 776; 1886.1; 2063; 3807.1; 3641.1   (below)</small>
47:21   "Although yours shall have divided out this land for yourselves amongst the

<small>3807.1; 7626; 3478   2050.1; it; 1961, 8804   yours; 5307, 8686</small>
47:22*   families of Israel,* it should have also been for those (Arabs) yours shall overthrow

<small>853 or 854; 1886.3; 871.1; 5159; 3807.1; 3641.1   2050.1; 3807.1; 1886.1; 1616</small>
(in order to keep) the inheritance property for yourselves. It, too, was for the ones

<small>cont.   1481, 8802   871.1; 8432; 3641.1   834   3205, 8689; 1121</small>
alienated that have been dwelling amongst yours, and who have begotten children

<small>871.1; 8432; 3641.1   2050.1; they; 1961, 8804; 3807.1; 3641.1; 3509.4; 249; 871.1   (below)</small>
in the midst of yours. Since they have been just as native born as your Israeli

<small>1121; 3478   854; 3641.1; they; 5307, 8799; 871.1; 5159   871.1; 8432</small>
children, they will divide out the inheritance property with (those) amongst the

| | 7626 plur. | 3478 | 2050.1; it; 1961, 8804 | 871.1; 7626; 834; 1481, 8804; 1886.1; 1616 |
47:23* families of Israel *that had existed with the alienated families, who have dwelled

853 or 854; 2050.2; 8033   yours; 5414, 8799; 5159; 2050.2
here with him [Jesus]. Yours must (also) give (him) back his inheritance property

                          5002, 8803   136   3069
as was (originally) stated in the Oracles of the Lord God."

Ezekiel 46:16-18

                  3541   559, 8804; 136; 3069
46:16   "This is what Lord Yahweh said:"

          3588   he; 5414, 8799; 1886.1; 5387   4979; 3807.1; 376; 4480; 1121; 2050.2; 5159; 2050.2; 1931
          "If the exalted one bequeaths an inheritance gift to each of his children, it should

          3807.1; 1121; 2050.2   it; 1961, 8799   272; 3963.1   (1931; 871.1; 5159)...
          go to his children. It should become their possession through the inheritance (from)

          cont.   2050.1; 3588; he; 5414, 8799   4979   (4480; 5159; 2050.2; 3807.1; 259; 4480; 5650; 2050.2)
46:17*   him. *But instead, if he shall bequeath the gift of his inheritance to one of his serv-

          cont.   2050.1; it; 1961, 8804   3807.1; 2050.2   5703 or 5704   (below)
          ants, when it should have been for his own (descendants), indefinitely, then after a

          8141; 1886.1; 1865; 2050.1   it; 7725, 8804   3807.1; 5387; 389; 5159; 2050.2
          year of the (servant's) release, it should have (been) returned as the exalted ones'

               cont.   3807.1; 1121; 2050.2   3807.1; 1992; 1961, 8799
          inheritance to his children, since it should be for them."

                              2050.1; 3808; he; 3947, 8799; 1886.1; 5387   4480; 5159; 1886.1; 5971
46:18   "Because the exalted one should never take the inheritance away from the people

                 4480; 3238, 8687; 3963.1   4480; 272; 3963.1   4480; 272; 2050.2
          by oppressively forcing them off of their property, then from his possession [that was

                                                                                (he; 5157, 8686)...
          wrongly taken from those exiled off their inherited property], he must (be) made to

                    cont.   853 or 854; 1121; 2050.2   (3807.1; 4616; 834; 3808; 6327, 8799; 5971; 2967.1)...
          bequeath the inheritance of his 'children' (back) to My people; on account that they

                    cont.   376   4480; 272; 2050.2
          should never scatter anyone off of their own property."

Ezekiel 45:8-11a

45:8   ^{3807.1; 776}   ^{it or that; 1961, 8799; 3807.1; 2050.2; 3807.1; 272; 871.1; 3478}
"In regards to the land in Israel that shall be for his own (people) as a possession;

^{2050.1; 3808; they; 3238, 8686; 5750}   ^(5387;2967.1;853;5971;2967.1;2050.1;1886.1;776;5414,8799)
they, consequently, must never again oppress My leaders (or) My people who would

^{cont.}   ^{3807.1; 1004; 3478; 3807.1; 7626; 1992}
(be forced to) surrender the land of their people over to the House of Israel."

45:9a   ^{(3541; he; 559, 8804)...}   ^{cont.}   ¹³⁶   ^{3068 or 3069}
"This is what he [Jesus] shall have relayed; 'The Lord, *Yahweh*, is the (true)

^{7227; 3807.1; 3641.1}
Master of yours.' "

^{5387; 3478; 2555; 2050.1; 7701; 5493, 8685}   ^(below)
[Jesus:] "Make Israel's leaders end the ruthlessness and violence; and (make

^{2050.1; 4941; 2050.1; 6666; 6213, 8798}   ^{(7311; 8685; 1646; 3641.1; 4480; 5921)...}
theirs) act justly and righteously. Put a stop to yours (causing) the dispossessions

^{cont.   5971; 2967.1}
of My people!" ^(N:22)

^(N:22) Since 1948, Israeli soldiers have unjustly forced numerous Arabs to leave their homes and possessions in Israel and the Israeli occupied Arab territories. At the time of this publication, at 10 of Jordan's official and 3 of their unofficial refugee camps, Jordan has accommodated over 2.3 million of Israel's Palestinian refugees registered with and aided by the United Nation Relief & Works Agency (UNRWA). [103] There are another 48 Palestinian refugee camps in other locations such as in Lebanon, Syria, and in the West Bank, where another 3.9 million Palestinians have been residing and being helped by UNRWA. [104] To this day, Israel continues to seize and occupy Arab territories, and according to Ezekiel 17:12-19, 30:4-19, 31:15-16, 32:30, 35:1-12, and 47:15-20, Israel will eventually also annex Egypt, and additional land from southern Syria, western Jordan, southern Lebanon, and from Palestine's West Bank and Gaza. As Israel continues to occupy Arab lands, Israel's Palestinian refugees have lost all hopes of obtaining independent statehood or returning to their homelands, and have a "long-building

anger" over Israel's continuing expansion of Israeli settlements on Arab territories, and Israel's poor treatment of its refugees. [105]

In retaliation against Israel, Hamas, which has been the Palestinian political and military body governing the Gaza strip since 2007, [106] has on several occasions launched hostile attacks against Israel, killing and injuring thousands of Israeli civilians over time. These Hamas attacks have, in turn, resulted in Israel brutally striking back each time, causing hundreds of thousands of Palestinian civilian casualties and the displacement of their people throughout the years. [107] Israel's merciless bombings over Gaza after each of the times Hamas fighters had fired missiles into Israel, may eventually lead to Israel occupying the Gaza Strip as indicated in Ezekiel 47:20.

45:9b   it; 5002, 8803   136   3068 or 3069
It was (clearly) stated in the Oracles, "The Lord is Yahweh."

45:10   3976; 6664; 2050.1; 374
"(On the Judgment Day, there will be) a set of scales for measuring righteousness,

45:11a*   6664   2050.1; 1324; 6664; it; 1961, 8799   3807.1; 3641.1 masc.   (below)
justly. It, indeed, will be a just unit of measurement for your (men), * as well as

1886.1 or 1886.3; 374 (gloom or a measurement); 2050.1; 1886.1; 1323 or 1324; 8506; 259; it; 1961, 8799   (below)
the(ir) gloomy womenfolk. One such means of measurement shall exist for when

3807.1; you or yours; 5375, 8800; per the passages in Section 3 of this book
yours rise up [from their graves for judgment]."

Ezekiel 37:15-28

37:15   2050.1; it; 1961, 8799; 1697; 3068 or 3069   413; 2967.1 559, 8800
Moreover, the Word of God shall come to Mine, saying:

37:16   (2050.1; 859)... cont.   1121 sing.   120   3947, 8798; 3807.1; 3509.2   (6086; 259)...
"You [Jesus], who are a descendant of Adam; take for yourself, one sheet made

cont.   2050.1; 3789, 8798
from wood [most likely a sheet of paper, which is made from wood pulp], and write

5921; 2050.2   3807.1; 3063
upon it, 'For Judah' [the west side of Jordan, the West Bank, including Jerusalem,

and the southern portion of Israel, including Dimonah and the Negev (Joshua 15)],

147

<small>2050.1; 3807.1; 1121; 3478; 2270; 2050.2</small>
'and for the companions of Israel's descendants.'"

<small>2050.1; 3947, 8798   6086; 259   2050.1; 3789, 8798; 5921; 2050.2   3807.1; 3130   6086 sing.   669</small>
"Then take another sheet, and write upon it, 'For Joseph; the sheet of Ephraim

<small>2050.1; 3605   1004   3478   2050.1; 2270; 2050.2</small>
that's all of the House of Israel, and its companion(s).'"

<small>2050.1; 7126, 8761; 853; 3963.1   259; 413; 259; 3807.1; 3509.2   3807.1; 6086; 259   (below)</small>
37:17   "After that, bring them together to you, one onto the other, into one stack, so

<small>2050.1; they; 1961, 8799; 3807.1; 259   871.1; 3027; 3509.2</small>
that they will be joined together in your hand."

<small>2050.1; 3509.4; 834; they; 559, 8799; 413; 3509.2; 1121; 5971; 3509.2   559, 8800</small>
37:18   "And when the descendants of your people speak to you; saying:"

<small>1886.1; 3808; you; 5046, 8686 3807.1; us; 4100; 428   3807.1; 3509.2</small>
37:19   "*Won't you explain to us what this means to you?*"

<small>1696, 8761; 413; 1992</small>
"Reply to them:"

<small>3541   559, 8804; 136; 3069</small>
"This is what Lord Yahweh said:"

<small>2009   589   3947, 8802   853; 6086   3130   834   871.1; 3027; 669</small>
"Behold! I am taking the sheet of Joseph, which was under the control of Ephraim,

<small>2050.1; 7626; 3478; 2270; 2050.2   2050.1; I; 5414, 8804; 853; 3963.1   (below)</small>
that's the people of Israel (and) its companion(s), and I have put them upon the

<small>5921; 2050.2; 853; 6086; 3063   2050.1; I; 6213, 8804; 3963.1   3807.1; 6086; 259   (2050.1; they; 1961, 8804)</small>
sheet of Judah, so that I have made them (joined) into one stack, and they have

<small>cont.   259; 871.1; 3027; 2967.1</small>
been united, under the control of Mine."

<small>2050.1; they; 1961, 8804; 1886.1; 6086; 834; you; 3789, 8799; 5921; 1992   (871.1; 3027; 3509.2)</small>
37:20   "Then after the sheets, which you (Jesus) shall write upon, have been in your

37:21* ^{cont.} ^{3807.1; 5869 plur.; 1992} ^{2050.1; 1696, 8761; 413; 1992}
hand, before their eyes, *also say to them:"

³⁵⁴¹ ^{559, 8804; 136; 3068 or 3069}
"This is what Lord Yahweh said:"

²⁰⁰⁹ ^{589; 947, 8802} ^{853; 1121 plur.; 3478} ⁴⁴⁸⁰ ⁹⁹⁶ ^(below)
"Behold! I am kicking out the descendants of Israel from among the foreign

^{1471 plur.} ^{per Ez. 47:15-20} ^(below)
nations [of Palestine, Jordan, southern Syria, southern Lebanon, and Egypt], who

^{834; 1980, 8804} ⁸⁰³³ ^{2050.1; I; 6908, 8765; 853; 3963.1; 4480; 5439 sing.}
had moved there. After I have gathered them together from the surrounding area(s),

^{2050.1; I; 935, 8689} ^{853; 3963.1} ⁴¹³ ^{127; 3963.1} ^{2050.1; I; 6213, 8804} ^{853; 3963.1}
37:22* and have brought them (back) to their own region, *I, then, shall have made these

^{3807.1; 1471; 259} ^{871.1; 776} ^{871.1; 2022} ³⁴⁷⁸
into one nation within the (Holy) Land, (to be united) with the hilly country of Israel;

^{2050.1; 4428; 259} ^{(he; 1961, 8799; 3807.1; 3605; 3963.1; 3807.1; 4428)...} ^{cont. (2050.1;it;3808;1961,8799;5750)}
and with one ruler. He [Jesus] will be the ruler of them all, and there shall no

^{cont.} ⁸¹⁴⁷ ¹⁴⁷¹ ³⁸⁰⁸
longer be the two (divided) nations [of the Israelis and their Arab neighbors]; nor

^{they; 2673, 8735; 5750; 3807.1; 8147; 4467 plur.; 5750}
shall they ever again be divided into two sovereignties."

37:23 ^{2050.1; 3808; they; 2930, 8691; 5750} ^{871.1; 1544 plur.; 1992} ^(below)
"Furthermore, they must never again defile themselves with their crucifixes, their

^{2050.1; 871.1; 8251; 1992; 2050.1; 871.1; 3605; 6588; 1992} ^{2050.1; I; 3467, 8689} ^{853; 3963.1}
abominations, and with all of their transgressions, once I have saved theirs (residing)

^{4480; 3605} ^{4186 plur.; 1992} ^{834; 2398, 8804; 871.1; 1992} ^{2050.1; I; 2891, 8765; 853; 3963.1} ^(below)
at all of their settlements, wherein they had sinned, and I have repurified them. Then

^{2050.1;they;1961,8799} ^{3807.1; 2967.1; 3807.1; 5971; 2050.1; 589; I; 1961, 8799} ^{3807.1;1992} ^{3807.1;410; 3963.1} ^(below)
37:24* they shall exist as My people, and I, Myself, shall exist for them as their God; *and

^{2050.1; 5650; 2967.1; 1732} ^{4428 sing.} ^{5921; 1992}
My beloved servant [Jesus] shall be the ruler over them."

149

     2050.1; 7462; 259 (one); he; 1961, 8799 3807.1;3605;3963.1 (2050.1; 871.1; 4941; 2967.1; they; 1980, 8799)...
    "When he is the sole ruler of all of these, and they shall follow by My Divine

    cont.   2050.1;2708;2967.1; they;8104,8799;2050.1; they; 6213,8804; 853; 3963.1 (2050.1;they;3427,8799 or 8804)
37:25* Laws and observe My Ordinances that theirs had (once) practiced, * then they will

    cont. (5921; 776; 834; I; 5414, 8804; 3807.1; 3290; 2967.1; 3807.1; 5650; 834; 3427, 8804; 871.1; 1883.3; 871.1; 1886.3; 1; 3641.1)
  dwell upon the land that I had given to My servant, Jacob, wherein your forefathers

    cont.   1992; 2050.1   1121; 1992   2050.1; 1121; 1121; 1992   (5704;5769)...
  had dwelt, as well as these, their children, and their children's children, for a long

    cont.   2050.1; 1732; 5650; 2967.1   5387 sing. 3807.1;1992 (below)
  time; and (where) My beloved servant [Jesus], the leader of these, (had dwelt) in

    3807.1; 5769
  ancient times."

       2050.1; I; 3772, 8804; 3807.1; 1992; 1285; 7965   (1285; 5769; it; 1961, 8799)...
37:26 "For I had (long ago) made a peace covenant with theirs, which shall (also) be an

     cont. 854;3963.1 2050.1; I; 5414, 8804; 3963.1 (2050.1;I;7235,8689;853;3963.1)
  everlasting covenant with these. After I have made (it with) these, whom I shall have

     cont.   2050.1; I; 5414, 8804; 4720; 2967.1
  multiplied, I, then, shall have assigned the holy sanctuary of Mine [located on top of

      871.1; 8432; 3963.1; 3807.1; 5769
  Temple Mount] to be in their midst from then on."

     2050.1; 1961, 8804; 4908; 2967.1 5921;1992 (2050.1;I;1961,8804;3807.1;1992;3807.1;410;3963.1)
37:27 "When the temple of Mine existed upon their (mount), I, indeed, had existed for

    cont.   2050.1; 1992; they; 1961, 8799; 3807.1; 2967.1; 3807.1; 5971 (below)
37:28* them as their God, and, now, these shall also be among the people of Mine. * The

   2050.1; 3045, 8804; 1886.1; 1471 plur. 3588;589 3068 or 3069 6942,8764 853;3478
  gentile nations that have known that I (Yahweh) am God, will be re-sanctifying Israel

    871.1; it; 1961, 8802; 4720 sing.; 2967.1   871.1; 8432, 3963.1 3807.1; 5769
  after the holy sanctuary of Mine is to (again) exist in their midst from then on."

Ezekiel 47:13b-14

     1454 (this) 1366 (834;yours;5157,8691;853;1886.1;776;3807.1;8147;6240;7626;3478)
47:13b [Israelis:] The following boundary is of the land to twelve of the tribes of Israel

      cont.   3130; 2256 plur. (2050.1; yours; 5157, 8804)

47:14* <u>that yours shall now possess</u>, which includes <u>Joseph's (double) portions</u> *<u>that yours</u>

   cont.

<u>acquired</u>.

  According to Genesis 48:5-6, Jacob had transferred the firstborn birthright to his pious son Joseph, leaving him double portions of land, of which, part of Joseph's portions was assigned to Ephraim and another portion was assigned to Manasseh; Joseph's two sons whom Jacob "adopted" as if his own. (N:23)

         853; 1886.3; 376 (Iyesh)   3509.4; 251 plur.; 2050.2 (834; I; 5375, 8804; 853; 3027; 2967.1)

It is <u>their Jesus' (land too)</u>, <u>just as (it was) his brethrens'</u>, to <u>whom I had lifted up</u>

  cont.   3807.1; 5414, 8800; 1886.3; 3807.1; 1; 3641.1

<u>My hand</u>, (and had extended it) <u>to give it to your forefathers</u>. (N:23 cont.)

Ezekiel 48

  After Jesus is returned, he will eventually be instructed by God to reveal the locations of land assigned to each of the twelve tribes of Israel. Since the allotments to the twelve tribes prophesied in Ezekiel 48:1-29 (which does not take into account the topography) is very different from that which was recorded in Joshua chapters 13-17, it seems that the following will be a reassignment of the land to the twelve tribes, based on the original, general placement of the allotments assigned by Jacob; prior to when Moses and Joshua had possibly reassigned the allotments. Regardless of where the land locations of the twelve tribes of Israel had been in the past, or will be located when disclosed by Jesus, Ezekiel 37:20-22 makes it very clear that in the near future, the Israelis and their neighboring Arabs will be instructed by God to live in peace amongst each other as one nation and under one sovereignty; with Jesus Christ as the ruler of them all.

     2050.1; 428   8034 plur. 1886.1; 7626 plur.

48:1 <u>Thus, these</u> are <u>the names</u> of <u>the tribes</u>, (including the general placement of each

of their inherited territories):

^{4480; 7097; 6828; 1886.3}   ^{413; 3027}   ^{1870; 2855}   ^{3807.1; 935, 8800}
From its northern end [of Israel] on the side of the Hethalon route, heading toward

^{2574 (Hamath)}   ²⁷⁰⁴   (below)
Hamah from the settlement of Enon [possibly Saida], (and down to) the northern

^{1366; 1834; 6828; 1886.3}   ^{413; 3027}   ²⁵⁷⁴   ^{2050.1; they; 1961, 8804}   ^{3807.1; 2050.2}
border of Damascus on the side of Hamah, shall have also been (inherited) to him

[i.e., to Joseph]. ^(N:23 cont.)

        ^{per Ez. 48:1}   ^{6285; 6921; 1886.1; 3220}   ^{1835; 259 (one)}   (below)
48:2*   (Then next to his land), east of the (Mediterranean) Sea was Dan's portion, *and

^{2050.1; 5921} ^{1366; 1835}   ^{4480; 6285; 6921}   ⁵⁷⁰⁴   ⁶²⁸⁵
next to Dan's territory, from the eastern border [of Dan's land] up to the edge of

        ^{3220; 1886.3}   ^{836; 259 (one)}   ^{2050.1; 5921}   ^{1366; 836}   ^(4480; 6285; 6921; 1886.3)
48:3*   its seashore was Asher's portion. *Then next to Asher's territory, from its east side

        ^{2050.1; 5704} ^{6285; 3220; 1886.3}   ⁵³²¹   ^{259 (one)}   ^{2050.1; 5921}   ^{1366; 5321}   (below)
48:4*   and up to its west side, was Naphtali's portion, * and next to Naphtali's land, from

        ^{4480; 6285; 6921; 1886.3; 5704 6285; 3220; 1886.3}   ^{4519; 259}   ^(2050.1; 5921)...
48:5*   its east side, up to its west side, was the one (for) Manasseh. *Moreover, next

        cont.   ¹³⁶⁶   ⁴⁵¹⁹   ^{4480; 6285; 6921; 1886.3; 5704; 6285; 3220; 1886.3}   (below)
to the territory of Manasseh's, from its east side up to its west side, was Ephraim's

        ^{669; 259 (one)} ^{2050.1; 5921}   ^{1366; 669}   ^{4480; 6285; 6921}   ^{2050.1; 5704} ^{6285; 3220; 1886.3}
48:6*   portion, * and next to Ephraim's territory, from the east side and up to its west side,

        ^{7205; 259}
was Reuben's portion.

        ^{2050.1; 5921}   ^{1366; 7205}   ^{4480; 6285; 6921}   ⁵⁷⁰⁴   ^{6285; 3220; 1886.3}
48:7   Then next to Reuben's territory, from the east side, up to its west side, was

        ³⁰⁶³ ^{259 (one)}   ^{2050.1; 5921}   ¹³⁶⁶   ³⁰⁶³   ^(4480; 6285; 6921; 5704; 6285; 3220; 1886.3)...
48:8*   Judah's portion, *and next to the territory of Judah, from the east side, up to its west

        cont.   ^{1961, 8799; 1886.1; 8641}   ⁸³⁴   ^{yours; 7311, 8686}   (below)
side, will be (where) the offering(s) occur that yours would provide, having a width

        ^{2568; 2050.1; 6242; 505; 7431}   ^{2050.1; 753}   ^{3509.4; 259; 1886.1; 2506}   (below)
of twenty-five thousand (cubits) and a length similar to this one's portion on its east

152

4480;6285;6921;1886.3;5704;3220;1886.3   2050.1; it; 1961, 8804; 1886.1; 4720; 871.1; 8432; 2050.2

side, up to its west side.   Also in its midst, (is where) the sanctuary has existed.

1886.1; 8641   834   yours; 7311, 8686   3807.1; 3068 or 3069   see also Ez. 48:19-21

48:9*   *The contribution(s) that yours would raise for Yahweh (will be for sustaining this

753   2568; 2050.1; 624   505   2050.1; 7431   6235   505

area) having a length of twenty-five thousand (cubits) and a width of ten thousand

6828; 1886.3   2568; 2050.1; 6242   505   2050.1; 3220; 1886.3

48:10b* (cubits); *its northside being twenty-five thousand (cubits long), its westside having

7341   6235   505   2050.1; 6921; 1886.3   7341   6235   505

a width of ten thousand (cubits), its eastside having a width of ten thousand (cubits),

2050.1; 5045; 1886.3   753   2568; 2050.1; 6242   505

and its southside having a length of twenty-five thousand (cubits).

2050.1; 3807.1   428   1961, 8799; 8641; 1886.1; 6944   3807.1; 3548

48:10a   But according to these, this sacred oblation area should belong to the priests,

2050.1; 1961, 8804; 4720; 3068 or 3068   871.1; 8432; 2050.2

48:10c*   *since (in ancient times) the sanctuary of God had existed in its midst, especially

3807.1; 3548; 6942; 8794; 4480; 1121; 6659   834   they; 8104, 8804

48:11*   *for the priests from the lineage of Zadok that were dedicated, who had observed

4931; 2967.1   834   3808; 8582, 8804   (871.1; 8582; 1121; 3478)...

My Ordinance(s), and who had not strayed when the descendants of Israel were

cont.   3509.4; 834   8582, 8804; 1886.1; 3881   (below)

48:12*   straying; such as when the Levites had gone astray.   *Thus, the most sacred portion

2050.1;1961,8804;3807.1;1992;8642;4480;8641;1886.1;776;6944;6944   413   1366 sing.   1886.1;3881 plur.

of the oblation region had also been for them; next to the section of the Levites

per Ez. 48:22

[which existed between Judah's and Benjamin's inherited properties].

2050.1; 1886.1; 3881; 5980; 1366; 1886.1; 3548   2568;2050.1;6242   505

48:13   The Levites' (section) adjoining the priests' region, was also twenty-five thousand

753   2050.1; 7341; 6235; 505   (3605; 753; 2568; 2050.1; 6242; 505)...

(cubits) long, and ten thousand (cubits) wide.   (Throughout) all of the twenty-five

cont.   2050.1; 7341; 6235; 505; 2050.1   3808; they; 4376, 8799

48:14*   thousand (cubits) long and ten thousand (cubits) wide (region),   *they would not sell

              4480;4480;2050.2   2050.1; 3808; 4171, 8686   2050.1;3808;5674,8686;7225;1886.1;776   (3588)...

(or profit) <u>off of it</u>, <u>nor would they exchange</u> <u>or export the land's firstfruits</u> <u>because</u>

     cont.   6944; 413; 3068 or 3069

<u>of</u> being <u>sacredly dedicated to God</u>.

          2050.1; 2568   505   1886.1; 3498, 8737   871.1; 7341   5921; 6440

48:15   <u>Also, five</u> <u>thousand</u> (cubits) <u>that was remaining</u> <u>of the width</u> <u>at the front of</u> the

       2568; 2050.1; 6242; 505   2455; 1931; 3807.1; 5892

<u>twenty-five thousand</u> (cubits long area) has been <u>common land of the city's</u> with

       3807.1; 4186   2050.1; 3807.1; 4054

<u>place(s) to dwell (or lodge)</u> <u>that's nearby open land</u> [such as a park, field, etc.].

           2050.1; 1961, 8804; 1886.1; 5892; 871.1; 8432; 1886.3   (2050.1; 428)...

    <u>Since (the ancient section of) the city shall have been in its midst</u>, these, there-

     cont.   4060; 1886.3; 6285; 6828;2568; 3967; 2050.1; 702; 505; 2050.1; 6285; 5045; 2568; 3967; 2050.1; 702; 505

48:16*   <u>fore</u>, will be <u>its dimensions:</u> *<u>The north and south sides (shall both be)</u> <u>four thou-</u>

          cont.   2050.1; 4480; 6285 (side); 6921

<u>sand five hundred (cubits long)</u>; <u>and from (both) the east and west sides, it shall</u>

       2568; 3967; 2050.1; 702; 505; 2050.1; 6285; 3220; 1886.3; 2568; 3967; 2050.1; 702; 505

<u>also be four thousand five hundred (cubits long, on each side)</u>.

        (2050.1; it;1961, 8804; 4054; 3807.1; 5892; 6828; 1886.3; 2572; 2050.1; 3967; 2050.1; 5045; 1886.3; 2572; 2050.1; 3967)

48:17   <u>And for the open land; it has been two hundred and fifty (cubits long on both)</u> its

      cont.   2050.1; 6921; 1886.3; 2572; 2050.1; 3967; 2050.1; 3220; 1886.3   (2572; 2050.1; 3967)

<u>north and south (sides)</u>, <u>and its east and west (sides have each been)</u> <u>two hundred</u>

   cont.

<u>and fifty</u> (cubits long).

     2050.1; 1886.1; 3498, 8737   871.1; 753   5980   8641; 1886.1; 6944

48:18   <u>As for the remaining</u> <u>of the length</u> that will be <u>alongside</u> <u>the sacred oblation area</u>;

      6235; 505; 6921; 1886.3; 2050.1; 6235; 505; 3220; 1886.3   2050.1; it; 1961, 8804

<u>its east and west (sides are each) ten thousand (cubits long)</u>. <u>Because it has existed</u>

     5980   8641; 1886.1; 6944   2050.1; it; 1961, 8804; 8393; 1886.3; 3807.1; 3899   (below)

<u>nearby</u> <u>the sacred oblation area</u>, <u>it has also become its (venues') food revenue</u> <u>for</u>

    3807.1; 5647, 8800 or 8802; 2967.1   1886.1; 5892   (2050.1; 1886.1; 5647, 8802; 1886.1; 5892; they; 5647, 8799; 2050.2)...

48:19* <u>(those) serving Mine (in) the city</u>, *<u>as well as being a work place (for) the city's</u>

154

48:20* workers who shall service it from (the help of) all the tribes of Israel, via *all the con-

tribution(s).

For (servicing) the city's twenty-five thousand by twenty-five thousand (cubits)

48:21* square property, yours shall present a sacred contribution, *as well as (provide fund-

ing) for the leader's remainder of the city's property on both sides of the sacred

oblation area, for the front of its twenty-five thousand (cubits^2 section), up to the ob-

lation region east and west of it that will be near the front of its twenty five thousand

(cubits^2 section); and for the area west of it, adjoining the portions of the leader's

that has existed (close to) the sacred oblation area and the temple's sanctuary,

within its midst.

48:22 Moreover, the property of the Levites, and the city's property (are) in the midst of

what shall belong to the leader. Between Judah's and Benjamin's territories, will

be for the leader.

48:23 Now, as for the rest of the tribes, (adjoining these) from its east side up to its west

48:24* side, was Benjamin's portion, *and next to Benjamin's territory, from its east side up

to its west side, was Simeon's portion.

155

48:25   Then, beside the territory of Simeon, from its east side up to its west side, was

_{2050.1; 5921   1366   8095   4480; 6285; 6921; 1886.3   5704   6285; 3220; 1886.3}

(line reference numbers above: 2050.1; 5921 — 1366 — 8095 — 4480; 6285; 6921; 1886.3 — 5704 — 6285; 3220; 1886.3)

48:26* the one (for) Issachar, *and next to Issachar's territory, from its east side up to its
(refs: 3485; 259 — 2050.1; 5921 — 1366; 3485 — 4480; 6285; 6921; 1886.3 — 5704 (below))

48:27* west side, was Zebulun's portion. *Moreover, next to Zebulun's territory, from its
(refs: 6285; 3220; 1886.3 — 2074 — 259 (one) — 2050.1; 5921 — 1366; 2074 — 4480 (below))

48:28* east side up to its west side was the one (for) Gad, * and beside Gad's territory, on
(refs: 6285; 6921; 1886.3; 5704; 6285; 3220; 1886.3 — 1410; 259 — 2050.1; 5921 — 1366; 1410 (below))

the south side, southward of it, is the territory that has existed from Tamar (up to)
(refs: 413; 6285; 5045 — 8486, 1886.3 — 2050.1; 1961, 8804; 1366 — 4480; 8559)

the waters of Meriba [the Sea of Galilee], its holy stream above the large, (Dead)
(refs: 4325; 4808; 6946 — 5158; 1886.3 — 5921 (1886.1; 3220; 1886.1; 1419))

48:29* Sea. *That was the land that yours shall allot as the inherited property to the tribes
(refs: cont. — 2063 — 1886.1; 776 — 5307; 8686 — 4480; 5159 — 3807.1; 7626)

of Israel, and those were their divisions as it was stated in the Oracles of the Lord,
(refs: 3478 — 2050.1; 428 — 4256; 3963.1 — it; 5002, 8803 — 136)

Yahweh. (N:23 cont.)
(ref: 3068 or 3069)

(N:23) A portion of the double allotment that Joseph inherited from his father, Jacob, was allotted to Joseph's sons, Ephraim and Manasseh, whom Jacob "adopted" as if his own (Genesis 48:5), making them two of the tribes of Israel.[108] Joseph's brothers, Judah, Asher, Naphtali, Zebulun, Gad, Issachar, Dan, Simeon, Reuben, and Benjamin each inherited one portion of land from their father.[109] Their brother, Levi, was set apart from these 12 tribes of Israel to serve in religious matters.[110] The Levites served on a plot of land (25,000 cubits long by 10,000 cubits wide) that was next to the plot of land of the priests' that were descendants of Zadok.

    According to God in Ezekiel 47:15-23, Jacob's land inherited to the Israelites (which never included Egypt), should have also been shared with Israel's Arab neighbors, who had, for centuries, lived in peace amongst the Israelis in Israel, Palestine, western Jordan, southern Syria and southern Lebanon. So after Prophet Jesus and his Turkish, Iranian, and Arab militia counterattack Israel and its annexed lands (which by then will include Egypt), according to Ezekiel 37:21-22, God will be making the few surviving Israelis that lived in the Israeli annexed

Arab territories to give the Arabs their lands back. Again, as a reminder, the following will be God's decree to the Israelis and their Arab neighbors regarding the rightful ownership of the Holy Land:

Ez. 37:21-22

"This is what Lord Yahweh said: Behold! I am kicking out the descendants of Israel from among the foreign nations [of Palestine, western Jordan, Egypt, southern Syria and southern Lebanon], who had moved there. After I have gathered them together from the surrounding area(s), and have brought them (back) to their own region, I, then, shall have made these into one nation within the (Holy) Land, (to be united) with the hilly country of Israel; and with one ruler. He [Jesus] will be the ruler of them all, and there shall no longer be the two (divided) nations [of the Israelis and their Arab neighbors], nor shall they ever again be divided into two sovereignties."

48:30   <u>Furthermore, this</u> will be <u>(the area within) the city's borders</u> [of Old City Jeru-salem], including <u>part of the north side</u> [above it]; its <u>area will be four thousand, five</u>

48:31* <u>hundred (cubits²).</u> (N:24) *<u>Also, the gates</u> of <u>the city</u> (will be named) <u>according to the</u> <u>names</u> of <u>Israel's tribes.</u> (For) <u>its three northern gates;</u> <u>one will be the Reuben Gate,</u> <u>another one will be the Judah Gate,</u> and <u>the other one shall be the Levi</u>

48:32* <u>Gate.</u> *Then, <u>on its eastern side</u> of the <u>four thousand, five hundred</u> (cubits² area), there <u>will also be three gates,</u> <u>and one gate will be Joseph's,</u> <u>another gate shall</u>

48:33* <u>be Benjamin's,</u> and <u>the other gate will be Dan's.</u> *<u>Likewise, on its south side (wall)</u> of the <u>four thousand, five hundred (cubits²</u> area), <u>along</u> it <u>shall also have three gates;</u>

157

     8179; 8095; 259   8179; 3485; 259   (below)
  one will be the Simeon Gate, another one shall be the Issachar Gate, and the other

     8179; 2074; 259   6285; 3220; 1886.3   2568; 3967; 2050.1; 702; 505
48:34* one will be the Zebulun Gate. *(On) its west side of the four thousand, five hundred

       8179; 1992; 8179; 8179; 1410; 259   (8179; 836; 259)...
(cubits² area), one of their three gates will be the Gad Gate, another one will be

   cont.   8179; 5321; 259
the Asher Gate, and the other one will be the Naphtali Gate. (N:24 cont.)

     5439   per Ez. 48:30
48:35 (The perimeter) all around (Old City Jerusalem's extended area of 4,500 cubits²),

  8083; 6240 505   2050.1; 8034; 1886.1; 5892   4480; 3117
will be eighteen thousand (cubits), and the name of the city, from that day (forward),

   3068 Shamah (or 8033;1886.3)
will be Yahweh Shamah [or Samah Allah, in Arabic]. (N:24 cont.)

(N:24) At the time of this book's publication, Jerusalem's Old City has been a relatively small, walled 0.35 miles² section within the modern city of Jerusalem, with a perimeter of 2.36 miles. [111] Its walls were built between 1536 and 1541 under the command of the Turkish Sultan Suleiman I, having the eight gates currently in use, and four other gates that have been sealed off. [112] From Ezekiel 48:30-35, it is implied in the prophesy that sometime around the time Jesus is returned, the border wall surrounding Old City Jerusalem will be extended to a perimeter of around 5 miles (18,000 cubits), with its area enlarged to approximately 1.28 miles² (4,500 cubits²). When this prophesy is fulfilled, God shall request that Old City be renamed 'Yahweh Shamah' (or 'Samah Allah,' in Arabic, which means God's Bounty), [113] and that the names of the 12 exterior gates be dubbed after Jacob's twelve biological sons - Reuben, Judah, Levi (3 north gates); Joseph, Benjamin, Dan (3 east gates); Simeon, Issachar, Zebulun (3 south gates); and Gad, Asher, and Naphtali (3 west gates).

CLOSING REMARKS

As explained in our translation of Ezekiel chapters 1-29 (*Preserved for the End of Time*, published in 2014), during our study of Ezekiel's revelation from God, because many of the events described in the previous Bible translations of Ezekiel were oddly stated, difficult to understand, or had not occurred as translated, our curiosity led us to investigate what the scriptures would disclose if we considered all possible word meanings of each Hebrew word occurring in the book of Ezekiel; ignoring the "centuries-later-added" vowel and punctuation marks, and discarding the illogical "waw-conversive rule." In continuing our research while translating Ezekiel chapters 30-48, we used the same process to find even more prophecies occurring within the 21st century.

In addition to the discoveries found in the first part of *Preserved for the End of Time* (Ezekiel chapters 1-29; 2014), where the coming Messiah (Son of Man; Iyesh, Jesus) would be returned to the Middle East sometime before the End of Time, more details emerged in Ezekiel chapters 30-48 about the bloodshed that will be caused by the rebellious Gog and Magog peoples, prior to and during the Messiah's return. Details point to evil zealot leaders of the Gog and Magog people being from Russia and Zionist Israel, who would continually conquer, plunder, and oppress those of their neighboring countries, until their eventual termination. These latter Ezekiel chapters (Ez. 30-48), thus, reveal even more descriptive characterizations of the evil, tyrannical Magog leader and the oppressive Russian ruler, Gog.

Also uncovered in the first 29 chapters of Ezekiel (2014), and confirmed in this second book, there will be two men in the Middle East claiming to be the prophetic ruler ordained by God (Yahweh); one being the actual Messiah returning for a second advent, and the other one being an imposter. Based on the timings uncovered throughout both parts of *Preserved for the End of Time*, the imposter Jesus, referred to in the Ezekiel prophecies as the "false prophet of Nazareth," and the "Pharaoh-like ruler of Egypt," shall appear on earth first; several years prior to the return of the actual Jesus. The imposter Jesus will temporarily be the ruler of Israel and Jerusalem, and of all the Israeli occupied territories, which, according to the Ezekiel prophesies, will also eventually include Egypt. The Israelis' imposter Messiah (ruler of the Zionist Magog people) will claim to be the Lord God, the Son of God, and to have died for the atonement of his followers' sins. Posing as God in the flesh, he will also falsely verify that the Israelis are still "His" chosen people, even though Lord Yahweh, according to the uncovered Ezekiel prophesies, refers to these particular Israelis, who shall have gone astray, as being rebellious and corrupt during these latter days. Unfortunately, because the imposter Jesus will be falsely confirming the incorrect beliefs and practices of his followers, many of today's Christians and Messianic Jews, and their converts, will be "deceived," and will not be heeding God's clear warnings uncovered in this translation of Ezekiel. It is clearly prophesied, however, that Israel's imposter Christ, will be committing numerous sins of his own and shall not be obeying or enforcing God's actual Commandments and Ordinances, and that he will be a tyrannical ruler to those opposing him.

The true Messiah (Iyesh; Jesus; Son of Man, a descendant of Adam), on the other hand, who is totally human according to the revelations discovered throughout all of the Ezekiel chapters, shall be returned to earth as God's prophet and messenger. He will worship God, shall devoutly and correctly follow all of God's Ordinances, Commandments, and instructions, and will be a doer of righteous deeds. Because the imposter Jesus will initially be ruling from Israel, once Jesus is returned to the Middle East several years after the fake Jesus' emergence, it is prophesied that he will rule from Babylon (Iraq, Syria, and the other allied nations), and will call upon the Arab countries, Turkey, and Iran to defend the oppressed Arabs exiled away from their Israeli occupied homelands. Followers of the true Messiah will include all of the believers in God who shall be correctly obeying God's Commandments and Ordinances, exactly as instructed, whether he refers to himself as a Jew, Christian, Muslim, monotheist, etc., or is nondenominational.

While the first half of Ezekiel (published in 2014) and several passages in this second book uncovered prophecies explaining that the real Messiah will come to correct the incorrect beliefs and practices of his people, and to condemn the harsh oppression against the Arab gentiles instigated by the House of Israel and by the imposter Jesus, the latter Ezekiel chapters also focus on Jesus' and his militia's counterattack battles against the evil Gog and Magog leaders and their haughty, corrupt followers; many of whom will eventually be destroyed by God's wrath. Also included in this second book are detailed architectural design descriptions of the most sacred houses of worship, sanctuary, and gates within the confines of Old City Jerusalem at the time of the Messiah's second advent. Because the architecture descriptions of these prophesied temples appear to match closely with the way Old City Jerusalem has evolved today, it's most likely that God included the tedious measurements foretold in this book to validate His prophesies revealed to Ezekiel, and to make it clear that His temple prophesies were not regarding the building of a massive, third Jewish temple on Temple Mount, but rather were the prophesied measurements of already existing houses of worship located upon and nearby the mount. The details of the Christian practices currently carried out at the sacred, galleried temple prophesied (i.e. at the Holy Sepulcher Church), and of the Temple Mount's once-again-practiced altar rituals (all of which will be observed by the Hebrew and gentile followers of the imposter Christ), as well as the prophesies regarding the drinking water resources for Israel, Jerusalem, and other Israeli occupied territories, are all astonishingly accurate!

Furthermore, because there has been much controversy between the Israelis and Arab gentiles over who the rightful inhabitants of the Holy Land should be, to correct the misapprehension that the Promised Land is exclusively for the people of Israel, God asserts in this second book that after the annihilation of the imposter Jesus and Gog, their troops, and many of the false Messiah's followers, their few survivors and future descendants must, from then on, live amongst their Arab neighbors in peace, as one united congregation and sovereignty. At that time, He shall also command that the Arab lands previously seized by the Israelis (which will also include the imposter Jesus' annexed Egypt), must be returned to the exiled Arabs after the destroyed cities are rebuilt.

Now that the Ezekiel prophesies uncovered in these two books of *Preserved for the End of Time* are unfolding before our eyes, with precision, it's time for all believers in God to prepare themselves for what's to come within the next few decades. No doubt, when the imposter Jesus (who is to be instructed and aided by Satan) arrives in Israel confirming the incorrect beliefs and practices of many of today's people, a large number of them in the Middle East will, unfortunately, not heed God's numerous warnings revealed throughout these uncovered prophesies and will sadly experience God's wrath. Again, Yahweh makes it very clear throughout Ezekiel that no one other than Him should be worshiped, and that mankind must strictly obey His Commandments and correct Ordinances that will be reiterated via God's returning messengers; Angel Gabriel and the true Jesus Christ.

God is also depicted throughout Ezekiel as being very merciful to those who solely worship Him, and promises in several of the Ezekiel passages that the sinners will be forgiven for all their past mistakes if only they would repent, mend their lives, correcting their incorrect beliefs and sinful actions, and would devoutly worship Him. He assures that those of us who believe in Him, worshiping Him, only in His Name, and who turn to Him in genuine repentance, pursuing righteousness from then on, will one day be resurrected from the grave to enjoy an eternal life in His presence. For salvation is achieved through not only the belief in and worship of God, but through ones' righteousness and by following God's guidance.

APPENDIX 1

Gregorian Equivalences of the Biblical Hebrew Months

	Hebrew Months	Gregorian Months
1st	Nisan	Mar. – Apr.
2nd	Iyar	Apr. - May
3rd	Sivan	May - June
4th	Tammuz	June - July
5th	Av	July – Aug.
6th	Elul	Aug. – Sept.
7th	Tishri	Sept. – Oct.
8th	Cheshvan	Oct. – Nov.
9th	Kislev	Nov. – Dec.
10th	Tevet	Dec. – Jan.
11th	Shevat	Jan. – Feb.
12th	Adar	Feb. – Mar.

APPENDIX 2

Biblical Measurement Conversions

Biblical Measurements	U.S. Customary Unit Approximations
1 handbreadth	4 inches
1 cubit	17 to 18 inches (1.41 to 1.5 feet)
1 reed	8.5 to 9 feet
1 homer	230 liters or 60 gallons
1 bath	23 liters or 6 gallons
1 shekel	11.4 grams
1 gerah	0.57 grams

REFERENCES

1. Mansoor, Menahem, *Biblical Hebrew, Step by Step*, Vol. 1, 2nd ed., Baker Book House, MI, 2000, p. 31.
2. Wegner, Paul D., *Journey from Texts to Translations*, Baker Academic, MI, 1999, pp. 177, 191, and 381.
3. Mansoor, Menahem, *Biblical Hebrew, Step by Step*, Vol. 1, 2nd ed., Baker Book House, MI, 2000, p. 187.
4. Ibid.
5. Young, Robert, *Young's Literal Translation of the Holy Bible*, Benedictions Classics, Oxford, 2012, p. 711.
6. Wegner, Paul D., *Journey from Texts to Translations*, Baker Academic, MI, 1999, pp. 102 and 167.
7. Reif, Stefon C., editor, *The Cambridge Genizah Collections: Their Contents and Significance*, Cambridge University Press, UK, 2002, p. xii.
8. Skehan, Patrick W., and Di Lella, Alexander A., *The Wisdom of Ben Sira*, Doubleday and Co., Inc., 1987, front matter page.
9. Kirkpatrick, David D., "Secret Alliance: Israel Carries Out Airstrikes in Egypt, With Cairo's O.K.", *The New York Times*, February 3, 2018, Article posted at: https://www.nytimes.com/2018/02/03/world/middleeast/israel-airstrikes-sinai-egypt.html.
10. TOI Staff, "Israel Carrying Out Secret Airstrike Campaign in Sinai to Help Egypt – Report," *The Times of Israel*, February 3, 2018, Report posted at: https://www.timesofisrael.com/israel-carrying-out-secret-air-strikes-in-sinai-to-help-egypt-report/#:~:text=Israeli%20drones%2C%20fighter%20je.
11. Tenney, Merrill C., *Zondervan's Pictorial Bible Dictionary*, Zondervan Publishing House, MI, 1967, p. 191.
12. McKenzie, John L. S. J., *Dictionary of the Bible*, Touchstone, NY, 1995, p. 523.
13. Editors of Encyclopedia Britannica, "Arab League," *Britannica Online*, Article Updated by The Information Architects of Encyclopedia Britannica, Updated September 11, 2023, Posted at: https://www.britannica.com/topic/Arab-League/additional-info#history.
14. McKenzie, John L. S. J., *Dictionary of the Bible*, Touchstone, NY, 1995, p.576.
15. Tenney, Merrill C., *Zondervan's Pictorial Bible Dictionary*, Zondervan Publishing House, MI, 1967, p. 815.
16. Tenney, Merrill C., *Zondervan's Pictorial Bible Dictionary*, Zondervan Publishing House, MI, 1967, p. 590.
17. McKenzie, John L. S. J., *Dictionary of the Bible*, Touchstone, NY, 1995, pp. 953-954
18. Tenney, Merrill C., *Zondervan's Pictorial Bible Dictionary*, Zondervan Publishing House, MI, 1967, p. 589.
19. Tenney, Merrill C., *Zondervan's Pictorial Bible Dictionary*, Zondervan Publishing House, MI, 1967, p. 85.
20. Tenney, Merrill C., *Zondervan's Pictorial Bible Dictionary*, Zondervan Publishing House, MI, 1967, p. 655.
21. McKenzie, John L. S. J., *Dictionary of the Bible*, Touchstone, NY, 1995, p. 865.

22. Momodu, Samuel, "Second Sudanese Civil War (1983-2005)," *Blackpast*, December 23, 2018, Article posted at: https://www.blackpast.org/global-african-history/events-global-african-history/second-sudanese-civil-war-1983-2005.html.
23. Simon, Scott, Host of Transcript, Reported by Batrowy, Aya, "Refugees Face an Uncertain Future in Egypt," *National Public Radio News*, June 10, 2023, News posted at: https://www.npr.org/2023/06/10/1181505832/hundreds-of-sudanese-refugees-face-an-uncertain-future-in-egypt.html.
24. Tenney, Merrill C., *Zondervan's Pictorial Bible Dictionary*, Zondervan Publishing House, MI, 1967, pp. 78-79.
25. Bullinger, D. D., *Sheol & Hades: Their Meaning and Usage in the Word of God*, The Open Bible Trust, Fordland Mount, Upper Basildon, Reading, RG8 8LU UK, 2019, p.32.
26. Ibid, pp. 15-18.
27. Ibid, p. 19.
28. Vermes, Geza, *The Complete Dead Sea Scrolls in English*, Penguin Books, London, 2011, pp. 169-170, 250-252, and 417-418.
29. Bullinger, D. D., *Sheol & Hades: Their Meaning and Usage in the Word of God*, The Open Bible Trust, Fordland Mount, Upper Basildon, Reading, RG8 8LU UK, 2019, pp. 7, 8, 15, and 30.
30. Ibid, p. 15.
31. Ali, Yusuf A., *The Meaning of the Holy Qur'an*, Surah 23:100, n. 2940, Amana Corp., MD, 1992, p. 860.
32. Broderick, Robert C., *The Catholic Encyclopedia*, Revised and Updated Edition, Thomas Nelson Publishers, Nashville, TN, 1987, p. 502.
33. Tenney, Merrill C., *Zondervan's Pictorial Bible Dictionary*, Zondervan Publishing House, MI, 1967, p. 240.
34. McKenzie, John L. S. J., *Dictionary of the Bible*, Touchstone, NY, 1995, p. 903.
35. Tenney, Merrill C., *Zondervan's Pictorial Bible Dictionary*, Zondervan Publishing House, MI, 1967, pp. 233-234.
36. McKenzie, John L. S. J., *Dictionary of the Bible*, Touchstone, NY, 1995, p. 811.
37. WebMD Editorial Contributors, Sheikh, Zilpah MD (Medical Reviewer), "Circumcision: Benefits and Risks," *WebMD*, November 10, 2023, Posted at: https://www.webmd.com/sexual-conditions/circumcision.html.
38. Taylor, Paul S., "Is circumcision a requirement for salvation for male Christians?" *Christian Answers. Net*, 2001, Answer posted at: https://christiananswers.net/q-eden/circumcision.html.
39. Abou-Ghazala, Yahya, "In Gaza, Palestinians Have No Safe Place From Israel's Bombs," *CNN Investigates*, October 12, 2023, Gaza, News posted at: https://www.cnn.com/2023/10/12/middleeast/gaza-airstrikes-warnings-invs/index.html.
40. Ibid.
41. McKenzie, John L. S. J., *Dictionary of the Bible*, Touchstone, NY, 1995, p. 783.
42. Rempfer, Kyle, "Israeli operations uprooted Palestinians in 1948. Many fear a repeat," *The Washington Post*, November 3, 2023, Article posted at: https://www.washingtonpost.com/history/2023/11/03/Israel-nakba-history-1948/.
43. Schmemann, Serge, "Mideast Turmoil; The Overview: 9 Palestinians Die in Protests Marking Israel's Anniversary," *The New York Times*, May 15, 1998, Article posted at:

https://www.nytimes.com/1998/05/15/world/mideast-turmoil-overview-9-palestinians-die-protests-marking-israel-s.html.

44. MEE Staff, "UN Approves Resolution to Commemorate 75th Nakba Anniversary," *Middle East Eye*, December 1, 2022, News posted at: https://www.middleeasteye.net/news/un-approves-resolution-commemorate-75th-anniversary-nakba.
45. Ibid.
46. Ong, Ruby, "Israeli Independence Day 2048: Shaharit's Centennial Celebration," *New Israel Fund*, April 26, 2012, Blog posted at: https.www.nif.org/blog/Israeli-independence-day-2048-shaharits-centennial-celebration/.
47. McKenzie, John L. S. J., *Dictionary of the Bible*, Touchstone, NY, 1995, p. 660.
48. Tenney, Merrill C., *Zondervan's Pictorial Bible Dictionary*, Zondervan Publishing House, MI, 1967, p. 191.
49. McKenzie, John L. S. J., *Dictionary of the Bible*, Touchstone, NY, 1995, p. 708.
50. McKenzie, John L. S. J., *Dictionary of the Bible*, Touchstone, NY, 1995, p. 319.
51. Barry, Jenny, "Former Soviet Union (USSR): What Happened to the 15 Republics Today," *Knowinsiders*, March 13, 2023, Article posted at: https://knowinsiders.com/former-soviet-union-ussr-what-happened-to-the-15-republics-today-334291.html.
52. Summers, Juana (Transcript Host), Reported by Maynes, Charles, "Former Soviet Republic of Georgia Walks a Thin Line Between Russia and the West," *National Public Radio*, November 27, 2023, Transcript posted at: https://www.npr.org/2023/11/27/1215470958/former-soviet-republic-of-georgia-walks-a-thin-line-between-russia-and-the-west.
53. Ibid.
54. McKenzie, John L. S. J., *Dictionary of the Bible*, Touchstone, NY, 1995, p. 896.
55. McKenzie, John L. S. J., *Dictionary of the Bible*, Touchstone, NY, 1995, p. 796.
56. Tenney, Merrill C., *Zondervan's Pictorial Bible Dictionary*, Zondervan Publishing House, MI, 1967, p. 211.
57. Kevas, A. A., and Walker, W. I., *Preserved for the End of Time*, New Uncovered Ezekiel Prophesies About Christ's Return, CreateSpace Independent Publishing Platform, SC, 2014, p. 206.
58. Borger, Julian, "Israel Expands Nuclear Facility Previously Used For Weapons Material," *The Guardian*, February 18, 2021, Article posted at: https://www.theguardian.com/world/2021/feb/18/israel-nuclear-facility-dimona-weapons.
59. Ibid.
60. McKenzie, John L. S. J., *Dictionary of the Bible*, Touchstone, NY, 1995, p. 82.
61. Ragg, Lonsdale and Laura (Translators), *The Gospel of Barnabas*, A&B Publishers Group, NY, 1993, pp. 213-214.
62. JHOM Staff, "Angels in the Talmud; Michael, Gabriel, Uriel, and Raphael: Four Angels of the Presence," *Jewish Heritage Online Magazine*, Article posted at: https://www.jhom.com / topics/angels/talmud_fourangels.htm.
63. Lumpkin, Joseph B., *The Book of Enoch: The Angels, The Watchers and The Nephilim*, Fifth Estate Publishers, AL, 2011, pp. 302-311.
64. Ragg, Lonsdale and Laura (Translators), *The Gospel of Barnabas*, A&B Publishers Group, NY, 1993, p. 62.
65. Ibid, pp. 239-241.
66. Vermes, Geza, *The Complete Dead Sea Scrolls in English*, Penguin Books, London, 2011, p. 611.

67. Ibid, pp. 412-413.
68. Peoples Dispatch Staff, "Palestinians Warn Against Israeli Proposal to Divide Al - Aqsa Compound," *Peoples Dispatch*, June 12, 2023, Article posted at: https://peoplesdispatch.org/2023/06/12/palestinians-warn-against-israeli-proposal-to-divide-al-aqsa-compound/.
69. Google Classroom, Khan Academy Staff, "The Dome of the Rock (Qubbat al - Sakhra)," *Khan Academy*, August 12, 2014, Information posted at: https://www.khanacademy.org/humanities/ap-art-history/west-and-central-asia-apahh/west-asia/a/the-dome-of-the-rock-qubbat-al-sakhra.
70. Shultz, Matthew, August 14, 2019, "The Importance of Temple Mount's Place in Jewish History," *Jewish Journal*, Article posted at: https://jewishjournal.com/commentary/analysis/303008/the-importance-of-temple-mounts-place-in-jewish-history/.
71. Editors of Encyclopedia Britannica, "Dome of the Rock Summary," *Britannica Online*, Summary posted at: https://www.britannica.com/summary/Dome-of-the-Rock.
72. Altein, Yehuda, "Korbanot: The Biblical Temple Sacrifices; A definitive guide to the animal sacrifices, meal and oil offerings, and wine libations," *Chabad.ORG*, Article posted at: https://www.chabad.org/library/artice_cdo/aid/4440323/jewish/Korbanot-The-Biblical-Temple-Sacrifices.htm.
73. Cohen, Dan, "What is the Temple Mount Movement? Jewish and Christian Zionist Movements call for the destruction of Muslim holy sites and the building of a third Jewish Temple," *Middle East Eye*, February 13, 2015, Article posted at: https//www.middleeasteye.net/features/what-temple-mount-movement.
74. Sharon, Jeremy, "Temple-ready Altar Dedicated on Last Day of Hanukkah by Activist Groups," *Jerusalem Post*, December 10, 2018, Article posted at: https://www.jpost.com/israel-news/temple-ready-altar-dedicated-on-lastt-day-of-Hanukkah-by-activist-groups.
75. Gomby, Rebecca, "The Story Behind Jerusalem's Sealed Golden Gate," *The Culture Trip*, December 3, 2023, Article posted at: https//theculturetrip.com/middle-east/israel/articles/the-story-behind-jerusalems-sealed-golden-gate.
76. Ibid.
77. Ibid.
78. "Haram al-Sharif," <u>Encyclopedia of the Modern Middle East and North America</u>, Retrieved November 15, 2023 from *Encyclopedia.com*: https://www.encyclopedia.com/humanities/encyclopedias-almanacs-transcripts-and-maps/haram-al-sharif.
79. Bin Thani Al Thani, Khalid, "The Concept of Animal Sacrifice," *The Peninsula*, October 18, 2013, Qatar, Article posted at: https://thepensulaqatar.com/article/18/10/2013/the-concept-of-animal-sacrifice.
80. Wiley, Henrietta, "Sacrifice in the Bible," *Oxford Bibliographies*, Last Reviewed August 18, 2021, Last Modified February 25, 2016, Article posted at: https//www.oxfordbibliographies.com/display/document/obo-9780199840731/obo-9780199840731-0121.xml.
81. Editors of Madain Project, "Al-Aqsa Mosque," *Madain Project*, Article posted at: https://madainproject.com/al_aqsa_mosque.
82. Editors of Encyclopedia Britannica, Revised by Petruzzello, Melissa, "Letters of Paul to the Corinthians," *Britannica Online*, Revised May 22, 2020, Article posted at: https://www.britannica.com/topic/The-Letter-of-Paul-to-the-Corinthians.
83. Editors of WHE, *World History Encyclopedia*, "The Gospels Timeline", Posted at: https://www.worldhistory.org/timeline/The_Gospels/.

84. Ibid.
85. Lake, Kirsopp, *The Didache*, Chapters 9 and 10 of *The Didache*, Cross Reach Publications, 2017, pp. 19-21.
86. Jacobs, Joseph; Ochser, Schulim (1905), "Symbol", *Jewish Encyclopedia*, Vol. S, Funk and Wagnalls Company, NY, p. 616.
87. Avi-Yonah, Michael & Gibson, Shimon, "Shiloah, Siloam," *Encyclopedia.com*, Article posted at: https:www.encyclopedia.com/religion/encyclopedias-almanacs-transcripts-and-maps/shiloah-siloam.
88. Hasson, Shlomo & Gilboa, Shaked, "Rosh Ha-Ayin," *Encyclopedia.com*, Article posted at: https:www.encyclopedia.com/religion/encyclopedias-almanacs-transcripts-and-maps/rosh-ha-ayin.
89. Issacs, Lisa, "Rosh HaAyin Forest," *Handmade in Israel-blogspot.com*, August 31, 2020, Blog posted at: https://lisa-handmadeinisrael.blogspot.com/2020/07/rosh-haayin-forest.html.
90. Agrawal, Priya, et al., "An Updated Review of Ziziphus Jujube: Major Focus on its Photochemicals and Pharmacological Properties," *Science Direct*, September 2023, Article posted at: https://www.sciencedirect.com/science/article/pii/s2667142523000830.
91. Ikram, Ali, and Khalid, Waseem, et al., "Nutritional, Biochemical, and Clinical Applications of Carob: A Review," *National Library of Medicine*, Published online June 9, 2023, Article posted at: https://www.ncbi.nlm.nih.gov/pmc10345664/.
92. "How Desalination Came to the rescue in Israel," *ISI Water*, Article posted at: https://isi-water.com/desalination-rescues-israel/.
93. Susannah, "Ein Gedi: The Complete Guide," *Hiking the Holyland*, September 22, 2020, Guide posted at: https://hikingintheholyland.com/2020/09/22/ein-gedi-the-complete-guide/.
94. Sanford, Jill, "How a Trip to the Dead Sea Can Benefit Your Health," *U.S. News – Health*, April 7, 2017, Article posted at: https://health.usnews.com/health-care/for-better/articles/2017-04-07/how-a-trip-to-the-dead-sea-can-benefit-your-health.
95. Phillips, Adam, "Tracing Roots: Uncovering the Descendants of Ishmael in Arabic History and Genealogy," *The Witness*, March 12, 2024, Article posted at: https://thewitness.org/who-are-the-descendants-of-ishmael/.
96. Lawler, Andrew, "DNA from the Bible's Canaanites lives on in the Modern Arabs and Jews," National Geographic, June 1, 2020, Article posted at: https://www.nationalgeographic.co.uk/history-and-civilization/2020/05/dna-from-the-bibles-canaanites-lives-on-in-modern-arabs-and-jews.
97. Ibid.
98. Phillips, Adam, "Tracing Roots: Uncovering the Descendants of Ishmael in Arabic History and Genealogy," *The Witness*, March 12, 2024, Article posted at: https://thewitness.org/who-are-the-descendants-of-ishmael/.
99. Tenney, Merrill C., *Zondervan's Pictorial Bible Dictionary*, Zondervan Publishing House, MI, 1967, p. 338.
100. "Regions of Jordan - Hauran," *Famous Fix*, Posted at: https://www.famousfix.com/list/regions-of-jordan.
101. McKenzie, John L. S. J., *Dictionary of the Bible*, Touchstone, NY, 1995, p. 867.
102. Editors of Encyclopedia Britannica, "Sea of Galilee," *Britannica Online*, Last updated December 19, 2023, Posted at: https://www.britannica.com/place/Sea-of-Galilee.

103. "120,000 Palestine Refugee Students in Jordan Return to UNRWA Schools," *United Nations Relief and Works Agency for Palestine Refugees in the Near East*, September 2, 2019, Article posted at: https://www.unrwa.org/newsroom/press-releases/120000-palestine-refugee-students-jordan-return-unrwa-schools.
104. Hollels, Jennifer, "Palestinians in the Middle East: Where and how do they live?" *DW*, November 29, 2023, Article posted at: https://www.dw.com/en/palestinians-in-the-middle-east-where-and-how-do-they-live/a-67583110.
105. Cook, Steven A., "Five Months of War: Where Israel, Hamas, and the U. S. Stand," Council on Foreign Relations, March 8, 2024, Briefing posted at: https://www.cfr.org/expert-briefing/five-months-war-where-israel-hamas-and-us-stand.
106. Editors of Encyclopedia Britannica, "Hamas: Palestinian Nationalist Movement," *Britannica Online*, Updated March 11, 2024, Posted at https://www.britannica.com/topic/Hamas.
107. Cook, Steven A., "Five Months of War: Where Israel, Hamas, and the U. S. Stand," Council on Foreign Relations, March 8, 2024, Briefing posted at: https://www.cfr.org/expert-briefing/five-months-war-where-israel-hamas-and-us-stand.
108. "What does Genesis 48:5 mean?" *BibleRef*, Posted at: https://www.bibleref.com/Genesis/48/Genesis-48-5.html.
109. McKenzie, John L. S. J., *Dictionary of the Bible*, Touchstone, NY, 1995, pp. 388-389.
110. Ibid, pp. 504-505.
111. "Jerusalem 101: The Walls of Jerusalem Today," *Generation Word*, https://www.generationword.com/jerusalem101/4-walls-today.html.
112. Ibid.
113. "Name Samah meaning in Arabic and English," Arabic meaning posted at: https://www.arabic-names.com/names/samah.

INDEX

Abraham
    Gentiles not practicing Abrahamic ordinance of Circumcision, 31
    Jewish belief Abraham attempted to sacrifice his son on the Temple Mount "rock", 84
    Muslims commemorate sparing of Abraham's son, 111
    As the ancestor of God's prophets, 49, 141

Adam
    Son of Man as a descendant of Adam, 8, 33, 60, 64, 90, 147

Altar
    Jewish Activists build altar for Temple Mount, 85
    Temple's sacrificial altar, 93-95
    Altar's ordinances, 93-95, 97-100
    Housing for the kohen safeguarding the sacrificial altar, 112
    Altar with a cross, 118
    Water on the south side of the temple's altar, 137

A'madians (Muslims)
    Israelis possess lands of neighboring A'madians, 32
    Jesus to aid Arab A'madians from Togarmah family, 54-56, 85

Amman
    Russian Gog's intention to invade Arab refugee lands such as Amman, 57

Arabia and Arabs
    God's helping hand to aid Arabs living amongst Jesus, 11
    Israelis' invasion of Egypt to cause anger amongst Arabians and Arabs, 12-16
    Israel muddies up Arabs' water supply, 24
    Israel's Arab neighbors have no bomb shelters or reinforced buildings, 33
    Israelis' perpetual hatred toward Arab Muslims, 42
    As Israel is destroyed, Arabians and Arabs will have overhead defensive protection, 54-55
    Arabia, Yemen and Turkey to question Gog's intentions to invade Arab refugee lands, 57-59
    Israelis ordered by God to share the land of Israel with its alienated Arabs, 144-145, 147-150

Ascension Site
    Jesus and the messenger spirit make ablution by the ascension site, 110
    Located within the Dome of the Rock Shrine where Muslims believe Prophet Mohamed's nighttime ascension into the heavens occurred, 84, 110

Asher
    General location of Asher's inheritance land, 152
    As a son of Jacob (Israel) and brother of Joseph, 156
    Future name of one of the west gates of Old City Jerusalem, 158

Assyria
> Imposter Jesus instructed to behold Assyria and contemplate on cedar allegory, 19
> Many of imposter Jesus' congregation to be buried throughout Assyria, 28

Atonement for Sins (as an erroneous teaching)
> Ezekiel foretold that Jesus had not died for the atonement of his people's sins, 8
> Israelis to again perform animal sacrifices for atonement of sins atop Temple Mount, 93-95 97-100, 111
> Jewish belief that animal sacrifices to atone for sins must be carried out on top of Temple Mount, 84-85, 97-99
> Isaiah, Jeremiah, and Amos passages revealing that animal sacrifices and offerings do not atone for sins, 99-100
> Jesus to tour Israelis' slaughter area atop Temple Mount for atoning of sins, 93-99
> Jesus to tour room where the holiest of holy priests receive the sacrament of the Eucharist, 120-121

Aven (vicinity of Cairo, Egypt)
> Young men of Aven will fall by a destructive weapon, 16

Babylon (Iraq, Syria, and other allied nations)
> Royal Ruler of Babylon to put an end to the false prophet and his congregation, 14-15
> God to strengthen the forces of the Royal Ruler of Babylon, 17-18
> Destructive weapon of the Royal Ruler of Babylon is to target Israel's army, 26

Barnabas
> Gospel of Barnabas passages that God wills for sinners to repent and mend their lives in order to be forgiven, 70-71
> Barnabas' accounts of the resurrections of Lazarus and the man from Nain, 76-78
> Barnabas' account of the Passover Supper, 127-128

Barzakh
> Arabic equivalent of Sheol, where deceased souls remain till the Resurrection Day, 23

Bashan (a region in east Palestine)
> Deceased sacrificial animals of Bashan, 65

Beasts (imposter Christ and his followers)
> God will cause the evil beasts to cease existence from the Holy Land, and for any of their survivors to dwell in the wasteland or woods, 39-40
> God's people will never again be the gentile beasts' prey, 40

Beirut (or Beruta)
> Part of the land that falls into the possession of the Israelis, 143

Benjamin
> The Levites', priests', and Israeli ruler's plots are located between Judah's and Benjamin's inherited properties, 153, 155
> General location of Benjamin's inheritance land from his father, 155
> As the brother of Joseph and son of Jacob (Israel), 156
> One of three east gates of renovated Old City Jerusalem will be named Benjamin, 157-158

Bomb Shelters (and reinforced buildings)
> Israelis within fortifications and cave-like holes that survive the destructive weapon will die by pestilence, 33
> Israel's Civil Defense Law makes bomb shelters mandatory, 33

Cedars
> Allegory about Lebanon's cedars having a beautiful branch, but overtaken by thick foliages, 19-20

Circumcision
> Fate of imposter Jesus' uncircumcised men and womenfolk slain, 23-24, 27-31
> Gentiles not practicing the ordinance of circumcision, 31
> Israelis allowing foreigners uncircumcised of spirit and/or flesh to enter God's sanctuary, 122, 132

Cloud of Smoke
> Caused by a destructive weapon that's to occur over Israel and its annexed lands, 12-13, 16, 25, 37, 59

Cross and Crucifix
> God will put an end to the crucifixes and idolatrous images originated from Memphis, 15
> Imposter Christ's followers will lift up their eyes towards crucifixes, 32
> Crosses and crucifixes at offensive worship places will be demolished, 45
> Holy Land defiled with crucifixes, 49-50, 91, 149
> God's anger that lifeless idols of Israel's imposter Jesus (crucifixes) are placed at the Houses of Worship, 91
> Priests serving their misled people in front of their crucifixes, 132

Cush (Saudi Arabia, Sudan and Ethiopia)
> Imposter Christ's army to cause anguish throughout Cush, 12-13
> Cush, Lud, and entire Arab League to counterattack against Israel's army, 13
> Cush will be safe when Israel and its annexed lands are counterattacked, 14
> People from Cush, Persia, and Put will have overhead defensive protection when going against Gog's army, 54-55

Damascus
> Land that fell into the possession of the Israelis, 143
> Was part of Joseph's inherited property, 152

Dan
- An eastern border of the Mediterranean Sea was Dan's inheritance land, 152
- As Joseph's brother and Jacob's (Israel's) son, 156
- One of the east gates of renovated Old City Jerusalem is to be named Dan, 157, 158

Dead Sea Scrolls (DSS)
- DSS have no vowel markings, 5
- As oldest available biblical fragments, and the years discovered, 7-8
- Few chapters and passages in the DSS were in different order as compared to King James version, 11
- DSS fragments regarding Sheol, 23
- DSS passages about the Resurrection, 80-81

Dedan (Arabia)
- Sheba, Dedan and Tarshish will question Gog's motives for attempting to invade Arab refugee regions, 57-58

Destruction
- Annexed Egypt's warning of future destruction, 12-18
- Oppressors in Israel and Egypt to be destroyed, 17-18, 20, 39-40
- Brutal armed forces of Egypt's and Israel's false Christ are to be destroyed, 18, 24, 26
- Arrogance in Egypt will be destroyed, 26
- Israel's exiles continually being destroyed were never cared for, 35-37
- Imposter Jesus orders destruction of God's people that tell him the Lord is Yahweh, 48-49
- Destructed cities in Israel and its annexed lands to be rebuilt by Jesus and God's people, 53

Destructive Weapon
- Israel's destructive weapon(s) to enter Egypt causing anguish, 13
- Israelis and gentiles following the imposter Jesus are to fall by destructive weapon(s), 13, 14, 16-18, 32, 41-42, 59-60
- Broken arm of Messianic Ruler in Egypt is to hinder him from firing off of a destructive weapon, 17
- A destructive weapon is to be provided to the Royal Leader of Babylon, 14-15, 17-18, 26
- Destructive weapon against Israel's oppressors put off long enough, 28, 61-62
- Congregation to fall by the destructive weapon had caused terror in Elam (Iran and Iraq), 28
- Tyrannical Sidonians to fall by destructive weapon, 30
- Israelis' destructive weapons target A'madians for their land and possessions, 32
- Annexed territories returned to Arabs by way of a destructive weapon, 56
- Russia's destructive weapon targeted against Arab refugee lands to be intercepted, 60-64
- God's warnings to the Israelis regarding counterattack via the destructive weapon not heeded, 68-69

Eden (Garden of Eden)
- Imposter Jesus' Garden of Eden, 20, 22, 23
- Trees of Eden and drinking water should have been for the morally best in Lebanon, 22

Eden (Garden of Eden), cont.
    Renovated lands previously war-destroyed to become like the Garden of Eden, 53, 142

Edom (south of the Dead Sea to the Gulf of Aqaba)
    Edom to be destroyed, 30
    God is against all of Edom for possessing the land of God's people, 43, 46

Egypt
    Ancient pagan tenets from Egypt in the Old Testament, 6
    Prophesy fulfilled that Israel would send troops to Egypt by the 40th year of peace, 10
    Commentary on Egypt's takeover by Israel led by the imposter Christ, 12
    Prophesy about Israel capturing Egypt, 12-13
    Egypt to be recaptured by Jesus and his militia, 13-18
    Egypt's defenders to include Turkey and the Arab League, 13
    Jesus to be instructed to put an end to idolatrous images originated from Memphis, 15
    Once Israeli annexed Egypt is recaptured, its arrogance and power will diminish, 13, 16, 26
    Egypt's Pharaoh-like ruler (imposter Christ), 17, 19, 24, 31

Elam (southern Iraq and western Iran)
    Israelis and allied gentiles to be destroyed for causing terror in Elam, 28

Enon (unidentified, possibly Sidon (Saida), Lebanon)
    Seashore settlement of Enon as part of Jacob's land, 143, 152

Erroneous Teachings or Beliefs
    Jesus (Son of Man) is human; not God (Yahweh), 8, 33, 41, 45, 60, 64, 90, 147, 160
    Worshippers are profaning God's name by praying in the name of others beside God, 9, 24, 50-52, 61, 64, 91
    God never required animal sacrifices (or the Crucifixion of Jesus) for the atonement of sins, 99-100
    Skeptics reassured that the dead will be resurrected, judged, and eternally rewarded or sentenced to the Pit (Hell), 21-23, 69-83
    Symbolically eating the body of Christ (bread) and drinking his blood (wine) was never actually requested by Jesus or God, and breaks God's covenant, 64, 122-130
    Land of Israel is to be shared with its Arab neighbors in peace, and as one united nation; is not solely for the Israelis, 145-150, 156-157

Eucharist (erroneous ritual of ingesting the body and blood of Christ)
    God is to satirically provide the flesh and blood of the imposter Jesus, Israelis and their neighboring gentile allies as a sacrificial offering to the areas' birds and land creatures, 21, 25, 32-33, 61, 63, 64-65
    Tour of sacred chamber where the holiest of priests consume the Eucharist, 120-121
    God's sanctuary defiled and His covenant broken when priests offer bread and wine to their congregation, 122-123
    Commentary on Pauline Eucharist, 123-124
    Passover Supper account in the Gospels of John and Barnabas do not include Jesus supposedly requesting followers to ingest his body and blood, 124-128

Eucharist, cont.
- Early Christian teaching of the Eucharist (in the Didache) as a meal gathering, giving thanks to God, 129-130
- Leviticus passages prohibiting the eating of human flesh and the drinking of blood, 130
- Kohanim (priests) would not eat carcass torn from birds or animals, yet will partake in the ritual of eating Jesus' torn flesh (broken bread), 135

Euphrates (and its tributary, the Khabur River)
- Euphrates region as land of the Togarmah family, 55
- Sightings to be seen nearby the Khabur River, 87

Extraterrestrials (God's spirit(s) and other celestial beings)
- Celestial beings that return Jesus to the Middle East, 8, 11, 87
- God's spirit(s) (the glorious one of God/ hand of God), 11, 51, 67, 73-77, 86, 87-93, 104-121, 136-138

False Prophet of Nazareth (Nebu-chad(b)-Nazzer); imposter Jesus
- False prophet of Nazareth, 8, 14, 19
- Because the people of the other Jesus capture the land(s) outside their boundary, a destructive weapon will appear above them, 68
- The Jesus who is deceiving, 98
- Atonements made by the temple (upon Temple Mount) will be carried out because of the deceitful Jesus' instructions, 98-99
- The priests of the imposter Jesus who will defile his followers will not pray for or approach the deceased people of God, 135-136

Famine (and hunger)
- Israelis trample over its exiles' pastures, destroying crops, 38
- God will cause gardens to grow for Israel's exiles suffering from hunger, 40
- God will provide food for the repented gentiles and Israelis suffering from famine, 52

Gad
- General location of Gad's inheritance land, 156
- As a son of Jacob (Israel) and brother of Joseph, 156
- Future name of one of the west gates of Old City Jerusalem, 158

God (Yahweh)
- The name of God in different languages, 9, 64, 79, 99
- The helping hand of God, 11, 73, 76, 86
- "I, Yahweh, am God," 14, 18, 27, 33, 40, 41, 42, 43, 44, 48, 53, 60, 79, 142, 150
- "The Lord is Yahweh," 14, 17, 20, 24, 25, 26, 27, 31, 36, 37, 39, 41, 46, 47, 48, 49, 52, 53, 56, 58 61, 63, 66, 67, 95, 131, 132, 133, 142, 146, 147
- As what Yahweh shall say or had relayed, 12, 13, 14, 15, 21, 32, 35, 36, 38, 41, 43, 45, 46, 47, 49, 50, 54, 58, 60, 68, 70, 71, 73, 74, 75, 78, 89, 90, 91, 93, 98, 101, 104, 105, 112, 118, 120, 131, 138, 141, 143, 147, 148-158
- God profaned by worshippers, 50, 61, 66

God, cont.
> God's spirit (His messenger, Gabriel), 5, 11, 51, 67, 73, 74, 75, 78, 79, 84, 87, 88, 89, 90, 93
> God's anger against the people in Israel and its annexed lands, 12-18, 41-44, 46-49, 58-60, 91

Gog (Russian ruler of Moscow and Tbilisi)
> Gog to send troops to the land of Magog (Zionist Israel), 54
> The destruction and damnation of Gog and his army, 55-56, 58-63
> God's wrath against Gog, chief ruler of Moscow and Tbilisi, 54-56, 59-60
> Gog's intention to seize and plunder the Arab refugees' lands, 56-58
> Gog's weapon to be struck off course, causing his and Israel's troops to fall instead, 61
> Burial site of Gog and his troops in a valley of Israel (Hamon Gog), 63-64

Gomer
> Army of Gomer to go against the family of Togarmah, 55
> Commentary regarding Gomer (Russia, Ukrain, Georgia, Moldova, and Romania), 55

Hamah (or Hamath)
> Part of the Syrian land that fell into the possession of the Israelis, 143
> As part of Joseph's inherited land, 150-152

Hamonah (Himonah) and Hamon Gog
> Region where Gog's army will be buried 63-64
> Hamonah (Himonah) is most likely Dimonah Israel, 63

Hauran Region (portion of S. Syria and N. Jordan, including land east of the Jordan River)
> Portion of land that fell into the possession of the Israelis, 143-144

Hethlon or Hethalon (probably Lebanon)
> Heading towards Hethlon, then from Beirut to Sadad - part of the land that fell into the possession of the Israelis, 143
> Description of where a portion of Joseph's inherited land was located, 151-152

Inheritance
> Israel drives God's people away to keep Abraham's and Jacob's land for themselves and to possess their personal inheritance, 46, 48, 95, 136, 141-142, 143-147
> Arab gentiles' argument that Abraham had occupied the Holy Land before Jacob, 141-142
> Regarding the inheritance gift to one's children, 145
> Original inheritance passed on to Jacob's sons, and to Joseph's sons, 150-156

Israel (House of)
> Cloud of smoke to cover over Israel and its annexed lands, 12-13, 16, 25, 37, 58
> As the rebellious house, 122
> House of Israel will refuse to listen to and obey God, 34, 36, 46, 68, 69, 71
> Israelis' wickedness and blaspheming, 14-16, 38, 42, 43-44, 45-47, 49-51, 66-67, 69- 70, 71-72
> Israel's warnings of destruction and damnation, 12-18, 20-33, 36-37, 41-44, 58-63, 64-67, 68-70
> God's people ruled by the Israelis with violence and cruelty, 35-37, 38, 42, 46-50, 144-145

Israel (House of), cont.
> Reasons for Israel's upcoming destruction, 45-52
> Demolished regions are to be rebuilt, 48, 53, 142
> Intention to build their temple upon Temple Mount, 84, 92
> Its sacrificial altar to be placed atop Temple Mount, 85, 92-99, 110-112
> Inherited land of the Israelites, 141-142, 150-156
> Jacob's inheritance land is to be shared with and ruled by Jesus and Israel's Arab gentiles, 142, 144-146, 147-150
> Israel must never again force God's people (its exiled Arabs) to surrender their land over to Israel, 146

Issachar
> General location of Issachar's inheritance property, 156
> Commentary regarding Jacob's inheritance to Issachar, 156
> One of Old City Jerusalem's south gates to be named Issachar, 157-158

Jacob
> God is to turn His face toward Israel's exiles cast out by Jacob's posterity, 66
> Followers of the true Jesus are to dwell on the land of Jacob, 150
> Jacob's inheritance properties to his sons and Joseph's two sons, 150-156

Jerusalem and Old City Jerusalem
> Prophesies to occur after Jerusalem is stricken by Jesus and his army, 11, 17, 18, 24, 27, 86
> Jerusalem's holy flock is to occupy the rebuilt regions, 53
> Jesus' outings to Jerusalem's and its vicinities' notable sites, 84-140
> Old City Jerusalem is to be renamed Yahweh Shamah (Samah Allah, in Arabic), 158

Jesus (Iyesh; also see "Son of Man")
> On the day of Israel's ruin, Prophet Jesus will only be accountable for his own life, 26
> Jesus will instruct people to heed God's Word that he relays, but they will not obey, 34
> God's glory is to be manifested following each of Jesus' battles, 65
> People of Israel will be judged based on Jesus' (righteous) ways, 73
> Jesus is to eventually be returned to Old City Jerusalem, 86-90
> Jesus' appearance, 86
> Temple Mount's east gate will be closed when God's spirit takes Jesus there, 88
> By an entrance to Temple Mount, Jesus will be introduced to worshippers who are to contemplate on what he will be showing them, 90
> Jesus to carry a measuring device for taking measurements, 86, 105, 137
> After touring Old City Jerusalem, Jesus is to be shown Jerusalem's and Israel's water resources, 136-140
> Jacob's inheritance to Israel's forefathers is also the true Jesus' inheritance, 151
> Jesus will reveal the locations of land assigned to Israel's 12 tribes, 151-156

Joseph
> Jesus instructed to write "Joseph; for Ephraim" (representing Israel) on a sheet of paper, and to unite it with the sheet of Judah (Palestine), uniting the two nations, 147-150

Joseph, cont.
> Land to the twelve tribes of Israel, including Joseph's portions, 150-156
> As a son of Jacob, 156
> One of the renovated Old City Jerusalem's east gates is to be named Joseph Gate, 157, 158

Judah
> Jesus is to write "For Judah" on a sheet of paper and is to place the sheet of Joseph upon it, demonstrating God's decree to kick out the Israelis from the neighboring foreign nations, 147-149
> General location of Judah's inheritance property from his father (Jacob), 152
> The Levites' section, priests section, and the city's property are located between the inherited properties of Judah and Benjamin, 152-155
> As a son of Jacob and brother of Joseph, 156
> One of the renovated Old City Jerusalem's north gates is to be named Judah Gate, 157, 158

Koran (Qur'an)
> Recitation from God's Testimony (the Qur'an) during the dawn prayer, 11
> Koranic quotes on the Resurrection and Judgment compared to the translated text and Dead Sea Scrolls, 81-83

Lamb
> Followers of "their male lamb" will be slaughtered, 21, 64-65
> Lamb, goat and bull sacrifices to again be erroneously carried out in Israel, 97-98, 102-103
> Comment regarding animal sacrifices and about Jesus as a sacrificial lamb replacement, 99
> Isaiah quote that God does not delight in the sacrifices made to him of lambs, bulls or he-goats, 100
> Gospel of Barnabas quote about Jesus and his disciples eating lamb during the Last Supper, 127-128

Lebanon
> Southern Lebanon as one of the lands of Jacob, 9
> As belonging to the Arab league, 13
> Allegory regarding Lebanon's Cedars, 19-20
> Many in Lebanon will mourn over the imposter Christ's death, 22
> Water and Lebanon's trees were meant for Lebanon's morally best people, 22
> Sidonians (of Saida Lebanon) will fall due to their shameful ways and terrorizing power, 30
> Southern Lebanon as part of the land possessed by the Israelis, 143
> Inhabitants of its annexed regions will be forced to move out, 144-146, 149

Libya
> Will be against Israel for seizing and annexing Egypt, 13
> As belonging to the Arab League, 13

Levi and the Levites
> Sin offerings given to the Levites' priests, 93-94
> Levites' section of land, 153-154, 155
> Levi was near to God in serving Him, 112

Levi and the Levites, cont.
> Regarding Levi's and his descendants' plot of land instructed by God to be used for serving in religious matters, 96, 132-133, 153
> Levites that strayed away from worshipping Yahweh, facing their crucifixes, 132-133, 153
> One of the north gates of renovated Old City Jerusalem will be named Levi Gate, 157, 158

Lud (Turkey)
> Will be against Israel for seizing and annexing Egypt, 13

Magog (Zionist Israel)
> Imposter Jesus will be the ruling Christ of the Gog and Magog people, 8, 12
> Gog will send allied troops to the land of Magog, 54, 56
> A raging inferno will be sent against Magog, 61-62, 63-64

Manasseh
> General location of Manasseh's inherited property, 152
> Jacob's grandson (Joseph's son), Manasseh, inherited one portion of Jacob's land, 156

Measurements (to be taken)
> Jesus carrying a measuring device, 86, 105, 137
> The sanctuary altar's measurements, 93
> Dimensions of the sacred properties within Old City Jerusalem, 95-96
> Dimensions of four enclosures with hearths, 104
> Measurements taken of Old City Jerusalem's gates' entrances, hall chambers, porticos and posts, 105-110, 112
> Measurements taken of the stone slaughter tables and hanging hooks, 111
> Measurements taken of the sanctuary building (Dome of the Rock Shrine), 112-116
> Measurements of the other temple (Al Aqsa Mosque) and the building beside it, 116
> Measurements taken of the temple with galleries (Holy Sepulcher Church), 116-121
> Spirit accompanying Jesus measures areas surrounding Holy Sepulcher, 121-122
> Estimated depth of the stream that supplies Jerusalem with water, 137-138
> God will judge fairly with a set of scales for measuring one's righteousness, 147

Meshech (Moscow) and Tubal (Tbil or Tbilisi)
> Deceased soldiers of Meshech and Tbil are to be sent down to the Pit, 29
> Gog, the chief ruler of Meshech and Tbil, 54, 60

Memphis (see Noph)

Migdol (a region in Egypt)
> The arrogance and power from Migdol to Syene will be terminated, 13-14

Mohamed (Muhammad)
> Reminder that a descendant of Mohamed and Shāphan will aid Jesus in his conquests, 55
> Mohamed's night ascension into the heavens, 84, 110
> Islamic belief that Mohamed and Arabs are descendants of Abraham and Ishmael, 141

Naphtali
> General location of Naphtali's inherited land, 152
> As a son of Jacob and brother of Joseph, 156
> One of the west gates of renovated Old City Jerusalem to be named Naphtali Gate, 158

Negev
> Negev area including Hamonah (Dimonah) will be destroyed by a raging fire, 63-64
> Jesus is shown the spring that provides water to the Negev Desert, 138

No (Luxor and Karnak, Egypt)
> God's punishment will be executed in No, 15

Noph (ancient Memphis)
> The crucifixes and idolatrous images of Noph will be destroyed, 15
> Noph will be rent asunder, 16

Pagan Customs and Beliefs
> Influenced the writings within the Old and New Testaments, 6
> Crucifix and idolatrous customs originated from ancient Memphis, 15

Palestine (and Jordan)
> The siege and annexing of Egypt by the Israelis angers the Arab League, 13
> Imposter Jesus tells the Israelis that these two nations belong to them, 44-45
> As part of the Togarmah family's land, 55
> Sacrificial animals of Bashan (E. Palestine), 65
> As part of the land that fell into the Israeli's possession, 143-144
> A portion was Judah's inheritance property, 147-149
> Arabs and Israelis will be ordered by God to share Israel and its annexed lands, 149-150

Passover and Passover Supper
> Followers of the imposter Jesus will celebrate Passover, 98-99
> During Passover, animal sacrifices and offerings will be carried out, 99
> Passover Supper according to Paul, 123-124
> John's account of the Passover Supper, 124-127
> Barnabas' account of the Passover Supper, 127-128

Paul
> Abrahamic ordinance of male circumcision was deemed unnecessary by Paul, 31
> The erroneous observance of the Eucharist evolved from Paul, 123-124
> Paul's account of the Passover Supper differs greatly from John's and Barnabas' account, 124-128

Peace Treaty
> Israel-Egypt Camp David Accord, 10
> Commentaries on the treaty between Jesus and the imposter Jesus, 12, 85

Pestilence
- Many in Israel within fortifications and bomb shelters will die by pestilence, 33
- Destructive weapon will cause pestilence, bloodshed, and an overflowing downpour, 60

Pit (Hell)
- As translated in the Old and New Testament, 22-23
- Imposter Christ and his followers will be sent down to the Pit, 20-22, 27-30

Prayer
- Jesus, celestial beings, and messenger spirit pray to Yahweh upon Christ's return, 11, 87
- Imposter Jesus will be worshiped instead of God, 44-45, 47-48
- Lord Yahweh demands that He alone must be worshiped, 53
- Gospel of Barnabas accounts that Jesus prayed in the name of God when requesting God to heal the sick and resurrect the dead, 76-78
- Commentary on the consequence of prohibiting Muslims from entering the Dome of the Rock Shrine, 84-85
- Exalted imposter Jesus prays with followers, 101

Priest(s)
- Levite priests from the line of Zadok, 94, 112, 133, 153, 156
- Priests throw salt on sacrificial offerings, 94
- Priests drop the blood of the sin offering on the temple's doorpost and altar, 98
- Priests prepare burnt and peace offerings whenever the imposter Christ enters Temple Mount, 101
- Jesus will be shown the place where priests cook the offerings, 104
- Jesus will be shown the priest's chambers, 112
- Jesus will be shown the sacred rooms where the holiest of the sacred priests would consume the Eucharist, 120-121
- Priests (wearing special linen garments) to minister at Temple Mount's sanctuary, 133-134
- Priests to stand for judgment due to straying from God's actual laws and ordinances, 133
- The priests' section of land next to the Levites' plot, 153-154

Purgatory
- As a place where the souls of the deceased are purified before entering Heaven, 23

Resurrection and Judgment of the Dead
- Sheol denotes a state of death till resurrection occurs, 22-23
- God's demonstration on how He will resurrect the dead, 73-75
- Gospel of Barnabas account of the resurrection of the young man from Nain, 76-77
- Gospel of Barnabas account of the resurrection of Lazarus, 77-78
- God's demonstration of resurrected bodies will be proof of the afterlife for skeptics, 79-80
- Quotes from Daniel, Isaiah, and the Dead Sea Scrolls regarding the resurrection, 80-81
- Koranic quotes regarding the Day of Resurrection and the Judgment Day, 81-82

Reuben
- General location of Reuben's inherited property, 152
- Commentary regarding Reuben inheriting one portion of land from Jacob, 156
- One of renovated Old City Jerusalem's north gates will be named Reuben Gate, 157, 158

Rock (within the Dome of the Rock Shrine)
    Its significance to the Jews and Muslims, 84-85

Salvation (as opposed to damnation)
    Forgiveness achieved through repentance and correcting one's life, 52, 53, 68-70, 71-72
    Gospel of Barnabas quotes of Jesus' teaching that sinners are not predestined to damnation if they repent and convert to penitence, 70-71
    One's righteousness will not save him if he goes astray, 71-72
    Isaiah quote that sacrifices and offerings to God do not do away with sinning, 100

Sacrificial Offerings (and other types of offerings)
    God's satirical sacrificial offering to the winged and land creatures, 64-65
    Israeli followers of the imposter Jesus to again carry out animal sacrifices and offerings, 93-95, 96-99, 102-103, 131
    Isaiah, Jeremiah, and Amos quotes that God never required and loathes sacrificial offerings made to Him, 99-100
    Imposter Jesus will present himself as a sin offering, 131
    Priests will consume the offerings, 120-121, 133, 135

Sadad or Sadadah (63 miles NE of Damascus)
    Part of the land that falls into the Israelis possession, 143

Sea of Meriba; believed by us to be the Sea of Galilee (Sea of Kinneret)
    Its region to fall in the possession of the Israelis, 144, 156
    As the holy stream in Palestine, 144, 156

Seir (Land between the Dead Sea and Gulf of Aqaba)
    Prophesy about the destruction of Mount Seir and its inhabitants, 41-44

Sheba (Yemen)
    Will question Gog's intention to invade Arab refugee regions, 57-58

Sibraim
    Land between Hamah and Damascus that fell into the Israelis possession, 143

Sidon (Saida, Lebanon)
    Sidonians causing terror will be slain, 31
    As possibly being the seashore settlement of Enon, 143, 152

Sightings (celestial crafts)
    God's angels will arrive in (space)ships to aid in Jesus' battles, 14
    Sightings of the messenger spirit's craft and the craft that returns Jesus, 87

Simeon
    General location of Simeon's inherited land, 155-156
    Brother of Joseph and son of Jacob inherits one portion of Jacob's land, 156

Simeon, cont.
    One of three south gates of renovated Old City Jerusalem will be named after Simeon, 158

Son of Man (also see Jesus)
    A descendant of Adam (i.e., human), 8, 33, 60, 64, 90, 147
    Instructed to prophesy about the destruction of Israel and annexed Egypt, 12-17
    Informed that the broken arm of annexed Egypt's ruler will hinder him from firing a destructive weapon, 17
    Instructed to relay God's message and allegory to the ruler of annexed Egypt, 19-21
    Instructed to relay a lamentation to annexed Egypt's ruler, 24-27
    Advised to only mourn over Egypt's noble women and army, 27
    Informed about the burial sites of the imposter Jesus' people and their final destination to the Pit, 27-31
    Instructed to relay a message to the imposter Jesus' people regarding their sinful actions and abominations, 32-33, 122-123
    Instructed to warn Israel (including annexed Egypt) about its upcoming destruction, 32-33
    Instructed to prophesy against those in Israel tending to God's flock, 35-41
    Instructed to prophesy against those occupying the annexed regions of Mount Seir, 41-44
    Instructed to relay reasons why Israel and Jerusalem will be in ruins, 45-50
    Is informed of God's wrath against those profaning his Holy Name and defiling themselves with their unholy ways, 49-53
    Instructed to prophesy against Russian Gog and his troops, 54-64
    Instructed to relate about God's satirical, sacrificial offering of Israel's slain, 64-65
    Instructed to relay that whoever doesn't heed God's destruction warnings will be held accountable; includes commentary, 68-71
    Instructed to relate about God's fair sentencing, 71-73
    Is shown how God resurrects the dead, 73-75, 78-79, 79-81
    Instructed to observe and comprehend everything explained and shown to him in Jerusalem, 86-99, 101-123, 130-136, 136-140
    Instructed to scold Israel for their temple design plan, 92
    Is informed and instructed to relay about the rightful inhabitants of Jacob's land, 141-145, 147-151

Sukkot Holiday
    Its festival begins on the 15th of the seventh month, 99
    Animal sacrifices and offerings carried out for seven days, 99

Syene (Aswan, Egypt)
    Assigned to utter ruins, 13-15
    As a refuge city, 16, 17

Syria
    A portion of Syria as part of Jacob's land, 9, 142, 149-150
    Commentary on Israel fighting against militants of Iraq and Syria (ISIS) in Egypt, 10
    Celestial beings take Jesus to Syria at dawn upon his return to Earth, 11, 87

Syria, cont.
    As part of Babylon, 8, 12, 14, 18, 19, 26, 55, 85, 159
    Belonging to the Arab League, 13
    Part of ancient Assyria, 19, 28
    Part of the Togarmah family's land, 54-55
    Syrian and Palestinian refugees in Jordan, 58, 145-146
    As part of the Hauran region, 142
    Inhabitants of its annexed regions will be forced to move out, 144, 148

Tahpanhes (A northern border of Egypt)
    Egyptians in captivity will move to Tahpanhes for refuge, 16

Tarshish (Tarsus, Turkey and vicinity)
    Will question Gog's intention to invade Arab refugee regions, 57

Temple(s) and Sanctuary
    Temple Mount - referred to by Muslims as the "Noble Sanctuary", 88
    Jesus instructed to focus on how to enter the temple at all of the sanctuary's entrances, 89
    Glory of God approaches the temple nearby the east gate, 88-90
    Israelis plan to rebuild their temple upon Temple Mount, 92
    Guide of the temple on Temple Mount and of the other Holy places, 92-139
    Animal sacrifices and offerings to be conducted outside the sanctuary shrine, 93-99, 101-103
    Jesus is shown a twenty-chambered temple ministered by the Levites, 96
    Israelis to again make atonements by the sanctuary temple, 97
    Jesus is shown the cooking area of a temple, 104
    Commentary on the destruction of the 2nd Jewish temple, 111
    Jesus shown the housing for the Kohen safeguarding the temple, 112
    Measurements of the sanctuary temple (Dome of the Rock Shrine), 112-115
    Measurements of the other temple upon Temple Mount (Al Aqsa Mosque), 116
    Measurements of the temple with galleries (Holy Sepulcher Church), 116-120
    Sanctuary temple to become defiled by worshipers partaking in the Eucharist, 120-130
    Prophesy about the priests ministering at the Temple Mount sanctuary, 131-136

Togarmah
    Russian Gog and his troops will go against the family of Togarmah, 55
    Location of the Togarmah territory, 55

Women
    Are to wail over the deaths of their multitude in annexed Egypt, 27
    Jesus instructed to only mourn the deaths of the noble, Egyptian women and men, 27
    Women and men that called out to their Jesus will be calling out to Yahweh in Sheol, 28
    Jesus prayed for the women afflicted by Lazarus' death, 78
    Israel's men and gloomy womenfolk will be judged fairly by God, 147

Zadok
    Righteous forefather of the Levite priests, 94, 112, 133, 153, 156

Zebulun
> General location of Zebulun's inherited land, 156
> As a son of Jacob and brother of Joseph, 156
> One of the west gates of renovated Old City Jerusalem to be named Zebulun Gate, 158

Zoan (a northern part of Egypt including the Sinai)
> A fire will be set in Zoan, 15

Made in the USA
Middletown, DE
06 July 2024